# Everything You've Always Wanted To Know About The

# LAW

but couldn't afford to ask

By Edward E. Colby

## DRAKE PUBLISHERS, Inc.
### NEW YORK

Published in 1972 by
DRAKE PUBLISHERS INC.
381 Park Ave. South
New York, N.Y. 10016


SBN: 87749-284-0

Manufactured in the
United States of America

To My Wife
ANITA COLBY

*True inspiration wrapped up in 104 pounds.*

# ACKNOWLEDGEMENTS

The primary aim of this book is to explain legal principles in nonlegaleze language. For specific law that applies to your state, the reader is advised to check on his local situation. It is not possible to offer advice on every conceivable legal problem because that would require volumes and volumes. Some of the more common and interesting subjects have been selected in the hope it will be helpful as well as entertaining.

Acknowledgement is made for research material emanating from American Jurisprudence 2d.

Acknowledgement is also made for "A Living Will" form furnished by the Euthanasia Educational Fund, 250 West 57th Street, New York 10019.

Last but not least, I wish to express gratitude to my wife, Anita Colby, for constructive criticism and understanding advice, that have materially contributed to the success of my literary efforts.

Edward E. Colby

*MADRID 1972*

# CONTENTS

# WHEN YOU
# BUY ON CREDIT

The dictionary defines "credit" as time given for payment for goods sold on trust. Modern American business has been built on the reasoning that the customer will buy more if he has the opportunity of paying his debt on the installment plan. As a result, buying on credit has become a way of life. In yesteryears, people used to brag about paying cash for anything and everything that they purchased. The public has been educated and encouraged to buy today and pay tomorrow, like $1 down and $1 per month.

*How to Establish Credit*

The easiest and best way to establish credit is by paying your bills promptly when they are due. The quickest way to hurt your credit rating is to be rated "slow pay" or even worse, to be sued for nonpayment of a bill. All creditors are concerned about the customer's record of payment.

Most retail stores require that a credit application be filled out with routine but necessary information as to place and length of employment; amount of income; where you bank; do you rent or own your home; other stores where you already have charge accounts and similar credit information. The person seeking credit is not privileged to question the right of the credit grantor to obtain this type of necessary background information.

Once your application has been approved, the credit grantor may see fit to limit the amount of credit. For example, you may be approved for a $200 limit, which means you can charge items totaling not more than $200. If you pay your charge accounts promptly when they are due, the same store will be glad to increase your credit limit at your request after a reasonable trial period.

If you have occasion to borrow money from your bank, it is recommended that you make your payments when they are due. Banks are delighted when customers pay a day or two ahead of schedule and they have the use of your money for the extra period of time. Months later, if you have occasion to borrow again from your bank, the loan officer will see from your record that you pay promptly and sometimes ahead of schedule. There is no substitute for good bank credit and one never knows when the need for a quick loan may arise. In addition to building up your bank credit, the use of your bank as a credit reference when you apply to others for credit, helps tremendously. Those that abuse their bank credit are only hurting themselves.

## Who Pays For Credit?

You do. The customer pays for credit that has been extended to him. Whether a large department store has its own credit cards for its customers or recognizes banktype credit cards is aside from the point. Someone has to pay for the cost of large credit departments and computer equipment that is used by large credit granting organizations.

A number of large chain stores that were successful over a long period of time have now discovered that in order to compete with credit granting competitors, credit must be granted. Even Mr. James Cash Penney, the founder of the J.C. Penney chain-stores, lived to see his cash and carry policy converted into a credit granting system.

## Cash Or Charge — Which Is Better?

With two exceptions, a person with established credit has advantages over the cash buyer. The exceptions are the persons who lack selfcontrol and buy more than they need or can afford to pay; and the wealthy person who never has a need for credit.

There is an important distinction between the person who operates on a cash basis and the person who has good credit and pays obligations promptly when due. Those that operate on a cash basis make it their policy only to buy something when they have accumulated the cash to pay for it. The person who uses credit intelligently can buy on the installment plan and pay for purchases over the agreed period of time. Very few persons would ever buy a car or a home if the privilege of paying for them on the installment plan was not available to them.

The advantages of buying on credit are numerous. The only way your name is known to any store is by your credit record. If you buy for cash, the store has no record of your name and you are not able to use them as a credit reference. Even if there is no need for credit, it is still a good idea to charge your purchases and then pay for them on the following 10th of the month. There are no carrying or interest charges and you suffer no penalties. Some stores have advance sales where merchandise is offered at discounted prices and this information is passed along to regular charge customers. If you are a cash buyer, you are unknown to the store. If a customer wishes to return merchandise for credit, it is easier to accomplish the mission if you are a charge rather than a cash customer. For those persons that operate their household on a budget, it is easier to regulate purchases on a credit basis because they have records at the end of the month as to just what they bought.

## Can Credit Be Abused?

Emphatically yes and some people cannot resist buying things that are really not needed, as long as they can pay for it on the installment plan. Those who are more experienced know that it is easy to buy things but there does come a day of reckoning and last month's purchases have to be paid this month or next. Many Americans are paying their home mortgage over a period of years which is understandable in view of the sum of money involved. Then come monthly payments on a car, one or more; then follow furniture payments which usually include a television set; appliances; and many other modern conveniences.

Where does the money come from to meet all of these commitments? If the income is sufficient then there is no problem. Unfortunately, in many cases where people refuse to face the financial facts of life, the monthly payments are greater than the income and now begins the problems. If the outgo is greater than the income, something has to give. Creditors want their money and financial problems cause family quarrels and life becomes very unpleasant.

With no intent to preach a sermon, those with limited incomes would be a lot happier and better off to drive a small inexpensive car rather than a large costly type. Cadillacs are nice if you can afford them but there is nothing wrong with a Ford, Chevrolet or even a compact that costs a lot less to own and operate. Trying to keep up with the Joneses doesn't really pay off.

## Carrying Charges And Interest

Many retail stores offer choices in connection with a charge account. The customer may pay a regular charge account on the 10th of the month following the purchase without any additional charge. Another choice is to arrange for a 3 months or six months budget account which means the customer agrees to pay equal monthly installments for the agreed time. The store makes a carrying or interest charge for the additional time given the customer to pay his obligation. Reputable stores show the interest charge on the statement so that the customer knows immediately that the monthly interest charge is 1 percent per month or whatever charge is made. If you think that 12 percent per year is too high and you can do better at your bank, then borrow the money from your bank and save the difference.

*Always Get A Receipt*

It is good business to always get a receipt when you pay cash. Your creditor is probably honest but it could save headaches later if you make it a point to always ask for and get a receipt. The written record speaks for itself and you do not have to trust your memory.

*Pay By Check Whenever Possible*

The big advantage of paying by check is that your cancelled check is a permanent record. No other receipt is really necessary. In addition, your cancelled checks may contain information that is needed for compiling your annual federal and state income tax returns. Some people use their check stubs for this important source of tax information.

*Get A Copy Of Whatever You Sign*

The reader cannot be urged too strongly to always get a copy of whatever paper or instrument you sign. You may have used poor judgment in signing the paper in the first place, but at least you have a copy. A copy gives you protection against any possibility of the other party making any unauthorized changes in the original instrument. It can and will save arguments later as to what the original instrument that you signed provided and it gives you protection to which you are entitled.

Even if your signing the original instrument proves to be a boner on your part and you then consult with your lawyer, he is able to advise you properly by examining the written instrument that you signed. Don't sign anything of importance without consulting your lawyer, but if you do, at least get a copy of the instrument you signed.

## Can You Dispute A Bill Without Hurting Your Credit?

Yes, most credit bureaus are fair if all of the pertinent information is furnished to them. If you have an honest dispute with a creditor you have a perfect legal right to refuse to pay the disputed bill and litigate the matter. In order to protect your credit, notify the credit bureau or local credit reporting agency in your community of the dispute so that this information will be placed in your file. If credit reports are later issued, your file will indicate that you were not delinquent in paying a bill but that you disputed the validity of the claim.

A few unscrupulous credit bureaus who handle collection of accounts as well as do credit reporting, try to intimidate a debtor into paying a disputed claim by threatening that his nonpayment of the disputed bill will hurt his credit record. This threat is false and the owner or manager of the credit agency will stop this procedure. If not, a complaint to the Better Business Bureau will get the credit agency in line in a hurry.

## Can Confidential Credit Information Be Sold?

The Congress of the United States as well as the general public were all shocked to learn that certain bookkeeping firms who charged for making out federal and state income tax returns, were selling confidential information to various mailing lists. This procedure is contrary to law and in violation of the customer's right to have his financial affairs be held in confidence. Fortunately, the largest firm offering this type of tax return assistance, issued its apology and assurance that this practise would stop immediately.

A different situation arises with requests for routine credit information from credit bureaus by a firm that you apply to for credit. By virtue of your application for credit, you authorize your credit grantor to obtain credit background information from the credit reporting agency in your area. Even your bank will be discreet in disclosing your average bank balance by using the answer "three figures or four figures, etc."

## Truth In Lending Act

The Congress of the United States recently enacted a new law that makes it mandatory for credit grantors, sellers of cars or merchandise on credit, banks and mortgage companies who lend money, etc., to advise the borrower exactly what the charges are for time payments.

Now the new car dealer must display a sign on the car, clearly stating the price of the basic car, extras, financing and whatever other charges are involved. If the gullible customer is not interested in examining how much it costs, he is not interested in being protected. Most people are very concerned with the various charges and how much each item costs. For example, if the financing charges appear to be high, check with the loan officer at your bank to find out how much the bank charges for an identical loan. If the bank deal is better, borrow from the bank and purchase your new car on a cash basis from the dealer.

Furniture, jewelry, and other credit granting stores have learned that the financing of their own accounts can be a bigger and more profitable business than the sale of the items involved. Once again, the knowledgeable customer will find out how much the furniture store is charging for financing. Then it will pay to check with your bank and find out if your bank small loan charges will represent a saving. In any event the time spent in obtaining this information is educational and one can learn how much he is being charged for financing.

## Credit Cards

The use of credit cards is now spreading all over the world. It is true as some people claim that a person can travel around the world without using money and credit cards are an acceptable substitute for money. Obtaining credit by the use of a credit card is all well and good as long as the user doesn't forget that the bill will have to be paid next month or so. The latest invention in connection with the use of credit cards is being perfected in Japan where the customer will have his handprints used as a substitute for his signature. Just as police authorities have successfully used fingerprints as a means of identification, it is claimed that handprints will be equally successful. The handprints of no two persons are identical and the computing machines will do the rest.

## Are Credit Cards Good?

Yes and no. In the hands of a responsible person, the ease in obtaining credit by use of an acceptable credit card has many advantages. Those who have difficulty in managing their financial affairs and paying their bills promptly when due, find that credit cards are as bad as liquor can be to a chronic alcoholic. These are the people who believe in living for today and let tomorrow take care of itself. They refuse to acknowledge that "charging today" means a bill to be paid within a month or so.

## Credit Cards — How Many?

There seems to be no limit to the issuance of new credit cards by various credit grantors, airlines, hotels, banks and credit card companies of many descriptions. Some people who like to impress others, will open their billfold and display credit cards in wholesale quantity. Such a vulgar display of credit proves nothing other than the ability to charge a lot of different services and merchandise.

Credit cards were issued by oil companies hoping to acquire new customers to buy their petroleum products. These credit cards represented personal business for the oil company involved and no outsiders had their finger in the pie.

Then came professional credit card companies whose cards were accepted by merchants, hotels and others, in various countries of the world. The credit card company paid the charged invoices, minus a service charge of around 6 percent. The gamble of collection fell on the professional credit card company.

The latest trend is credit cards that are issued by large banks who make a similar service charge of about 6 percent. One large California bank gambled by issuing credit cards in a limited amount to every person listed in the telephone directory. They soon learned that the granting of credit indiscriminately, resulted in high collection losses and now credit cards are issued only to those who have good credit.

## Is The Cash Buyer Penalized By Credit Cards?

A qualified yes. Certain customers who enjoy excellent credit and buy merchandise and present a bank credit card are pleasantly surprised at being approached by the credit grantor. For example, the customer buys $200 worth of clothing at a men's shop where he is well known. The customer presents a bank credit card which means the merchant will receive $188 from the bank in return for his $200 invoice. The merchant then proposes to the good customer that he pay for his purchases reduced to $188 and bypass the bank charges. The customer has saved $12 and the merchant has gained the appreciation of a good customer. The merchant only makes this proposal to customers whose credit is rated high and for those that are shaky he uses the bank financing and pays the 6 percent discount and the bank has the gamble of collecting their bill.

### What If A Credit Card Is Lost Or Stolen?

In the early stages of credit cards, the matter of lost or stolen credit cards presented a serious and worrisome problem. The credit card victim telephoned or wired the credit card issuer so that steps could be taken to prevent its use by a thief or a forger.

Changes have been made that solve this serious problem for all practical purposes. New federal laws have been enacted that protect the innocent victim of a credit card loss and subsequent use by a thief or forger. The new law limits the liability of the credit card holder to a nominal sum and further provides that the burden is on the issuer of the credit card to prove that the customer ordered the credit card. This protects the innocent credit card holder victim who did not order or even want the credit card in the first place.

So many credit cards have been sent to people unsolicited that the recipient uses scissors frequently to destroy those credit cards that are not of interest. Even special credit card containers are not large enough to hold the rash of credit cards mailed by companies in wholesale quantities.

American Express and a few other large and respected firms have been successful in making a nominal charge for the issuance of a credit card.

### Credit Cards And Computers

Credit cards and computers seem to go together like ham and eggs. They both are comparatively new inventions and are revolutionizing the business world. Even the large stock exchanges are discovering the serious problems in handling a vast volume of paper work and are turning to computers.

Computers have been known to make mistakes until a correction is made regarding information that is fed into it. Credit cards have not been infallible, however, their use is being constantly improved. The fact that more and more banks throughout many countries of the world are issuing credit cards to their own customers as well as purchaser of services and merchandise from others, proves the success of their use.

If the use of credit cards is not abused by the individual, they have many advantages.

### Life Memberships — Whose Life?

Frequently, advertising claims are made by various clubs or health organizations offering a life membership. The price sounds inexpensive and the prospective customer thinks of his long life ahead of him. The next thing that happens is that the new member has changed his mind and he is either bored or disappointed with the services offered and he wants to get out of the deal.

For the first time, the disenchanted member reads the written contract that he signed and he scratches his head in wonderment. He contacts his attorney hoping there is some legal technicality that will enable him to get out of what is now a bad deal. Some courts have ruled that the contract is unenforceable because the club offers no assurance as to the length of time they are going to be in business. Thus the contract can be cancelled because the life expectancy of the member is one thing but the life expectancy of the club is vague and indefinite.

### Establishing Credit In A New Community

If you have lived in one community for many years, your credit is easily established and there is no problem. When you move to a new community, it is difficult to establish credit because you haven't lived there very long.

Some people who are astute, immediately contact a bank in the new community and borrow a nominal sum of money even though there is no need for the use of the money. The interest charges are nominal and the prompt repayment of the personal loan starts you off with a favorable record at your new bank. If you are smart enough to pay off your loan a few days ahead of schedule, the bank is delighted and your credit record is enhanced. Your name is now known to the bank and you are no longer a stranger, even if you are fairly new in the community.

# REAL ESTATE
# AND MORTGAGES

Are you thinking about buying a home for the first time in your life? If so, it will probably be the largest money transaction during your life. Every married couple should discuss the matter in great detail because it is an important financial step. Do you want a small or large house? Do you want to live in the city proper or join the thousands who have moved to the suburbs? Have you accumulated enough money to handle at least a minimal down payment? Are you financially able to make the monthly payments that do not end with the payment that is applied to principal and interest?

With no intent to frighten a prospective purchaser, it is important that he understand the money outgo that is involved. Most mortgage lenders require the borrower to pay monthly impounds. The estimated bill for fire insurance permiums and real estate taxes are due each month on the basis of one-twelfth of the total. Then at the end of the year the money has been accumulated and the mortgage company pays your insurance and tax bill for you. Sometimes taxes or insurance premiums are increased and if so, the monthly impound payment must be raised.

Even if you have your own furniture, moving into a new home always involves the purchase of additional items, such as curtains, drapes, appliances, rugs, garden equipment, and numerous other necessary things.

People have argued for years whether it is cheaper to pay rent or own your own home. It costs less to be a tenant even though the rent money seems to go down the drain. The argument that the home owner accumulates an equity in his property and is thus saving a portion of his payments is not accurate.

Living in your own home is a luxury involving advantages and disadvantages. There is no substitute for the privacy and joy that go along with the labor involved in occupying your own home. The cost of maintaining your own home is far greater than paying rent for an apartment.

Money has a value which we all learn when we go to the bank to borrow and pay interest. Many owners overlook the value of the money which they have tied up in buying or owning their own home. When you add the cost of the money being used to the normal operating expenses, you soon learn that the joy of owning a home is not inexpensive.

## Buying A Home?

Time and patience are two very important attributes for home buyers that will pay dividends in the long run. Those that buy in a hurry are taking a gamble and may later regret their speedy actions. The amount involved in any purchase of a home is very substantial and careful thought and planning should be given, rather than acting in a hasty manner.

One of the decisions that has to be made when a couple decide to purchase a home is whether to employ an experienced real estate broker or find a home on their own. The real estate broker's commission is paid by the seller and not the buyer. It is true that if buyer and seller get together with no real estate broker involved, the owner saves the broker's commission that run around 6 percent of the total purchase price. From the buyer's point of view, unless he is an experienced homeowner, he will be better off being represented by a real estate broker.

There are many factors involved and pitfalls to be avoided, which can be explained by a competent and experienced real estate broker. He knows the zoning laws for the area; the plus and minuses of the neighborhood; location of schools and necessary stores for shopping; the true value of comparable homes in the area as compared with the seller's asking price; whether the home you are interested in is the most expensive home in the neighborhood which is not good for resale purposes and many other factors.

## Neutral Professional Appraisal

Some homeowners arrange for a friendly appraisal from a real estate broker and then tell the prospective buyer about the value. This type of appraisal may or may not be accurate. The buyer should not rely on the seller's appraisal but should arrange for a neutral appraisal by a professional, such as those offered by the Veteran's Administration, Federal Housing Administration, or a qualified independent appraiser. The cost of the appraisal is $35 for a VA or FHA type and a bit more for a private independent appraiser. Considering the amount of money involved, the nominal appraisal charge is cheap insurance.

Some buyers of less expensive homes, protect themselves by having the real estate binder agreement provide: "subject to V.A. or F.H.A. appraisal approval." Then if the official appraisal is lower than the proposed selling price, the deal is off. The parties may get together on a new and lower price.

## Restrictions

In years gone by, some land developers who subdivided large tracts and sold individual lots, featured the fact that if you bought a lot, the deeds contained restrictions that appealed to well-to-do whites. The main restriction prohibited the sale of any of the lots in the subdivision to any person other than members of the caucasian race. It was sometimes worded the other way, namely a prohibition of sale to any negro or oriental, but the net result was the same. The United States Supreme Court has ruled that this type of restriction is void and in violation of the Constitution of the United States. Today, any person, regardless of race, color or creed, can buy a home or land anywhere, providing the owner is willing to sell.

Other popular restrictions limit the use of the lot to one or two stories residences; minimum liveable area; no animals other than domestic variety; no housetrailers and similar taboos. These restrictions are legal and binding upon present and future owners for the period of time named.

Another advantage of using a qualified real eastate broker to locate your future home is his knowledge of the various residential areas and possible restrictions that may be very important.

## Cash Or Terms?

The old saying, "Money talks" is particularly true in connection with the purchase of a home or other real estate. Many sellers are anxious to receive cash for their equity in the home for sale and are willing to adjust the price downward. This does not come under the category of "chiseling" but is merely good business.

If you are working through a real estate broker, let him know the extent of your cash payment available so that he can find out from the seller what the price is for the installment plan and how much of a discount for a lump sum cash payment.

In connection with terms for payment of the purchase price or the owner's equity, the rate of interest ought to be discussed. The most important item for benefit of the buyer is a provision in the written agreement for any installment payout, that gives the purchaser the right to make two or more payments at any time without penalty. This means that the buyer has the right to pay the entire remaining balance at anytime without any penalty. For example, the contract will provide that the buyer's monthly payments are $150 including interest, OR MORE. The two magic words, or more, protect the buyer in his option of paying ahead of schedule or paying the entire remaining balance without penalty. Some sellers of homes or financial institutions that lend money on mortgages provide for penalties if the buyer wants to pay his balance ahead of schedule.

### Don't Be An Anxious Buyer

If you are a prospective home buyer, with or without a real estate broker and see a house that you like, hide your emotions within reason. If the seller observes your enthusiasm and excitement, you are hurting any chances for getting the asking price reduced. Most sellers of homes ask for a higher price, knowing that the buyer will offer a lesser sum of money. If the asking price includes a $900 figure above a certain number of thousand dollars, the true gross price is usually at least $900 lower than the quoted price. Often there is still another one, two, or even three thousand dollars that can still be lopped off the asking price. It is a rare seller or real estate broker who will not reduce his price.

Every seller has the right to ask any price that he wishes. Any prospective buyer has the right to make a counter offer for any lesser sum that he wishes. If the seller is not interested in the counter offer, he can refuse it or name a new inbetween price. Neither party has a right to become indignant or annoyed, even if the parties do not get together as buyer and seller.

If the buyer makes an offer in writing and his offer is accepted in writing by the seller, the parties have entered into a legal and binding contract of sale. If the buyer revokes his written offer before acceptance by the seller, the deal is off.

### Owner's Equity

Owner's equity is the difference between the agreed selling price and the balance due on the mortgage. Most home sellers are only concerned with their equity because the purchaser assumes and agrees to pay the mortgage balance. Before assuming any other person's mortgage, the buyer ought to find out the identity of the lender and all of the pertinent provisions of the mortgage itself. Aside from the rate of interest provided in the mortgage, it is important for the buyer to find out if he can pay the mortgage balance without penalty. If the mortgage provides for penalties, the amount of the penalty is a factor that should be considered by the buyer. The money market changes and rates of interest that are common today, may be high three years from now. If the mortgage provides for a payoff ahead of schedule at any time without penalty, there may be advantages in refinancing later at a lower rate of interest.

## Check The Neighborhood

After the buyer has looked at the house and has checked it out carefully inside and out, and is interested in buying under the terms offered, he should check the homes on either side, across the street, and the entire immediate neighborhood. A close examination of the entire area and the appearance of the other houses may prove to be of interest. If you go to a bank, savings and loan association or insurance company to borrow money for a mortgage, their appraiser is required to do this in order to determine the mortgage limits of the home you want to buy.

## Title To Land

Some people like to gamble when buying a home or land a la "Russian roulette." Their home purchase involves thousands of dollars and they decide there is no need to check the title to the property they are about to buy. Some think that the seller looks like an honest person. Others rely on the mortgage lender and feel that if the title were bad, the financial institution would not have loaned mortgage money. This is poor reasoning because the title may have been good when the mortgage was placed on record, but things happened afterwards that could create liability on the buyer.

No one can afford to buy a home or land without having the title checked. It is not only sound business to know that you are getting merchantable title but this procedure is routinely followed by financial institutions before they agree to lend any mortgage money.

Having the title checked is neither complicated nor expensive. In some states, abstracts of title are still used as a means of checking anything affecting the title to your land purchase. The seller is obligated to pay for having the abstract of title brought down to date. The buyer pays for having his attorney check the title and issue a written opinion. If there is anything of record that affects the merchantability of the title, your attorney's opinion will list it. For example, the county records indicate an old improvement or paving lien; (if it has been paid a release should be filed of record) a pending mechanic's lien filed by a plumber for an alleged unpaid bill, etc.

In many urban areas, title companies issue title insurance policies as a modern substitute for the old-fashioned abstract of title. Many insurance companies and other mortgage lenders now require title insurance policies as a replacement for abstracts of title. The cost of the title insurance policy is based upon the amount of money involved in the real estate or home purchase. The figure used by the title insurance companies for their bill is not the owner's equity but the total amount including the mortgage balance. The cost is usually paid by the seller because it is his obligation to provide proof of ownership. The title insurance policy will list all items of record that may affect the title. If there is any question about the exceptions, a buyer should have his attorney check it. Like other insurance policies, it provides that if anyone should challenge the title and you have to pay money to clear it, the title insurance company will handle the lawsuit for you and reimburse you for any monies paid out.

## Real Estate Taxes

Inflation has affected the value of houses and land as well as taxes. It behooves the buyer of a home or land to find out and verify the amount of taxes. In many sections of the country, real estate taxes have reached a sizeable sum. Just as an informed buyer needs to know the cost of utilities (particularly heat), accurate information about taxes is also a must. The information is available from the county assessor or tax collector. It is not good business to rely on the seller's statement as to the amount of taxes for last year.

## What Kind Of Deed?

There are two different deeds to land. The most popular is a

Warranty Deed and the other is a Quitclaim Deed. In a Warranty Deed, the seller warrants to the buyer that he has a valid title and that if the title proves to be otherwise, the seller will make the purchaser whole.

In a quitclaim deed, the seller makes no warranties as regards the title. It is like a used car dealer selling a jalopy "as is". Legally, under a quitclaim deed, the seller says: "Whatever interest I have in the land, I pass along to you." Obviously, a buyer ought to receive a warranty deed from the seller in return for his money unless there is some unusual reason for a quitclaim deed.

Once a deed has been delivered to the buyer, it is very important that it be recorded at the County Clerk's office promptly. Some people have formed the bad habit of keeping a deed, which has not been recorded, with their personal papers. The reason that it is important to record your newly acquired deed to land promptly, is that it is notice to the world of your claim to title to the land. Many things can happen to the seller that could adversely affect your claim to title. For example, the seller fails to pay his taxes and Internal Revenue Service files a tax lien against all of his real estate. Another example of what can happen if you delay recording your deed is a judgment against your seller and a transcript is recorded which amounts to a lien against his real estate.

## Termites — Whose Problem?

In California and some other states, the problem of termites is prevalent in many homes. Termites are ant-like insects which infest lumber. They gnaw tunnels in it and breed. Their community life and habits make an interesting story but we are only concerned with their damage to buildings.

The termite problem is basically the sellers and not the buyers. Under the laws of some states, a pest control operator is required to examine the premises and if there is not visible signs of infestation by termites, to issue a "termite clearance." If there is termite damage or dry rot, the seller has to pay for it.

## Do I Need A Lawyer?

Emphatically, YES! Never sign anything or pay money without consulting your lawyer first. Buyers do not realize how heavily weighted and rigged most broker-drawn contracts of sale are in favor of the broker first, the seller second and guess who runs a poor third. Some binders are so worded that the buyer could not only forfeit deposit money, but might be forced to go through with the real estate transaction. Other binder agreements provide that if the buyer changes his mind and decides not to go through with his purchase, that his deposit money will be equally divided between the real estate broker and the seller.

The time to see and consult with your attorney is BEFORE you sign any papers and BEFORE you make any deposit. The more you are told that the property may be sold to another, the more hesitant you should be about signing or paying any money. If the deal can't wait for you to obtain protection through the advice of your lawyer, it isn't good for you so let it go.

Unlike the real estate broker who hopes to earn a substantial brokerage fee, or the anxious seller who wants to make a sale, your lawyer has only your interests in mind. Most lawyers will not discuss the price of the home or real estate values because that is not a legal function. Whether you are making a good or bad deal is your decision. But your lawyer is concerned with all of the legal ramifications and mainly whether his client is receiving protection to which he is entitled. Some years ago, a client asked me to prepare the necessary papers for the sale of his home. He gave me the figures of the total price of $11,000 with nothing down and a $50 monthly payment. I pointed out to my client that with interest at 6 percent per annum, the monthly payment left nothing to be applied to the principal balance and that at that rate the buyer would never pay out his real estate contract. The parties then agreed to increase the monthly payment so that the buyer would have a possibility of paying off the contract in many years to come.

Whenever you sign anything of consequence, whether it be a real estate binder; a deposit agreement; agreement to buy or sell; or similar contract; ALWAYS GET A SIGNED COPY. Don't permit a fast-talking real estate salesman or anyone else to tell you that he will deliver a signed copy later. You wouldn't give a stranger a blank signed check and permit him to fill in the amount because that would be poor business and dangerous practise. It is bad enough if you sign an important document without consulting your attorney first, but you are compounding your boner and hurting yourself if you fail to get a signed copy of whatever document you signed. Visualize a victim of some bad business deal who consults with his lawyer too late. The victim tells the lawyer about the verbal statements that were made and when asked for a copy of the written instrument, says, "He didn't give me a copy." Failure to get a copy is the fault of the signer and obviously handicaps his lawyer in trying to help the inefficient client.

## What Is The Statute Of Frauds?

The Statute of Frauds is universal law that requires every agreement pertaining to land to be in writing in order to be enforceable. In real estate transactions, until the verbal agreement is down on paper and signed by the parties, there is no binding agreement. Samuel Goldwyn, the famous movie producer is reputed to have said, "A verbal agreement isn't worth the paper its written on." Experienced real estate brokers say that a deal has not been completed until the money is paid and the check has cleared the bank. In other words, don't count your chickens before they hatch.

## How To Handle Personal Property

Frequently in buying a house, the parties agree that certain appliances, curtains, drapes and other furnishings are included in the price. A Warranty Deed is used only for land and not for personal property. A Bill of Sale should be used for personal property, properly signed by the seller and his wife in favor of the buyer and his wife. An itemized list of the various personal property items should be included in the preliminary binder agreement.

## Proration Of Taxes And Insurance

Real estate taxes are invariably based on the calendar year. When the parties are ready to close their deal, the real estate broker or title company will prorate the taxes between the parties. The seller is responsible for taxes for the time he owned the property and the buyer is responsible for taxes for his period of ownership. If both parties desire, the fire insurance premiums can be prorated between the parties on the same fair basis. If the buyer wishes to purchase his own insurance through his insurance agent, that is his privilege and the seller has to cancel the old policy when the new owner takes over. Proration is really simple arithmetic and is fair to both sides and results in a series of credits and debits.

## Closing Statements

Every real estate transaction eventually reaches the stage where it is ready to be completed. If it is a cash deal, the seller wants his money and the buyer wants his deed and possession to the home or land. If it is an installment purchase to be paid out over a period of time, there are still down payments and credits and debits to be worked out, together with a real estate contract setting forth the terms agreed upon by the buyer and seller.

Usually, a title company acts as escrow agent and handles the money and papers that are involved. The title company employees are trained and experienced and are fair to the buyer as well as the seller. When the transaction is ready to be completed, the title company delivers a closing statement to the buyer and seller as well as real estate broker, if he is involved. The closing statement lists all of the charges and credits and debits. The charges for services rendered by the title company is usually split between buyer and seller.

The main function of an escrow agent is to be neutral in handling money and important papers for buyer and seller. In addition to giving the seller his portion of the money due him, the escrow agent also pays off other obligations, such as commission due the real estate broker, past due taxes and recording fees, etc. They even record the deed for the buyer which saves him a trip to the County Clerk's office. They are efficient and render a valuable service.

## Purchase Of Land In General

The preceding portion of this chapter discussed problems pertaining to the purchase or sale of a home. The same general rules of advice would also apply to the purchase of real estate or raw land. By raw land is meant land that is unimproved and produces no income. Farm land is not raw land because it has crops and does produce income. Any land that has a home or building on it is improved land.

Fortunes have been made and lost in land speculations. Puffing statements sometimes made by glib real estate salesmen to the effect that land can only go up in value, is simply not true. The value of land is subject to the same law of economics and supply and demand, as is the stock market.

Land promoters have been successfully prosecuted by federal authorities for using the mails to defraud and making false representations to the gullible public, some of whom buy land in another section of the country without ever having seen it. A typical advertisement showed a picture of the city of Phoenix, Arizona with statements of its phenomenal growth and increase in real estate values. However, the land that was being offered for sale was not located anywhere near Phoenix but was some 400 miles distant and had no water available. A buyer of this valueless acreage who lives in Connecticut, who says, "The acreage price is so cheap that even if I lose my $500, it was still a good deal" is impossible to protect from a fraudulent land promoter.

## Mortgages

Professional money lenders claim that the life of the average home mortgage is eight years, even though it was made originally for a much longer period of time. This does not mean that the mortgagor, the borrower, struck it rich and paid off ahead of schedule. It merely means that the mortgage was refinanced. The majority of home owners go through an entire lifetime with a mortgage of some type on the family home.

With inflation that has been going on for some years, the value of homes has increased, both old as well as new and as a result the amount of home mortgages has steadily increased. The borrowing of money for the purchase of a home, secured by a note and mortgage, is usually the largest financial transaction ever entered into by the average person. Some buyers ignore the important factors of interest rates and other charges and are only concerned with the amount of the monthly payment. This haphazard method of doing business can be very expensive and cost a lot of extra money over a period of years.

## Where To Borrow Mortgage Money?

Banks, savings and loan associations, and insurance companies are the most popular financial institutions for mortgage money. The vast difference in their charges can be as great as the interest they pay for deposits. Many banks are not interested in lending bank money for home mortgages that provide for payments for 20 or 25 years. These banks prefer to make short term commercial loans with a constant turnover of their money. However, many banks are lending agents for insurance companies and after the loan is completed in the banks' name, the note and mortgage is assigned to the insurance company that is providing the money. Then the banks continue to collect the monthly payments for the insurance company which is called "servicing the mortgage."

More home mortgages are made by savings and loan associations than by any other financial institution. The main reason being that they are better geared to serve the mortgage borrower and their depositors leave their money for long periods of time.

Some insurance companies have gone in for home mortgage loans in a big way, whereas other insurance companies prefer to make large commercial mortgage loans for apartment houses, shopping centers, and other commercial structures.

## How Much Interest?

The important thing to remember is that lending institutions are competitive and vary in their charges. Don't go to the first one and arrange to borrow your mortgage money. Shop around and make the best deal you can. If you think that a variation of one percent interest charge is not very important, you are in for a rude awakening. For a $25,000 mortgage payable over a period of 25 years, a difference of one percent in interest can amount to much more than a thousand dollars.

In addition to normal interest charges, many financial institutions have added a variety of other charges, some with fancy names. A charge for appraising the value of a prospective borrower's home is in line. So is a reasonable charge for obtaining a detailed credit report on the borrower. Sometimes, it becomes necessary to hire a surveyor to make a plot plan of the house on the lot or a survey of the land to be pledged, and this charge is a proper one.

Banks and savings and loan institutions have discovered a new source of income. It is called "points" or a fee that is charged to initiate the mortgage loan. Each point is the same as one percentage point of interest. A one point charge on a $25,000 mortgage means a $250 charge. Two points would mean $500 and so forth. It is merely a fancy name for an additional charge and if you can find a lending institution that does not charge any points or initiation fees, you are that much ahead of the game. During periods when money is tight, lending institutions are not hungry for customers and take advantage of the situation. When you are ready to buy a home on the installment plan, the cost of borrowing your mortgage money should be given serious consideration.

## Open End Borrowing

Some lending institutions offer "open end borrowing" features to good customers that pay promptly. This means that if you borrowed $25,000 on your mortgage and have paid off $5,000 and now owe a $20,000 balance, you are privileged to borrow any sum up to the original amount, under the same terms and conditions.

## Penalty For Lump Sum Payoff

Beware of the lending institution that makes a penalty charge for the privilege of paying off your mortgage balance ahead of schedule. In addition to asking this important question, you are privileged to examine the printed mortgage form to read what it says about paying two or more payments at anytime, or paying off the entire remaining mortgage balance without penalty. Reputable lending institutions make a normal profit on regular charges and don't gouge a customer with this additional charge. Unfortunately, some mortgage borrowers never bother to inquire and wake up too late and then are compelled to pay the penalty when an incoming buyer wants to refinance the mortgage elsewhere.

A few insurance companies vary the pre-penalty payment charge by providing that the mortgage borrower is privileged to pay off no more than 20 percent per year, without penalty. This means a 5 year payoff without penalty. The original mortgage might have been for many more years.

## Why A Note And Mortgage?

A mortgage is a legal instrument that is used to make property security for the payment of a loan. A promissory note is a separate legal instrument that is used as evidence of the obligation. The mortgage instrument is recorded and placed of record. The note is not recorded and is held by the mortgagee, the money lender, until it is paid. The note marked paid in full is then given to the mortgagor, the borrower, and the mortgage is released.

## Real Estate Contract Or A Mortgage?

If the house seller owns his home clear with no mortgage, he can permit the buyer to purchase under a real estate contract or under a note and mortgage. There is a technical difference between the two that occurs only in the event of default in payment by the buyer. For all practical purposes, the result is the same if the buyer pays as agreed. Under a real estate contract, the important paper is the warranty deed that is placed in escrow, waiting for the buyer to pay the agreed sum of money before he gets his deed. In the case of the note and mortgage, the buyer gets his warranty deed at the beginning and issues his note and mortgage in favor of the seller, as security for the obligation.

If a buyer fails to pay as agreed under a real estate contract, the seller is required to give him notice in writing, usually 30 days, before attempting to oust the buyer from possession. The buyer can cure this defect by making the delinquent payment, one or more, before the 30 day notice period has expired.

Under a note and mortgage, if the buyer fails to pay as agreed, the mortgagee can file a lawsuit for foreclosure and the real estate mortgage note provides for reasonable attorney fees that will normally be assessed against the delinquent mortgagor.

### Foreclosures And Deficiency Judgments

Most financial institutions that lend money on a home mortgage will bend over backwards to avoid filing a foreclosure lawsuit against the delinquent mortgage borrower. If the borrower is unable to pay as agreed, he should promptly notify his creditor and talk to them in person. If he explains his problems openly and honestly, they will work with him to every reasonable extent. If there is need and if it will help to solve his problems, they are privileged to permit him to pay interest only for some months to help out. In dire cases, the customer can be granted a moratorium, which means no payments at all for a given period of time.

If the borrower wants to give up the house voluntarily and if the mortgage company thinks they can resell the house and break even on the loan, they will accept a quitclaim deed from the borrower and release him from any further liability.

If the mortgage company thinks they cannot collect all of their money from a sale of the mortgaged home, they are privileged to file a lawsuit to foreclose and under the terms of the mortgage, the house will later be sold at public auction to the highest bidder. Usually, the only bidder present is the mortgage company representative and their attorney and they buy the house for a lesser sum than is due. They are then awarded a deficiency judgment against the borrower. Collecting the deficiency judgment is not easy because the borrower is usually not in good financial shape. If he were, he wouldn't have financial problems and be unable to pay as agreed.

## Impounds

Impounds are the monthly payments that are made by the mortgage borrower to the lending institution to apply on his annual bill for fire insurance and real estate taxes. Many borrowers like this arrangement because instead of receiving a staggering bill at the end of the year for insurance premiums and taxes, he has already accumulated the money during his 12 previous monthly impound payments. It is true the mortgage company gets the free use of this money during the year, however, they keep the records and pay the taxes and fire insurance premiums as a service to their customer.

# LANDLORDS AND LEASES

Printed form leases refer to landlords as Lessors and to tenants as Lessees. The relation of landlord and tenant is created by contract, oral or written. A guest, boarder, or lodger is not a tenant. A tenant has the exclusive legal possession of the premises and is responsible for its care and condition. A lodger has a right to the use of the premises, but the landlord retains control.

*Do You Need A Lawyer?*

No, there is no law that makes it mandatory for a lawyer to prepare a lease. If the landlord and tenant involved, think they are knowledgeable enough and have the ability to do so, they can buy a form lease at a stationery story and fill in the blank spaces. Whether they are wise in acting as their own attorney is something else. Most business men have learned from experience that they are money ahead to have their leases prepared or checked by their attorney.

I have seen people obtain someone else's old lease and they decide to copy and adapt the essential features to their own lease. Frequently, this copying routine boomerangs and the dispute winds up in a courtroom and the legal expense is greater than it would have been if a competent attorney had been employed initially.

*Can You Break A Lease?*

A lease is a contract. It can be broken only for good and valid reasons.

A valid reason for breaking a lease could be material misrepresentations by the landlord to the serious detriment of the tenant. Destruction of the leased building by fire or other causes and the landlord refuses to rebuild promptly, is another example.

An actual example occurred to one of my clients who had a long term lease for his autobody painting and repairing business. The electrical wiring system in the building was in bad shape and the city building inspector redflagged the building, which meant it was unsafe for occupancy unless repaired. My client then requested that the landlord make the necessary repairs. The landlord refused and my client broke his lease and moved out. Although the problem was never presented to any court, I am confident that the judge would have ruled that the tenant had good reason to break the lease.

It is simple for a tenant to move out in violation of the terms of his lease but the important question is the extent of his legal liability if the landlord should file suit for breaking his lease. Sometimes, the tenant will gamble and move out and the landlord will decide not to pursue his legal remedies. This happens frequently on apartment leases where the apartment is furnished and the tenant moves out under the cover of darkness. Legally, the tenant is in the wrong but the landlord decides that it isn't worth the time, money and effort to file suit against the transient tenant who moved out by loading up his car with his personal belongings.

### Should A Lease Be In Writing?

Yes, it is good business to put the terms of any business agreement in writing. The laws of many states provide that any lease for over one year must be in writing to be valid. Many disputes between landlords and tenants could be avoided if the terms of their lease are in writing, with all important provisions spelled out in detail. An oral lease for less than one year is valid and binding on the parties, however, when a dispute arises the landlord claims one thing and the tenant another and the judge has to be a "Solomon" to decide the case.

An unusual situation arose with a commercial lease to a national chain store organization in connection with a location in a shopping center. Usually, most written leases provide for the period of years and the amount of rent, together with other routine terms. Then, if the location did not work out well for the large chain store, they were privileged to close the store and pay the agreed rent for the remaining portion of the lease. This astute landlord decided that the closing of any store in his shopping center would adversely affect the business welfare of all of his other tenants. The landlord then presented this unusual lease that provided that no tenant may close their store and pay the agreed rental but were obligated to keep their store open for the period of time provided in the lease. This provision was novel and unique but it was perfectly legal and binding.

## Can Fraud Affect A Lease?

Yes, if one of the parties makes fraudulent representations of consequence, the innocent party can declare the lease void. A Georgia court held: "A tenant's misrepresentations as to the parentage of her children and her failure to report the birth of another illegitimate child authorized the landlord to cancel the lease." In another case, the landlord of a home knew that it had secret defects and conditions rendering it unfit for a residence, and the court ruled that the tenant was justified in breaking the lease and leaving the home. The defrauded party must act promptly when he discovers the defects and rescinds his contract because if he "sleeps on his rights," he forfeits his claim to fraud. To rescind is to cancel.

## Can A Lease Be Illegal Or Immoral?

In cases where the landlord has knowledge that the use of the premises by the tenant involves illegal or immoral activity, the landlord cannot collect his rent. An English court ruled: "Where a landlord let a flat to a woman whom he knew to be the mistress of a certain man, the landlord supposing that the rent would be paid with the man's money and would come through her being a kept woman, and the landlord knew the man went constantly to the flat to visit her, the landlord could not recover the rent, since the flat was let for an immoral purpose." Many American judges have ruled that the mere knowledge on the landlord's part that the tenant will use the premises for an unlawful purpose does not make him a participant. Some judges say: "The tenant may change his or her mind and use the leased premises for a lawful purpose." With these conflicting opinions, the reader can better understand why most experienced lawyers refuse to predict the outcome of the average disputed lawsuit.

The majority rule is that where the lease is executed with the knowledge and intent of the parties that the premises will be used for a gambling house, or the illegal sale of liquor, or operating a house of prostitution, then it is invalid and unenforceable.

## Unusual Exceptions

A person may occupy premises as a tenant and yet be an employee of the owner. There is no inconsistency in the relation of employer and employee with that of landlord and tenant.

An Indiana court ruled: "A Roman Catholic priest, in charge at the will of the bishop, and occupying a home belonging to the church, was a servant and not a tenant, and that his right of occupancy ceased with his services." This same ruling applied to ministers of other denominations who occupy the parsonage as an incident to their services.

In addition to members of the clergy, other persons are furnished with living quarters in connection with their employment. Logging camps and mining in remote areas, frequently result in employees being furnished with their living quarters by the employer. This is usually one of the fringe benefits included in their employment contract. When the employment terminates, the living quarters terminate at the same time.

Internal Revenue Service has ruled that for income tax purposes, the rental value of the home furnished by the employer, is taxable income just as is the base salary.

### A Lease For How Long?

In the absence of any state law to the contrary, a lease may be made for one day or ninety-nine years or even nine hundred and ninety-nine years. Leases for a thousand years stand upon the same footing as those for one year. A Delaware court upheld the validity of a lease for two thousand years.

Some states have laws that restrict the length of a lease of agricultural lands to ten or twelve years. One case held that a lease of farming land for mining purposes is not within the time restriction that applies to an agricultural lease.

### When Does A Lease Terminate?

Under normal conditions, a lease terminates at the time provided in the contract. Death of the tenant or landlord before the expiration date does not terminate the lease. The estate of the dead person would be responsible for the rent or other provisions of the contract.

In the average lease that provides for monthly rental payments where the tenant stays on with the knowledge and approval of the landlord, the tenancy is deemed to be from month to month. Under these conditions, the liability of the tenant can be terminated by the tenant giving one month's notice to the landlord and the same holds true in reverse. The effective date of the notice depends upon the rental period. If you rent by the month, the termination notice would start thirty days from your next rent due date. For example, if the landlord wants you to vacate your rented home or apartment that you rent beginning the first day of each month, his notice would be effective thirty days after the next rent payment falls due. He cannot give you notice on the second of the month to vacate that same month because you are entitled to a full thirty days' notice. The requirement of notice is the same for the tenant as it is for the landlord.

## Are Options Good?

Options that are granted to the tenant are good for him, provided they are clear and meaningful. A provision in a lease that provides for an option to the tenant to "renew the lease for the same period of time at terms to be agreed upon between the parties" is absolutely meaningless. It really gives the tenant no protection and might just as well not have been included. If the original lease called for rent of $250 per month, and the tenant wants to renew at $250 per month and the landlord says he wants $500 per month, the option had no teeth in it and did the tenant no good.

If the same tenant wanted protection, the option should have provided "renew the lease for the same period of time under the *same terms and conditions* as contained in the original leasehold period." Even if the lease provided that the option for renewal was granted to the tenant at a rental "to be determined by an appraisal committee of the local board of realtors" it would provide some protection to the tenant against any unreasonable demands on the part of the landlord.

The same reasoning applies to options granted to the tenant to purchase the property under lease "at a price to be agreed upon by the parties." From the viewpoint of the tenant, this option gives him no protection against any unreasonable price set by the landlord. If the option named an agreed price, the tenant would have the privilege of exercising or ignoring the option. I have always disliked the granting of any options, unless the recipient, usually the tenant, was paying a reasonable sum of money for the privileges obtained under the option. An option in a lease gives the tenant a free ride with no obligation on his part to exercise the option.

For example, when an oil company is interested in buying or leasing a commercial location for a gasoline station, they may want an option for a fixed period of time but they are willing to pay a reasonable sum of money for the privilege of tying up the land. During the option period, the optionor or land owner may not sell or lease to another. The recipient or optionee is paying for the rights obtained under the option. If the company does not exercise the option, then the landowner is entitled to keep the option money and sell or lease to another.

## Should A Lease Be Recorded?

For an ordinary house or apartment lease there is no need to have the instrument recorded. In the case of important commercial leases where large sums of money are involved, it is considered desirable to have the pertinent information recorded. In order to withhold the confidential information that may be contained in a lease, mainly the amount of monthly rental paid or the time factor, etc., the pertinent details are deleted from the recording notice. For example, the Woolworth Company might decide to record a notice that they are leasing their location at 400 Central Avenue from John Jones and Mary Jones, his wife, and omit all other detailed information. The recording serves as notice to the world of the existence of a lease. A recording is accomplished by taking the instrument or a substitute to the County Clerk where the property is located and where it is filed for record. A search of the County Clerk's official records would reveal the contents of the document that was recorded or placed on record.

## Exclusive Mercantile Rights

In many modern shopping centers, the granting of exclusive rights to conduct a certain type of business is quite common and binding on the landlord. This situation occurs when the tenants of a shopping center each handle their own category of merchandise and the landlord represents there will be no duplication of such exclusive rights. A Mississippi judge ruled: "A landlord is under an implied obligation not to conduct a supermarket on his adjoining property which competes with the tenant's business." This identical restriction can also apply to the tenant.

## What About Attorney's Fees?

It is not uncommon for parties to a lease to make provisions for the allowance of reasonable attorneys' fees in the event of a default.

An award of attorneys' fees may go to the landlord or to the tenant, depending upon who was found to be at fault. If the lease is silent in regards to any award of attorneys' fees they may not be assessed. Some leases state that if the tenant does not pay as agreed and the landlord hires an attorney, then the tenant is obligated to pay reasonable attorneys' fees. This provision ought to be worded to protect both sides. The judge determines the amount of a reasonable attorney fee award.

## Who Furnishes Utilities?

What does the lease provide? A landlord may agree with a tenant to assume the payment of charges for water, gas, or electricity furnished upon the premises. Sometimes, there is local custom as to which party pays for which utility. In order to avoid any arguments, the lease should spell out who pays for what.

## Tenant's Rights

If the tenant pays his rent as agreed, he is entitled to use the premises as if he were the absolute owner for all practical purposes for the term granted. The landlord has no authority to enter or disturb the tenant in any manner or interfere with his rights. The law says that a lease is a grant of an interest in the land and is not a mere license.

Most printed form leases give the landlord the right to enter and make repairs as are necessary to prevent waste. The printed form leases favor the landlord over the tenant to the extent of about ninety percent.

If the tenant gives notice to his landlord that he is terminating his tenancy, then the landlord has a right to show the premises to prospective tenants, provided the right is exercised in a reasonable manner. This includes the landlord's right to place a "for rent" sign on the property.

## Keeping Animals

A provision in a lease forbidding the keeping of animals is not unreasonable. If the lease prohibits the keeping of an animal, violation by the tenant entitles the landlord to judgment, on unlawful detainer. Unlawful detainer is legal jargon for kicking the tenant out. In an Illinois case, the landlord permitted the tenants to keep their dog in his leased premises for five years and accepted the rent without objection. Then the landlord had a change of heart and sued to oust them. The judge ruled that the problem should have been submitted to the jury and any jury would vote for the dog-owning tenants under those facts.

### Who Pays For Insurance?

Usually, the landlord pays for fire insurance on his building and the tenant pays for whatever insurance coverage he wants on his personal property. In order to answer the question intelligently, one has to read the written lease contract between the parties. The parties may agree on anything that they wish, pertaining to insurance or anything else.

### Who Pays For Taxes?

If the lease does not specify details regarding the payment of taxes, the parties are on their own. The customary rule is that the landlord pays the land tax on his building and real estate and the tenant pays the personal property tax for his items.

Some landlords that build a special commercial building for use of the tenant have their lease provide that the landlord will pay the tax for his bare land only and the tenant pays that portion of the tax assessed for the building as well as the contents. It is up to the parties involved to agree on all details and once agreed upon, all of the conditions should be in writing and spelled out so that there will be no future misunderstanding.

### Who Provides Public Liability Insurance?

The purpose of public liability insurance is to protect against a claim of a person who is injured or killed while on the leased premises. In retail stores, these accidents are commonly referred to as "slip and fall" cases. The injured person will usually file a lawsuit against the tenant as well as the landlord. As a result, both the tenant and the landlord find it desirable to protect themselves by having coverage for this eventuality. The cost of public liability insurance is not expensive. The amount should be determined by your insurance advisor. Even if the customer was at fault, it is expensive to defend a lawsuit and prove that you were not negligent and therefore not legally responsible for the person's injuries.

In the case of a leased home or apartment, the usual "home owners policy" should include public liability coverage.

## Can The Tenant Or Landlord Assign Or Sublet The Lease?

Unless it is prohibited by the lease, a tenant may assign or sublet his premises to another, however, the original tenant remains primarily liable under the lease. If the new subtenant does not pay as agreed, the original tenant is still responsible and liable to the landlord. Under this arrangement, the landlord loses none of his rights and actually has gained another party, namely the sublessee. The only way the original tenant can get off the "hook" as regards his liability under the lease, is to get the landlord to agree in writing to accept the new subtenant as a substitute for the tenant. If the landlord thinks the incoming subtenant is as good financially or better than the original tenant, he may agree to the substitution and then the future rent payments are up to the landlord and subtenant.

The landlord can always assign his interest in the lease to an outsider without obtaining the permission of the tenant. The reason being is that the tenant is not harmed and it does not matter to him who receives the monthly rent payment. The incoming party who is called the assignee, takes the lease under all of its terms and conditions. The one who assigns is called the "assignor." For example, if the original lease gave the tenant an option for renewal of the lease, this option is still binding on the incoming assignee. The new assignee cannot say: "I was not a party to the option and I refuse to honor its terms." To assign a lease means to transfer all of your right, title and interest involved. If the lease says that the tenant may not assign or sublet, then it is binding upon the tenant.

## Percentage Leases

Percentage leases only occur in connection with commercial leases for the operation of a place of business. There are different types of percentage leases and one must turn to the lease to determine the rights and liabilities of the tenant and landlord. The reasoning behind a percentage lease is that if the landlord's location works out well for the tenant, the landlord is entitled to share a portion of his good fortune.

The most popular percentage lease provides for a low guaranteed amount as a minimum and then a percentage of the gross receipts over and above a certain sum. For example, a percentage lease of this type could say: "The agreed monthly rent is $500 per month, plus three percent of the gross receipts in excess of $10,000 per month." Using this example, if the monthly gross receipts were $9,500, the tenant would only owe the base rent of $500. If during the next month, the gross receipts totalled $15,000, the tenant would owe the base rent of $500 plus 3 percent of the additional $5,000 or $150.

Another type of percentage lease that is popular for supermarkets is a straight percentage lease. The tenant and landlord agree under the terms of the lease that the monthly rent shall be a certain percentage of every dollar taken in, which is a simple definition of gross receipts. If the tenant does well, the landlord shares in the results. If the tenant does poorly, the landlord shares the burden.

## Landlord's Lien

Under the laws of most states, if the tenant does not pay the rent as agreed, the landlord has a lien on all of the personal belongings of the tenant that are located in the leased premises. There is a variance between the states, but the overall effect is the same. In some states, the landlord's lien is automatic. In other states, the landlord is required to give written notice to the tenant advising that the landlord is asserting his lien for nonpayment of rent and instructing the tenant not to move his personal belongings under penalty of law. This is called a statutory lien because it is created by the legislative acts of the state. Payment of the past due rent by the tenant naturally dissolves any lien asserted by the landlord. The landlord's lien is an effective tool afforded the landlord in collecting his rent from a past due tenant. In a similar vein, many states have laws making it a criminal offense to move out of a hotel or motel without paying your bill.

## Who Pays For Repairs?

If the parties use the usual form type of lease, it favors the landlord and provides that the landlord is responsible for the roof and tenant is responsible for all other repairs. If the tenant wants other provisions for repairs, then the lease ought to be prepared by an attorney and include arrangements agreed to by the parties.

Practically all leases provide that at the end of the leasehold period, the tenant agrees to return the premises to the landlord in the same condition that he received it, reasonable wear and tear excepted.

Aside from all of the technical provisions of a lease, I have always been concerned with the attitude of the landlord. If the landlord is a fair and reasonable person and if the tenant is a fair and reasonable person, the lease presents no problem. If the landlord is the other type, every T ought to be crossed and every I dotted.

*Evicting A Tenant*

It is not easy to evict a tenant and some knowledgeable tenants can give the landlord fits while he is trying to get them out. The usual reason for eviction is the failure to pay rent on the part of the tenant.

The laws of most states provide that if a tenant fails to pay his monthly rent as provided in the lease or agreed upon verbally, the landlord must serve him with a notice, entitled: "Notice to pay past-due rent or to quit." After the required waiting period of three to five days, the landlord may then file a lawsuit against the tenant, entitled: "Unlawful detainer." Some tenants are past masters in the use of delaying tactics. If a member of the household is ill, he obtains a doctor's certificate advising that the patient's ill health makes it impossible for him to be moved and the delay game is on its way. They disqualify the judge designated on the grounds that he is prejudiced and cannot fairly decide the disputed lawsuit. This means that a substitute judge has to be appointed and meanwhile the delay of days are going into weeks. Eventually the trial is held and of course, the delinquent tenant has no valid excuse for failure to pay the agreed rent. The judge awards a judgment in favor of the landlord and finally, after a long delay, the tenant moves out in the dead of night. By this time, the landlord is so happy to get rid of the undesirable tenant, that he usually is willing to forget his lost rent money. His judgment is a valid one but collecting from this type of debtor is not a simple task.

During a depression many years ago, an apartment tenant became friendly with the managers of the apartment house. The tenant was out of work and was eight months behind in his rent. The friendly manager offered to drive him around town to locate another apartment and his offer included forgiveness for the back rent. Whereupon the delinquent tenant became very indignant and refused the offer and said: "I wouldn't think of leaving my apartment owing you money."

# SEX AND THE LAW

*Rape*

SEX is the most basic force in every human being. People are as preoccupied with their sexual desires as they are with food and sleep. The impulsive need for sexual intercourse was as strong in prehistoric man as it is for people in modern life today. The desire and need for sex is as powerful in women as it is in men. Some people are embarrassed to talk about sex but they really should not be; sex is not dirty and can be beautiful. The beauty or ugliness of sex is strictly in the mind of each individual.

Rape is the most uncivilized form of sexual assault on a female.

The rules of law governing rape; statutory rape; assault with intent to commit rape; and attempt to commit rape; are the same as those related to all other crimes. In prosecutions for crime, the accused is entitled to a public trial. The courts are not in harmony as to what constitutes a public trial. Some judges have ruled that the testimony of the female victim, who is called the prosecutrix, is immoral, shocking and obscene, and they exclude all spectators other than the defendant, the attorneys, witnesses and court officials. This ruling is unconstitutional in that it violates the defendant's right to a public trial. More important, the attorney for the defendant wants to embarrass the prosecutrix by forcing her to answer pertinent questions in the presence of courtroom spectators. Examples might be, "Did he insert his penis into your vagina?" "Were you a virgin?" "What, if anything, did you do by way of resisting?" and similar. The embarrassment of this type of cross-examination frequently is the reason for a rape victim and her family to drop criminal charges.

## What Is Rape?

Rape is unlawful sexual intercourse by a male with a female by force and without her consent. Penetration is necessary to complete the crime of rape. The offense is committed if the male organ enters the labia of the female organ. Rupture of the hymen is not necessary, nor is laceration of the vagina. The essence of the crime is the injury to the person and the outrage to the feelings of the victim.

### Is Force Necessary?

Yes, force is a necessary ingredient in the crime of rape. The amount of force can vary with different situations. Force can be varied as when the man plies the woman with intoxicating liquor or takes advantage of her while she is asleep. The female must resist to the best of her ability. She is equipped to interpose most effective obstacles by means of her hands and legs and kicking and squirming and the use of her pelvic muscles. The female must resist the consummation of the act, and must persist until the offense is consummated.

The sexual act must be committed against the will of the woman, and without her consent, or it will not be rape. Consent given at any time prior to penetration defeats the charge of rape.

### Is Submission Equal To Consent?

Yes, consent may be express or implied. In the ordinary case, when the woman is awake, of mature years, of sound mind, and not in fear, a failure to oppose the sexual act constitutes consent. Although a woman objects verbally to the act of intercourse, yet if by her conduct she consents to it, it is not rape.

### Can A Prostitute Be Raped?

Yes, a prostitute has a legal right to be protected from a rapist.

### Is Rape A Serious Offense?

Yes, the crime of rape is a very serious offense and in some states, the punishment provided by law is close to murder. Rape is the easiest offense for a female to charge a male with and the most difficult for the male to disprove. Usually, the male and female are alone and eye witnesses are not available. The female lifts her skirt and lowers her panties and shouts "RAPE." Only the two persons involved know the entire truth as to what transpired between them earlier. The moral is: "Do not enter without permission."

### Can There Be A Female Rapist?

Yes and no. Females have been found guilty of rape, by virtue of being an accessory to the man who is committing the crime. This occurs where the female defendant holds the victim and assists her male companion to accomplish sexual intercourse. Females have been known to take advantage of certain males but their aggressive actions do not constitute rape.

### Statutory Rape

The laws of all of the states provide that female under a certain age may not legally give her consent to sexual intercourse, because her consent is the same as "no consent." The term "jail bait" has been used for generations by males, as applied to young girls who are under the legal age of consent. Every male in his right mind should "run" from any offer or chance of sexual intercourse with a female under the legal age of consent. The fact that the girl "looked old enough" does not protect the defendant because her actual age is the controlling factor. The only proof required in the court trial is that the man's penis penetrated the vagina of the underage girl and force or consent is not a factor. The law seeks to protect young girls and having sexual intercourse with them can result in heavy punishment. The punishment for statutory rape is more severe than ordinary rape.

The age of the young female who may not legally consent to sexual intercourse varies from ten to eighteen years. Some states use the age of puberty, or twelve years, as the controlling age. Other state's laws provide that the young female is protected only if she still retains her virginal chastity.

### Assault With Intent To Commit Rape

An assault and an intent to commit rape are both essential elements for the crime of assault with intent to commit rape. The mere existence of intent without perpetration of an assault is not sufficient. Touching the hand of a sleeping woman to awaken her to solicit sexual intercourse is not an assault with intent to commit rape. A man who gets a woman drunk so that she has no power of opposing sexual intercourse, and of then having sexual intercourse with her, is guilty of assault with intent to commit rape.

### Attempt To Rape

An attempt to rape is distinct from rape or an assault with intent to rape. A specific intent to rape is an absolutely essential element to an attempt to rape, and must accompany the means used to effect the crime.

### Can A Husband Rape His Wife?

No, a husband cannot be guilty of an actual rape, or of an assault with intent to rape his wife by reason of having sexual intercourse with her forcibly and against her will. A wife gives her matrimonial consent when she enters into the marriage contract and she cannot retract.

### Can A Boy Under 14 Commit Rape?

The laws of different states vary in this regard. In some, the rule prevails that a boy under fourteen years of age is conclusively presumed to be incapable of committing rape. In other jurisdictions, this presumption is debatable.

### Can Rape Be Committed On A Female Of Any Age?

Yes, puberty in the female is not a necessary element.

### Is Impotency A Defense To Rape?

Yes, impotency is a defense to a charge of rape. However, this defense is not available to males over fourteen charged with assault with intent to commit rape. The essence of the crime is the violence to the person and feelings of the female.

### What About A Drunk And Rape?

Voluntary intoxication is no defense to a criminal act. Drunkenness, if severe enough, may render a man incapable of sexual intercourse. Slight intoxication often increases the passion and desire for sexual intercourse which lead to rape.

### Can A Woman Sue Her Rapist?

Yes, the criminal prosecution of a rapist does not preclude the female victim from suing him for damages. In addition to the rights of the victim, her husband may bring a separate lawsuit against the rapist for damages for the rape of his wife.

### What About Rape Resulting In Pregnancy?

Even though the odds would appear to be against it happening, a few unfortunate females have become pregnant as a result of being raped. Some years ago, Illinois law provided that the female victim of rape resulting in pregnancy was not privileged to have a legal abortion. Modern abortion laws in many states would solve this problem today.

### Adultery

Any married person who has sexual intercourse with one who is not his or her spouse is guilty of adultery. The laws of each state vary greatly and the reader who is concerned should learn the laws of his particular state. Some states follow the rule that a married man is not guilty of adultery by reason of sexual intercourse with an unmarried woman. When the state law does not expressly mention single persons of either sex, it has been held that a single person, male or female, who has intercourse with a married person of the opposite sex is not guilty of adultery. Other states have enacted laws declaring that a single person who has sexual intercourse with a married person is guilty of adultery. To add to the confusion, some state laws are directed only against married men who have illicit sexual intercourse with married women. In other states, only a married person can commit the offense, and the act of intercourse between a married person and an unmarried person is adultery in the former and fornication in the latter.

Adultery is made a crime in most states by statutes which make it a felony and in some cases a misdemeanor.

### Divorced Persons And Adultery

A valid divorce dissolves the marital ties of both husband and wife and for purposes of sexual intercourse, they have the same rights as single persons.

### Fornication Or Copulation

Fornication is sexual intercourse between two unmarried persons, male and female. Fornication and copulation are synonymous. A few states attempt to prosecute offenders, however, most state authorities are not concerned unless the parties become a public nuisance by their conduct. In some states fornication requires a continuous relationship and the law is not concerned with the "overnight stand."

During puritanical periods years ago state legislators felt

obligated to conserve the public morals "by the prevention of indecent and evil examples tending to debase and demoralize society and degrade the institution of marriage." The object of these old-fashioned laws was "to prohibit the public scandal and disgrace of the living together of persons of opposite sex in a notorious illicit intimacy which outrages public decency." This was called "Illicit Cohabitation" and is now known as "Shacking Up."

## Seduction

Seduction is the offense of a man who induces a woman to surrender her chastity, usually on promise of a future marriage. Comedians have rephrased this definition by saying: "I'll gladly marry you tomorrow for a honeymoon tonight." When enticement is absent and both participants have engaged in intercourse voluntarily for the purpose of gratifying their physical desires, seduction is not committed. Most states have laws making seduction a criminal offense. The requirement that the female be a virgin eliminates many seduction claims. A Washington court said: "A chaste female is one who has never had sexual intercourse, who yet retains her virginity; a virtuous female is one who has not had sexual intercourse unlawfully."

## Incest

Incest consists of sexual intercourse or marriage between persons who cannot be lawfully married because of blood relationship. It is a serious criminal offense in all of the states. Sexual intercourse between father and daughter, mother and son, uncle and niece, grandfather and granddaughter, and, in many states, between first cousins, is punishable as incest. Relations of the half blood, as well as the whole blood, are generally included under statutes using the word "brother" or "sister." Furthermore, the statutes do not distinguish between legitimate and illegitimate relationships. An adopted daughter is not a daughter within the statute against incest.

Consanguinity is relationship by blood, and affinity that by marriage. A husband is related by affinity to his wife's brother, but not to that brother's wife, and sexual intercourse between them is not incest. Stepparents are related by affinity to their stepchildren, and sexual intercourse between them is incestuous under statutes including relationship by affinity. If the natural mother of a stepdaughter dies and the stepfather then starts to have sexual intercourse with his stepdaughter, it is not incest.

## Miscegenation

Miscegenation is the intermarrying, cohabiting, or interbreeding of persons of different races. As a criminal offense, it is entirely statutory. Recent rulings of the United States Supreme Court have nullified the laws of states who prohibited a person of one race from marrying a person of another. Now, people are free to marry anyone they desire and individual states are powerless to do anything about it. Early miscegenation laws provided that only members of the white race were liable to punishment for the offense.

## Abortion

Abortion statutes penalize the unjustified causing of a miscarriage, or the administering of drugs or the use of instruments for that purpose. The terms "abortion" and "miscarriage" are used synonymously by the law to describe the expulsion of the fetus. The terms in themselves do not connote illegality, since it is the circumstances under which the act occurs which determines its legality.

Some of the states have already enacted legislation legalizing abortions and many of the old laws are now archaic and unenforceable. The pregnant woman now controls her own fate and she can bear her child or abort her pregnancy. She no longer has to patronize some out of town quack doctor or person who operated outside of the pale of the law and charged accordingly. The new laws permitting legal abortions are safe, quick and inexpensive. Happily, it put all abortionists out of business.

Birth control pills and devices which prevent the female from becoming pregnant have materially reduced the need for abortions. The law says that pregnancy exists from the moment of conception until the delivery of the child.

## Sodomy

Sodomy is sexual intercourse of human beings in other than the natural manner. When defined so as to include "buggery," it extends to the intercourse of a man or a woman with an animal. "Buggery" consists in the intercourse by a human being with an animal. Many state statutes designate the offense as "the crime against nature," "the bestial crime against nature," "the infamous crime against nature," "unnatural intercourse," and similar. In many states, sodomy is a felony.

The offense of sodomy requires the penetration by the male sex organ. Because of the requirement of penetration, sodomy cannot be committed by two women. Some courts hold that sodomy cannot be committed by penetration in the mouth but must be rectal. When sodomy is so defined as to include buggery, it has been held that it is immaterial whether the penetration of the animal was vaginal or anal.

## Prostitution

Prostitution is the indiscriminate offering by a woman to engage in sexual intercourse for money. Illicit intercourse with one man does not make the female a prostitute. Normally, this type of woman is called "a kept woman." The terms "nightwalker" and "streetwalker" mean a prostitute who solicits men on the street. Any female, including a married woman, may be guilty of being a prostitute. In lieu of prohibiting prostitution, it is in the power of a state or city to regulate such activity.

## Disorderly House

This name has nothing to with the appearance or cleanliness of a home. It is also known as "a house of ill fame or repute." Old laws used to call it a house which is kept for the purpose of public resort for thieves, drunkards, prostitutes, or other idle and vicious people. An Iowa court ruled: "Bawdyhouse" and "house of ill fame" are synonymous terms, having no reference to the form of the house, but denoting the fact of promiscuous illicit sexual intercourse thereat." Both male and female may be guilty of the offense of keeping a disorderly house.

## Pandering Or Pimping

Any act of exploiting the prostitution of a female is known as pandering or pimping and is prohibited by statute. The pimp is sometimes paid by the male customer but more often shares in the money received by the prostitute. In some states the pandering statute applies only to men. The prostitute is honest about her services rendered but the pimp is the lowest of the low. Pandering is frequently made a felony.

## Can A Husband Place His Wife In A House Of Prostitution?

Even though a few husbands might like to do so, the law says no. Statutes in many states make criminal the placing of one's wife in a house of prostitution. The crime is predicated upon a lawful marriage. The fact that the defendant's wife was a prostitute before marriage is no defense.

## What Is The Mann Act?

A number of years ago, a Congressman by the name of Mann sponsored a new federal law to stop white slave traffic and this law has been called "The Mann Act" as well as "Federal White Slave Traffic Act." It basically prohibited the interstate transportation of a female for immoral purposes. In order to evade the law, some men would require the woman riding in his car, to walk across the state line and then reenter his car so that he did not technically transport her across the state line. The federal authorities are only after the professionals and not the ordinary male who has a female companion for a weekend.

## Homosexuals

Certain males limit their sexual desires to one of their own sex. In other words, a homosexual is not interested sexually in a female. Many homosexuals refer to members of their own group as "the gay set." Even though they represent a minority as regards their sex habits, they argue vehemently that the majority is not automatically right. Recently, a group of homosexuals in San Francisco and New York protested illegal tactics used by police officers in violation of rights granted by the Constitution of the United States.

England has enacted modern legislation providing that two consenting adults, regardless of sex, are privileged to engage in any sexual activity that they wish, in the privacy of their bedroom.

## Lesbians

Lesbians are female homosexuals. They are interested in satisfying their sexual desires only with another female. Just as the homosexual is not interested in sexual intercourse with a female, a lesbian is not interested in any sexual activity with a male.

## Bisexuals

This group possesses peculiar sex habits in that they participate sexually with males and females. A male who is bisexual may have sexual intercourse with a female and then continue sexual activity with his fellow homosexual. The identical ability may be used by a lesbian who has sexual intercourse with a male and then returns to her lesbian companion.

A recent California lawsuit was filed by a wife against her husband because he changed his sex by surgery from male to female, against her will and she is asking for money damages for the loss of her sex life. It will be interesting to learn what the courts do with this unusual and unique problem. My curbstone guess is that the wife will not prevail in her lawsuit for money damages. I would recommend a divorce and another husband that is all man.

## Birth Control

Experts have issued warnings that there are too many people and that unless "population explosion" is controlled, serious food shortages will face the world. Progress has been made by the use of birth control pills and a worthwhile non-profit organization, named "Planned Parenthood." As indicated by the name, Planned Parenthood, disseminates free information to women who are interested in avoiding unwanted pregnancies and planning the birth of wanted children. In addition to birth control pills, they recommend the use of intra-uterus devices, diaphragms, and pills for the male, etc.

## Obscenity

Obscenity means offensive to morality or chastity, indecent, or nasty. Various acts and forms of obscenity are also made criminal offenses by statute or ordinance. The statutes concerning obscenity are usually broadly worded so as to cover all possible methods of bringing the attention of decent persons to obscene papers, pictures, or articles. All the authorities agree that obscene matter are not protected by constitutional guarantees of free speech and press. It is difficult to define obscene matters.

## What Is The Roth Test?

Under the definition of obscenity in the Roth case, three elements must blend: it must be established that (1) the dominant theme of the

material taken as a whole appeals to prurient interest in sex; (2) the
material is patently offensive because it affronts contemporary
community standards relating to descriptions or representations of
sexual matters; and (3) the material is utterly without redeeming
social value. In the following cases the Roth test was consistently
recognized: The French film "The Lovers" was not obscene; a film
portraying illicit and perverted sexual relations was not obscene; the
book "Lady Chatterley's Lover" was not obscene; picture book of
nude women not obscene; the novel "Tropic of Cancer" was not
obscene; motion picture depicting act of male masturbation, fellatio,
oral copulation, voyeurism, nudity, sadism, and sodomy, was held to
be obscene; silent peepshow movies, without story, showing a naked
woman, simulating sexual intercourse were obscene; a book entitled
"The Sex Addicts" held not obscene; the motion picture "Garden of
Eden" depicting the experiences of non-nudists in a nudist colony was
not obscene; the book "Fanny Hill" was not obscene.

## Sex And Obscenity

Sex and obscenity are not synonymous. Obscene material deals
with sex in a manner appealing to prurient interest. The portrayal of
sex, in art, literature, and scientific works, for example, is not itself
sufficient reason to deny material the constitutional protection of
freedom of speech and press. The mere fact that adultery or other
sexually immoral relationships are portrayed approvingly cannot serve
as a reason for declaring a work obscene without running afoul of the
First Amendment. Nudity is not necessarily obscenity.

Opinion is divided as to whether the Roth test limits the meaning
of obscenity to "hard-core pornography." The United States Supreme
Court held that the book entitled "Tropic of Cancer" by Henry Miller
does not constitute hard-core pornography and thus is not obscene
within the meaning of the obscenity statute.

## Indecent Exposure

Indecent exposure is the intentional or negligent exposure of the
private parts of the person to public view. Such conduct is prohibited
on the basis that it tends to scandalize or to excite lascivious desires.
Under some statutes it is made a special offense to commit indecent
exposure before a child, whether male or female. A Michigan court
peculiarly ruled that an operator of a nudist camp who goes about

privately without clothes among both male and female members of the camp on his own property is guilty of violating a statute against indecent exposure.

## Dress

In some instances, statutes and ordinances relate to decency as regards wearing apparel or the lack of it. People can dress as they please and wear anything, so long as they do not offend public order and decency.

## Pictures and Art

Mere nudity in painting or sculpture is not obscenity.

# INSURANCE

Back in the tenth century, Portugal and Italy required every shipowner to contribute 2 percent of the profits of each voyage to a common fund to pay losses. The next step was that of insurance by payment of premiums. Contrary to general belief, it is not banks who control the wealth of the world but insurance companies.

Insurance policies are contracts between the insured and the insurance company. Most insurance contracts agree to indemnify the insured against a loss. Indemnify means to reimburse or guaranty a loss. Examples could be a fire insurance policy; real estate title insurance; fidelity bonds for employees; and other insurance contracts offering protection in the event of a loss.

Life insurance policies fall into a separate category because some have investment features. A life insurance policy is a contract to pay the beneficiary a certain sum of money when the insured dies. Some people argue that the name "life insurance" is wrong and that the correct name is "death insurance." No money is paid by the insurance company during the insured's lifetime. To many people, the word "death" is distasteful and unpleasant and as a result it is easier for an insurance agent to sell a policy called life insurance for the protection of the insured's family.

## Workmen's Compensation Insurance

All states have enacted laws for the protection of an employee who is injured or killed while on the job. There is variance between the various states as to many facets of protection. Some states have laws requiring workmen's compensation insurance for every employer of three or more persons. The amount of money paid to an employee who is injured or killed on the job will vary greatly in different states. The state agency who handles claims of injured employees is sometimes called "Industrial Accident Commission" and in other states, the claims are handled by regular courts and judges.

Some large employers offer various fringe benefits to their

employees in the form of group health, hospitalization, and life insurance. These fringe benefits have nothing to do with the required protection for the employee who is injured or killed while on the job.

The cost of workmen's compensation insurance falls on the employer and he may not bill the employee for any part of the bill. Some employers offer group insurance of various types to the employees on a basis of dividing the cost between management and employee.

The laws of some states provide that certain large employers such as public utilities and comparable are exempted from posting a workmen's compensation insurance policy and may be self-insured. From the viewpoint of the employee, the result is the same.

## What Are Annuity And Endowment Contracts?

An annuity policy of insurance differs from ordinary life insurance. In life insurance contracts, the insured pays his premiums at regular intervals, usually quarterly, semi-annually or annually. In annuity contracts, the insured pays the total amount of the annuity to the insurance company in a lump sum at the time of entering into the agreement. The agreement usually provides that upon the annuitant's death, the insurance company agrees to pay his beneficiary a certain sum of money annually until the named amount has been paid in full. It further provides that if the annuitant is alive at an agreed age, the insurance company will pay him an agreed sum of money annually until a certain sum has been paid. The insurance company has the use of the annuitant's money for an indefinite period of time and assumes the risk of how long the annuitant will live. For all practical purposes, annuity contracts are used only by those who are wealthy enough to pay sizeable sums of money in a lump sum to the insurance company. The annuitant is the person who is insured and pays the money in a single payment.

An endowment policy starts off similar to an ordinary life insurance contract in that it agrees to pay X dollars to the beneficiary of the insured upon the occasion of his death. The endowment contract further provides that if the insured does not die during the agreed period of years, then the insurance company will pay him the policy amount in a lump sum. An example would be a 20 year endowment for $5,000. The insured pays his premiums for 20 years and if he does not die, the company will pay him $5,000 in a lump sum. If he dies during the 20 years, the company will pay the $5,000 to his named beneficiary. Don't worry about how the insurance company can afford to take this risk. The insurance company has the use of the premium payments for periods varying from 20 years down to one and make a profit on the transaction.

## What Law Governs An Insurance Policy?

The general rule is that the state in which the application is made, the premium paid, and the policy delivered is the place where the contract is entered into. The law says that a contract of insurance is deemed to be executed at the place where the last act is done which is necessary to complete the transaction and bind both parties.

If the insurance policy provides that it shall not be valid until it is countersigned by an officer or agent of the company, the place of the countersigning is held to be the place of the making of the contract. The only time it is important is when the parties have a dispute and wind up in court. The state laws of the home office of an insurance company can favor them more than your state.

## Are Insurance Companies Regulated?

Yes, every state has laws that regulate and control insurance companies who are authorized to do business in that state. Insurance business affects the public interest and are subject to strict control for the general good of the people. Most states have an Insurance Commissioner whose main function is to see to it that the insurance companies comply with the state laws and protect the people of his state. If you ever feel that you are not being treated fairly by an insurance company doing business in your state, a complaint to your Insurance Commissioner will bring some action. Your complaint may not be decided in your favor but it usually will not be ignored. If a company is guilty of some unfair practise and if enough people complain, some good will result. Many people used to forget their grievance and say: "You can't fight city hall" but Ralph Nader and his Nader Raiders taught us otherwise.

## Are Insurance Agents and Brokers Licensed?

Yes, many states prescribe the qualifications for the granting of a license to insurance agents and brokers. Most states are concerned with their fitness and moral character. Whenever a state has the power to issue a license, it also has the right to revoke the license for cause. Some insurance agents and brokers have had their license revoked for the following reasons; withholding or misappropriation of premiums; illegal or improper conduct; incompetency to act as agent; the offering of a rebate to prospective customers; and the selling of insurance at rates varying from those filed with the insurance commissioner.

### What Are The Three Types Of Insurance Companies?

The three types of insurance companies are stock, mutual, and mixed. A stock insurance corporation is privately owned and operated by its board of directors, just like any other corporation engaged in business for profit. A mutual insurance company is a cooperative enterprise, where the members all pay premiums or assessments, to a fund for the payment of losses, and where the profits are divided in proportion to their interest. Dividends are paid by a mutual insurance company out of their profits. A mixed insurance company embodies the characteristics of both stock and mutual. A certain portion of the profits of a mixed insurance company are paid to the stockholders and a portion is divided among the insurers.

### Dividends, What Are They?

Insurance companies say that dividends represent a portion of a surplus which they have accummulated. A former insurance executive claims that dividends are a partial refund of an overcharge. The surplus of a life insurance company is derived from income investments, mortality savings, savings from the amount by which policy premiums are loaded to meet expenses and extraordinary losses, and gains from forfeited policies.

### Your Insurance Man — Who's Agent?

This question is difficult to answer in a few words because it depends upon a number of factors. Under certain circumstances and for certain purposes, an insurance broker may be the agent of both the insurer and the insured. If he is an employee of one insurance company and you are billed by the company, he is clearly the company's agent. If he is an independent insurance broker and you order fire insurance coverage and specify no particular company and he placed the coverage with a company of his choice and he bills you directly, he is your agent. An insurance broker may properly be an agent for both factions if there is no conflict in his duties.

Many people who deal with independent insurance agents for their insurance needs, rely on their agent for coverage with a company of his selection. The main time when you need help is when you have a claim and you are being pushed around by your insurance company. If your agent has your interest at heart, it is up to him to use his influence with the insurance company to see to it that you receive fair treatment. If he takes the position that your insurance claim is none of his concern, you are ready to find another insurance agent who will look out for your interests. Thanking you for payment of your insurance bill is only a part of his job and not an important one from the customer's point of view.

### Is An Oral Contract Of Insurance Valid?

Yes, an oral contract of insurance which is otherwise binding and contains all of the elements essential to a contract is valid. As far as the law is concerned, an insurance contract does not differ from other contracts. A common example occurs when a person buys a new car and telephones his insurance agent for coverage by giving him the motor and serial number and his insurance is effective from the moment he drives his new car. The written insurance policy may not be delivered for days or even a week, yet if he had an accident minutes later, the policy is in effect. Temporary insurance coverage is usually called a "binder."

### What Is The Difference Between Insured And Assured?

None, the words "insured" and "assured" are synonymous.

### Who May Be Insured?

Anyone capable of entering into a contract may order insurance. The mere fact that a man is a convicted felon does not make him uninsurable. However, an insurance company has a right to choose its customers.

### Can The Insurance Company Cancel Its Policy?

Yes, most insurance contracts provide that fire insurance and other contracts of insurance may be cancelled by the insured or by the insurance company. Most contracts provide that the company must give five days notice and refund the unearned portion of the premium paid by the insured. Some insurance companies cancel after the customer files his first claim for a loss.

## Insurable Interest

The law says that you cannot take out life insurance on a stranger because you have no insurable interest. The same reasoning forbids insuring some strange person's property. If this rule did not exist, some people with evil intent would insure a stranger's life and then do him in. Insurance companies do not issue insurance contracts in any case where there is no insurable interest. There was a case where a stranger took out a life insurance policy on a child, and then murdered the child to collect the insurance proceeds. An exception to the insurable interest rule permits parents to take out life insurance policies on their children and children to insure their parents lives.

Insurable interest in property is very common. When you borrow mortgage money on your home or car, the insurance coverage is payable to you and financial company involved. Because the balance that you owe on a mortgage constantly changes, the insurance policy provides that any loss payable to the mortgage company is in the amount "as their respective interest may appear." For example, if you had a fire loss in the amount of $15,000 and owed a $10,000 mortgage balance, you would receive $5,000 from your insurance company and the other $10,000 would be paid to your mortgage company.

A husband and wife have an insurable interest in each other. After divorce, the insurable interest ceases. One has an insurable interest in the life of another whom one is engaged to marry. Sisters and brothers have an insurable interest in the life of each other. Partners have an insurable interest in the life of a copartner.

A policy of life insurance taken out without the knowledge or consent of the insured person is against public policy and unenforceable. A wife, for example, is not permitted to obtain insurance on the life of her husband without his knowledge and consent; such a practice, might be a fruitful source of crime.

## Don't Overinsure

If you overinsure or overvalue your home or anything else and suffer a loss, your insurance company will not pay you the face amount of the policy but only the fair value of the property stolen or destroyed by fire. If your car is destroyed by fire, your insurance company will replace it with a comparable car or at their option, pay you the fair value of your car as of the date it was destroyed. If you pay $30,000 for your home and the lot is valued at $5,000, don't insure your home for $30,000 fire insurance because you are overinsuring and in the event of a total loss your claim will not be paid for the face amount. Even if the home was totally destroyed down to the ground, your lot cannot burn and it will still have the value of $5,000.

If the insured by mistake has grossly overvalued and overinsured the property, without negligence or fraud on his part, he is entitled to a rebate of the excessive proportion of premiums paid.

## Photographs And Appraisal Of Jewelry

All women are urged to have their jewelry appraised by a reputable jeweler who will also photograph valuable pieces. Your insurance agent will arrange to have the appraisal and photos attached to your insurance policy. Then if a loss should occur, you avoid the inconvenience of trying to satisfy the insurance adjuster who wants detailed information about each item of jewelry. All of the necessary information has been obtained in advance and your claim will be quickly honored by your insurance company. Valuable furs fall in the same category although they depreciate.

## Can You Have More Than One Fire Insurance Policy?

No, most insurance companies will not permit the insured to order additional coverage without their knowledge and approval. They are afraid of deliberate claims if the insured were permitted to overinsure. Most policies provide that if additional coverage has been placed with another company, the original policy is void.

## Is The Medical Examiner The Company's Agent?

Yes, the doctor who examines an applicant for life insurance to see if he meets the insurer's requirements is the agent of the insurance company. If the applicant is guilty of fraud or deceit in answering questions pertaining to his past condition of health, the insurance company would have a good chance of having the court declare the policy voidable. Under these facts, the insurance company says that they would not have issued the life insurance policy if the applicant had been truthful.

## What About False Answers Suggested By The Insurance Agent?

An applicant is cleared who reveals a history of previous illness to the agent and the agent states that such illness is of no importance. The law does not require the applicant to question the authority or judgment of the agent and the company cannot void the policy. If the insured is a party to the fraud of an insurance agent or medical examiner, he will not be allowed to profit thereby.

## Are There Any Restrictions On Insurance Coverage?

No, the parties may make any insurance contracts that they choose. The only prohibition would be those that would be repugnant to public policy. Lloyds of London have received international publicity in connection with their insurance policies to cover unusual situations. Some examples are: insurance coverage against rain for an athletic event; protection for the legs or nose of prominent actresses; vocal cords of opera singers and similar.

## Life Insurance

A life insurance policy can be matured by one event only, namely, the death of the insured. The insured receives no money during his lifetime and the contract provides that certain benefits will be paid to the named beneficiary. Some life insurance policies provide for certain exceptions, as by a provision that the insurance company will not pay if death occurs while piloting private aircraft; while engaged in military service; while violating the law; while using narcotics; and the like.

## Double Indemnity

Some insurance contracts provide that in case of accidental death, the company will pay double the amount named. Frequently, there are legal hastles to determine whether death was or was not accidental, to qualify for double indemnity.

## Unusual Exceptions

A few life insurance policies may contain particular provisions excepting certain causes of death from the risk assumed. An insurer may provide that there shall be no liability on its part if the insured dies within a year from some cause or disease excepted from the contract of insurance. For example, an insurer may except liability for death when the insured is participating in the transportation of explosives. The killing by a husband of his wife's paramour, although classified by the law as justifiable homicide, is not at the "hands of justice." The paramour's insurance contract exempted the company from liability if the death of the insured is caused at the hands of justice. An exception of death caused by a duel relates to a quarrel of two persons to settle an old grudge and does not refer to death while engaged in combat in sudden heat and passion.

## Death Penalty And Life Insurance

Where the death of the insured is the result of his leagl execution there can be no recovery on the policy. The legal reasoning is that his criminal offense was against public policy and that death in this manner is not one of the implied risks assumed by the company.

## Suicide

If life insurance is taken out in contemplation of suicide, the law says that suicide is a defense notwithstanding the lack of any provision in the contract. The legal reasoning is that suicide in such a case is a fraud on the insurer, and that to permit a recovery would be against public policy. If a policy contains no provision, the suicide of the insured while insane is as much insured against as death resulting from any other affliction.

In order to prevent a person who is despondent or heavily in debt from perpetrating a fraud on the insurance company, many policies provide against liability for death by suicide for a named period of time, usually either one or two years. After that, the company is liable under the insurance contract even if the insured took his own life. This would seem to solve the problem in a manner that is fair to both sides. In some states it is against the law to attempt to take your own life. If the person is successful, there could be no enforcement of this law. If unsuccessful, the enforcement of the law would not be very popular. The alleged law violator needs medical help and not jail confinement.

## Term Insurance

Term insurance is life insurance without any fancy trimmings. As the name implies, the insurance contract is for a specified period of time, usually one year at a time. In effect you are making a wager with the insurance company and you say you will die during the named year and they say you will live. If you are still alive at the end of the designated year, the company won and you lost your premium money. It is comparable to paying a fire insurance premium and if you have no fire during the year, you lost and the company won.

The one big advantage of term insurance over ordinary life is that you get about 2-1/2 the amount of protection for your premium dollar. Premiums will naturally vary with the age of the insured but the estimate is reasonably accurate. On that basis you can buy $25,000 worth of protection for the cost of $10,000 in ordinary life insurance.

The disadvantage of term insurance over ordinary life is that you are not building up any cash values or reserves. For certain young couples with small children and limited income, term insurance is more desirable than ordinary life. Consult with your insurance expert and then decide for yourself.

*Health Insurance*

Health insurance is an undertaking by an insurance company to indemnify a person for losses caused by illness. It has nothing to do with health problems caused by an accident. The fact that the insured's indiscretion or vice caused his sickness will not prevent a recovery where indemnity is broadly provided for in case of sickness or inability to work. Insanity is regarded as sickness or disability within the meaning of a health insurance policy.

*Is Chronic Alcoholism Or Drug Addiction A Disease?*

Yes and no. As to whether chronic alcoholism or drug addiction is a disease within the meaning of a disability policy, the rule is that neither of them is considered to be a disease as such term is used in the policy. If the use of intoxicants by the insured results in a change of his organic condition which disables him from pursuing a gainful occupation, then the insured will be held disabled by disease within the meaning of the policy.

*Accident Insurance*

The parties to accident insurance contracts have the right and power to contract as to what accidents and risks the company shall and shall not be liable for, and the courts may not make new or different contracts for them. The wide variety of accidents which may befall an insured has resulted in a notable extension of the law of insurance in this respect. Many accident policies are hedged around with exceptions which greatly limit liability.

## War And Military Service

While the cases are not all agreed, a majority of them have taken the view that death or injury of an insured in battle or in the military service is "by accident" or "by accidental means" within contractual stipulations of an accident policy or an increased indemnity provision. Some judges rule that in a battle it is to be expected that a number of soldiers will be injured or killed by enemy fire but the fact that a particular soldier, the insured, was injured or killed by a particular missile fired by the enemy is an unforseen circumstance. Other judges have ruled the other way, stating that it is not unusual or unforeseen, but the expected thing, that a person going into battle will be injured or killed.

## Death Or Injury While Traveling

Some accident policies provide coverage for death or injury incurred while the insured is traveling or is in or on a train, streetcar, automobile, airplane, elevator, etc., or while he is a pedestrian or is on a highway. The desire for protection of the insured, or for exclusion of liability of the insurer, have led to double or treble indemnity provisions. Many policies spell out the specific items that are covered and those that are excepted and both sides understand the contract clearly. If a policy states that you are covered if injured or killed while on a public street, a court battle follows to decide what is a public street or highway. For example, a school child accident policy provided coverage while the child is "enroute between the home and the school." The child's father, intending to drive him to school, struck the child while he was standing inside the garage by the father's car and the child was killed. The court battle resulted in a ruling favorable to the family and against the insurance company.

A number of courts have considered the question when and under what circumstances the insured is "in," "on," "in or upon," "within," or "inside," a motor vehicle within the meaning of accident policies. If it takes the proverbial "Philadelphia Lawyer" to figure out what coverage the policy does or does not offer, it is not a very desirable insurance contract.

## Airplane Passenger's Trip Policy

Airplane passengers' trip insurance policies are policies of insurance against injuries or death to an insured resulting from a particular airplane trip. They are usually sold at insurance counters located within airports or through vending machines. In an unusual case, the court held that an airplane trip insurance policy covers the death of the insured who was killed while a passenger on a non-scheduled airline despite the fact that a sign on the vending machine from which the policy was purchased as well as in the policy itself limited the coverage to scheduled airline flights. It appeared that the vending machine stood in front of the ticket counter where tickets were sold for nonscheduled airlines and a lighted sign above the machine contained the words "airline trip insurance."

### Fire Insurance

Some people are lucky enough to go through a lifetime, and never have a claim for a fire loss. This is good for the fire insurance company and is really not bad for the insured. Among those that have had a fire loss, some think they will wind up with a profit in connection with their claim. They are in for a rude awakening and if they manage to come close to breaking even they will be quite fortunate.

Did you know that there is a "friendly" and a "hostile" fire? A friendly fire would include a fire lighted in a furnace, fireplace, stove, incinerator, and used for heating, cooking, or usual everyday purposes. A hostile fire is unexpected, unintended, not anticipated, and in a place not intended for it to be. A fire originally friendly, by escaping can become hostile, and the resulting damage is recoverable.

A policy insuring against losses by fire cover every loss, damage, or injury to the insured property of which fire is the proximate cause. Most fire insurance policies today contain "extended coverage" or "comprehensive" provisions bringing additional risks within the coverage of the policy.

### Malpractice Insurance

A form of liability insurance in common use is one which protects a doctor, lawyer, dentist, pharmacist or any other professional person against liability while practicing his profession. It protects the individual against claims of malpractice, error, or mistake. Doctors have been known to leave surgical sponges in the patient's stomach after surgery and lawyers have made mistakes that are costly to the client. If these mistakes represent negligence then the claimant has a valid claim against the professional person and the loss is covered by malpractice insurance.

## Public Liability Insurance

Public liability insurance protects the owner, occupier, or operator of real property against liability, incident to his ownership or to the use of the premises. Such public liability policies provide for protection for liability for "accidental" or "bodily" injuries. Many people who slip and fall, sue the tenant as well as the property owner for their injuries, claiming negligence. The cost of this type of insurance is nominal and businessmen cannot afford not to have this coverage. In the case of a homeowner, this protection is frequently covered in a "Homeowner's Policy."

## Notice And Proof Of Loss

The purpose of the requirement for notice and proof of loss is to allow the insurance company an opportunity to form an intelligent estimate of its rights and liabilities. Over a period of years, many frauds have been perpetrated against insurance companies and they are privileged to investigate the claim and to prevent fraud upon it.

## Autopsy

An autopsy is an examination of a dead body to determine the cause of death. Provisions in life or accident policies giving the insurance company the right and opportunity to make an autopsy in case of death are valid. Such a provision is necessary in accident insurance to afford protection against fraudulent claims and also against claims which are invalid. In an unusual case, the insured's widow did not know of the policy before the cremation and the court ruled the insurance company's inability to request an autopsy did not bar recovery. Unless the policy so provides, it is not necessary that the insurer call the attending physician to make an autopsy; the company may call its own physician for such purpose.

## Fraud Or False Swearing

Policies of fire and property indemnity insurance usually provide that any fraud or false swearing on the part of the insured, whether before or after loss, shall relieve the insurance company from liability. This rule is applicable to the following: an overvaluation of the property insured; false statements as to the ownership of property destroyed; the inclusion in the proofs of property not destroyed; and the "padding" of an inventory of merchandise by false entries of articles not on hand.

If a false statement is knowingly made by the insured, with regard to a material matter, the intent to defraud will be inferred. Some insurance companies are inclined to be overly technical and not very liberal in honoring a legitimate claim. Some claimants try to chisel and defraud the insurance company.

### Who Controls Insurance Litigation?

The insurance company has the right to make such investigation, negotiation, and settlement of any claim as it deems expedient. The insured is not privileged to voluntarily assume any liability, settle any claim, incur any expenses, or interfere in any legal proceedings, unless with the consent of the insurer. If you are involved in an accident, don't be overly talkative. You can courteously tell the other party that you will report the accident to your insurance company and they will handle all details.

Your insurance company will do most of the deciding as regards settling a claim or fighting it in the courts. You have no legal right to advise your own company and if they want to settle a claim against you, that is entirely up to them.

If the other party's claim can be settled within the limits of your coverage, you have some important legal rights in the matter. For example, you carry $25,000 public liability insurance and the person injured is willing to settle for $15,000. Your own insurance company is stubborn and refuses to settle, advising that they prefer a jury trial to settle the lawsuit. The final result of the jury trial is a verdict in favor of the claimant for $30,000. You can protect yourself in this type of situation by placing your own insurance company on notice that if they fail to settle for an amount within your policy limits, you hold them responsible for any amount in excess of your policy limits. In the example noted, your insurance company is legally obligated to pay the entire $30,000.

### Duty To Forward Lawsuit Papers To Insurer

Liability policies contain an express provision requiring the insured, if he is served with summons or other legal papers, to forward them promptly to the insurance company. The purpose of such requirement is to enable the insurer to defend itself promptly concerning the claim. If the insured fails to comply, he can lose his benefits under his insurance policy. Basically, the insurance company controls the litigation and the insured must cooperate with his own company. If you are unhappy with your own insurance company, you are privileged to change when your policy expires.

## Accident And Health Insurance

Health and accident insurance policies, and life insurance policies with disability features, usually provide for the payment of a certain sum of money in case of specified injuries, or for periodical payments in case of total, permanent, or partial disability. Many people laugh while reading provisions of an accident insurance policy that spells out the amount of money a claimant will receive for the loss of both hands, both feet, or one hand and one foot, and half of that amount for the loss of either hand or either foot, etc. It sounds gruesome but that happens to be the insurance contract that applies.

## Insurance Adjusters

An adjuster is an employee or agent of an insurance company whose function is to settle claims. If the adjuster works for one insurance company only, he is their employee. If the adjuster hires out to many insurance companies to settle their claims, he is an independent adjuster and is their agent with limited authority.

Some adjusters have been accused of contacting the injured claimant "before the blood has dried," trying to make a quick settlement in an effort to save money for the insurance company. Some adjusters tell the claimant, "There is no need for you to hire a lawyer and if you do, my offer will be withdrawn." Reputable insurance companies do not approve or permit any such sharp practices.

If you have a claim against an insurance company due to a loss either of property or one involving personal injuries, you have certain rights. Listen to the adjuster's offer of settlement and do not make an immediate decision. Take your time and think about it. If there is any doubt in your mind as to whether the offer is a fair one, discuss it with your attorney. If your attorney advises you to accept the offer, follow his advice. If your attorney thinks the offer is not enough, he should handle your case and charge no fee for the amount offered by the insurance company. He should base his fee on any overage he is able to obtain for you.

## Beneficiaries

A beneficiary is the person who is designated in a contract of life, health, or accident insurance as the one who is to receive the benefits which become payable, upon the death of the insured. Where an insured names one of his family as beneficiary and retains control of the policy, the transaction is not to be judged as a business affair.

The rights of the beneficiary to receive the proceeds of the policy, are in no way affected by the fact that the parties are divorced after the issuance of the policy.

## Right To Change Beneficiary

Unless the policy reserves to the insured the right to change the beneficiary, no such right exists. Many state laws confer on the insured the right to change the beneficiary on the granting of a divorce between the insured and beneficiary of a policy.

## Who Should Own A Life Insurance Policy?

Sometimes for tax reasons, ownership of a life insurance policy on the husband should be changed to the wife, even though the wife is already named as beneficiary. If the couple are fairly wealthy and there is a danger of using up the federal estate tax exemption of $60,000 per person or $120,000 for husband and wife, it is advisable to have the wife designated as owner of the life insurance policy on the husband's life. If there is any doubt in your mind, check with your life insurance representative and discuss the matter. In certain cases, there are tax advantages to removing the life insurance policy proceeds from the husband's portion of his estate upon the occasion of his death. It might also be advisable to discuss this problem with your accountant and attorney in connection with any estate planning that is being followed. Changing the ownership of life insurance policies is only important in cases where the family estate assets exceed the $120,000 federal estate exemption.

## Group Insurance

Group insurance is the coverage of a number of persons by means of a single or blanket policy. It is cheaper which enables the insurance company to sell its services at lower premium rates than are available to individuals for the same protection. A group life insurance contract is made by the insurer and employer, rather than between the insurer and the employees covered. A group insurance policy affects four parties; the insurer, the employer, the insured employee, and the beneficiary. One who is not an employee is not covered by a group insurance policy. Some group policies include coverage for the employees' dependents. Some employers pay the entire premium while others pay part and require the employee to pay part.

## What Happens If The Insured Disappears?

Universal law provides that there is a presumption of death which arises from unexplained absence of the insured for 7 years. One insurance company tried to change this rule by having their policies state that 7 years absence unexplained was insufficient to prove the death of the insured. The court ruled against the insurance company and said the company's special provision is contrary to public policy and void.

## Incontestability Provisions

Some insurance companies have gone too far in trying to cancel an insurance contract where they claim the insured gave untruthful answers to questions pertaining to his background or health. Their insurance contracts provided that if the insurance company ever discovered that the insured gave false information they could cancel the contract at any time. In some cases, the insurance company had collected premiums for a number of years.

In order to put a stop to this unfair situation, many states enacted laws limiting the time in which an insurance company could complete their investigation of the insured's statements. This time limit is usually one or two years. The insurance company has had a reasonable opportunity of completing their investigation and if they accept the insured's premium money for one or two years, they no longer have a right to cancel the insurance contract. In this situation, it does not matter if the insured gave truthful answers or not because the law says the insurance contract becomes binding.

## What Is Grace Period?

Days of grace are extra time granted to an insured in which to pay his insurance premium. Most insurance policies grant 30 days as a grace period. This means that a late payment within the grace period is legal and not subject to any penalty.

## Cash Or Loan Value

Contracts of life insurance frequently stipulate that upon the insured's failure to pay a premium when due or within the grace period, the insurer will automatically pay the premium in his behalf and charge it as a loan against the policy. This is only done in those cases where the policy is old enough and the reserve value is sufficient. Otherwise, the policy is lapsed for nonpayment of premiums. This is another way of saying that the insurance contract has been cancelled for nonpayment. Reinstatement procedures vary widely with different companies.

## Policy Loans

Some states have enacted laws requiring all life insurance policies to contain provisions for loans by the insurer on the security of cash equities that have been accumulated. This right in many instances is a potent factor in inducing the taking of a policy. It is a part of the life insurance contract, and the insured is entitled to a loan and to a renewal thereof, based upon premium payments already paid. Money borrowed from an insurance company upon a policy does not create a debtor and creditor relationship and imposes no personal obligation upon the insured. The insurance company does charge interest on the loan and if it is not repaid by the insured, eventually the borrowed money plus interest will be repaid in the final settlement of the policy when death occurs.

## Cash Value

Life insurance policies that have existed for many years accumulate cash values. If you paid insurance premiums for ten or twenty years and then wanted to quit paying, your life insurance policy has a cash value and you can draw down the money and cancel the insurance contract or you can keep it in force for the reduced amount of insurance coverage. Most life insurance policies have a table giving this information based upon units of $1,000. If it is not clear, contact your insurance representative for more detailed information. The important fact to remember is that your policy does have a cash value.

# THE FAMILY CAR

In order to know the law that applies to a given situation, we must turn to the statutes of the particular state involved. Similarly, in order to be able to answer the question, "Am I covered under my insurance policy" — we must turn to the automobile insurance policy contract to learn the coverage. Many people complain about the length and fine print that is usually contained in most insurance policies. Even lawyers can have trouble in understanding the complicated legaleze gobbledygook that ends with the phrase "everything to the contrary notwithstanding." Some insurance companies deliberately issue policies which are impossible to understand without the help of the proverbial "Philadelphia lawyer." The complaint is justified and some of the larger and more reputable insurance companies are now simplifying the policy language so that ordinary people can understand its provisions. I appreciated the following ruling of a New York court in a lawsuit over an automobile insurance policy: "It is not the construction or interpretation that the company gives to a policy that governs, but the plain meaning understandable to "Joe Doakes, the average person" that counts."

Frequently, a person buys a new car and makes arrangements with his insurance man to have the car covered immediately as he drives it away from the new car dealer's place of business, by telephoning the motor and serial number and similar information. This oral contract of insurance is called a "binder" and it is legal and effective. An insurance agent may bind his insurance company by an oral contract.

## What Is Compulsory Insurance?

Every state, other than Alaska, has some type of law directed to the problem of the financially irresponsible motorist. In a number of states, laws have been enacted which make the carrying of liability insurance mandatory before a car may be operated upon the public highways. Other states have passed laws called "financial responsibility" which require a motor vehicle driver involved in an accident with no insurance, to prove his financial responsibility for the future before he can drive his car on the highways. This means the first accident was "on the house" and the victim is usually unable to collect for his injuries or property damage because the person responsible carried no insurance. At least, the second accident victim of the same driver will be protected because he is forced to comply with the financial responsibility act by providing automobile insurance. People who drive cars without any insurance are usually difficult to collect damages from, because they are not in very good financial shape. Public liability insurance protects the car owner in case one or more persons are injured or killed.

Most state laws provide that the driver of the uninsured vehicle that was responsible for the accident and failed to pay the victim's claim, has his driver's license revoked until he complies with the financial responsibility act by having insurance. It won't help victim number one but it will protect number two.

### What Does $5,000/10,000 or $10,000/20,000 Mean?

It means that if one person is injured or killed, the insurance company limits their liability to $5,000 and if two or more persons are injured or killed, the policy limits are $10,000. The same formula holds true for $25,000/50,000 or $100,000/200,000 or any other amount of coverage. Since inflation and high jury verdicts are in vogue, the coverage of $5,000/10,000 is totally inadequate and should not be bought. Why pay money for what you think is adequate insurance coverage, only to discover after the accident that you have to hire your own lawyer to defend the lawsuit filed against you for $100,000 damages?

Although the cost of automobile insurance in general has gone sky-high, the difference in cost of public liability coverage that is woefully inadequate and a more realistic amount, is very small. Just for the fun of it, call your insurance agent and ask the difference in cost between $10,000/20,000 and $50,000/100,000 and you will be pleasantly surprised in the small additional cost for the higher amount. You cannot afford to drive without adequate public liability insurance and you can ill afford not to have adequate coverage. To copy a TV deodorant slogan, "Don't be half safe" with inadequate public liability insurance coverage.

Some of the newer policies issued by large and reputable insurance companies have completely solved the problem of deciding what is adequate insurance. For a few dollars more than you are now paying for $25,000/50,000 or even $50,000/100,000, the new policy protects you for $300,000 per accident, regardless of whether one or more persons are injured or killed. You can rest easily because you know that you are adequately protected against any reasonable lawsuit.

## The High Cost Of Insurance

The $15-billion-a-year auto-insurance industry is of universal concern, affecting every driver. "When a guy is paying $650 a year to insure a $350 car that he's taking to a $150-a-week job, there's something wrong." The casualty insurance companies claim they are losing money but have managed to increase their total assets by nearly 65 per cent, to a total of $50 billion. The insurance companies now point the finger of blame at Detroit and the car manufacturers that they claim are producing fragile automobiles. Many in the insurance field feel that government-backed insurance for most auto owners will result if the insurance companies continue to raise their premiums and cancel policies indiscriminately.

The immediate problem is how to keep your insurance cost down to a reasonable figure and still have adequate protection. The most expensive item on your car insurance bill is the collision premium. If your policy provides for $50 deductible, it is more expensive than $100 deductible. For the uninitiated, this means that if your car is damaged in an accident, you pay for the deductible amount and your insurance company will pay any amount in excess. Thus, all fender bumps and comparable are paid for by the car owner.

From personal experience, I can recommend that each car owner act as his own insurance carrier for collision coverage only. The cost is so great, I can now afford to pay my own property damage out of the premium money I have saved. This involves a gamble of having to pay any and all damages to your car.

For all other insurance coverage of your car I recommend that you have complete coverage. The cost of fire and theft and comprehensive is minimal and is a good investment. Ditto for property damage which protects the other car. Many insurance policies covering public liability for personal injuries or death, also cover property damage, usually to the other car. Property damage is not restricted to the other car, it may be to a gasoline pump or to a building. Medical expense coverage for the driver and up to five passengers is not terribly expensive and is desirable protection. Finally, the most important is public liability insurance which the average person just cannot afford not to have, regardless of the cost. Actually, the cost of public liability insurance is not too bad, not nearly as rough as collision insurance.

With many automobile insurance companies canceling policies at any excuse, it is wise not to file a claim for a small amount. If someone steals your hubcap, you are better off replacing it at your own expense, in order to keep your claim record as clean as possible. Once you are cancelled out by one insurance company, it becomes more difficult to get another company to insure your car.

Many countries all over the world are now requiring that tourists arriving at their border in automobiles have insurance coverage to protect their citizens in the event of an accident causing injuries or property damage in their country.

One of my Clients was charged with DWI (driving while intoxicated) when his vehicle caused about $500 property damage to a wall and shrubbery. His insurance agent urged him not to file a claim under his policy on the grounds "it will hurt your insurance record because of the pending criminal charges against you." In due course of time his trial resulted in a verdict of "not guilty" on a finding that he was ill and not intoxicated. I then recommended to my Client that he disregard the statement of his insurance agent and file his claim for the $500 loss. There is no point in paying insurance premiums for protection and then paying a substantial sum out of your own pocket, when your loss is covered under the policy.

*Property Damage*

Property damage insurance coverage protects the car owner for any and all damage to the other car or any other property. For example, if your car went out of control and hit a store front or gasoline pump or a building, the damages would be covered by your property damage insurance coverage. Obviously, your insurance company will pay only if it is determined that you were at fault. If the other driver was at fault, his loss is his problem and not yours.

The punchline of my entire automobile insurance philosophy is to gamble by acting as your own insurer for one item only, the deductible collision insurance for damages to your own car. The cost is so high that if you drive carefully, it is a good gamble. If you lose the gamble, you have to pay for repairing your car, if you were at fault. If the other driver was at fault, there is a possibility that you can recover your loss, if he is insured.

Your gamble is limited to this one item only and all other insurance coverage is all inclusive. You are protecting your passengers, the other driver and the other car and your limited gamble is restricted to damage done to your car.

## Insurance When Renting A Car?

Most of the larger car rental companies charge anywhere from $1 to $1.50 per day for complete automobile insurance coverage. This does not seem like an unreasonable charge, however, the rental companies do not explain all of the pertinent facts. If you don't order the car insurance, they usually require that you initial the line marked no insurance desired. The attractive young lady who is employed by the car rental company does not tell you that if you do not order car insurance and are responsible for damage caused by an accident, her company automatically carries complete coverage except for $100 deductible. Thus, you are paying $1 or $1.50 per day against the maximum possible loss of $100.

## What Is Comprehensive?

Car insurance policies for fire and theft usually include protection against "comprehensive loss." If your policy doesn't, it should. A comprehensive loss is the unexpected and unusual. The most common examples are: windstorm; hail; earthquake; flood; explosion; vandalism; malicious mischief; missiles; lightning; smoke or smudge; pitted windshield or glass breakage; falling objects; civil riot or commotion; etc.

A Missouri court held: "An automobile policy which does not include coverage under which loss or damage by flood or rising waters is set out does not cover damage to an automobile when the insured, because of a heavy rain and sudden rise in the river where he was fishing, was unable to drive his car to safety and was compelled to leave it, as a result of which it was completely covered by rising water and sand and other material causing damage to it." Another court ruled: "Where a 3-year-old child released the brakes of the insured car when it was parked on a hill and steered it down the hill for more than a block, when it collided with another car, the proximate cause of the damage was the act of vandalism on the part of the child and the circumstances that the immediate or incidental cause of the loss was a collision did not prevent recovery under a comprehensive policy." A New Mexico court decided: "Damage to the parked automobile of the insured by a motorist who drove into the parked car while the motorist was intoxicated and was driving in a wanton, wilful, reckless manner, was held not to be "malicious mischief" within an automobile policy covering loss resulting from malicious mischief, but was held damage resulting from a "collision" between the two automobiles for which the insured was not covered.

If the last two cases appear to have resulted in opposite rulings, don't get excited because this situation happens quite often in a court of law. One judge rules one way and another judge rules another way and the facts may be similar but are never identical. This is a good example of why experienced lawyers refuse to predict the outcome of a litigated lawsuit. Unfortunately, some insurance companies through their claim agents, are overly technical against the customer's claim and they can quote 84 reasons why the insured is not covered under the terms of the policy.

## Who Is Covered — You Or Your Car?

Many American families own more than one motor vehicle. Double garages are being replaced by garages that hold 3 or even 4 cars. In the more affluent families, dad has his car, mom has her car; junior has his car and sister may have her car. Junior may ask permission to drive the family car for his big date on Friday night because his jalopy is not flashy enough for junior's new girl friend. Members of the same family may have occasion to drive family cars other than their own.

The better insurance companies issue an automobile policy that offers protection to all members of the family, regardless of which car they are driving. In other words, in the example of the 4 family cars, the insurance policy protects the 4 cars while being driven by any member of the family or any authorized driver. You may shudder at the cost of insuring 4 family cars, including two teen-age drivers, but the only way to hold that cost down within reason is to gamble on the $50 deductible or collision part of the protection. Some state laws require the "omnibus" clause in an automobile liability insurance policy, which means that all other authorized drivers of your cars are covered.

## Uninsured Motorist Coverage

"Uninsured motorist" coverage provides that the company will pay to the insured all damages resulting from an accident caused by the operator of an uninsured automobile. It further provides that this coverage includes the insured, his spouse, relatives living in his house, operators with permission, and all occupants of the vehicle. Sometimes the operator of the uninsured car is a hit-and-run character whose identity is unknown. A number of states have passed laws requiring this type of coverage. It has become a fairly common feature inserted in standard automobile insurance policies by reputable companies.

This provision means that you are protected in the event the other driver is uninsured or runs away. Your company is not really giving anything away because you are paying the premiums and if your insurance company loses money, the premiums go up.

## What To Do If You Have An Accident

There are any number of things to do when you are involved in an accident. First and most important, REMAIN AS CALM AS YOU POSSIBLY CAN. If you or anyone else is injured, try to get medical help or an ambulance as fast as is reasonably possible. Don't talk about the cause of the accident with the other driver or anyone else. Your insurance company will have issued you a card of instruction and it is headed: DON'T TALK ABOUT THE ACCIDENT. If a police officer approaches, be courteous and answer all of his questions honestly and to the best of your ability. If you don't know your speed at the moment of impact, say so. Don't guess and say "I am not sure but I think I was going X miles per hour."

If there are any witnesses available, approach them and ask if they saw the accident and if they would be kind enough to give you their name, address and telephone number. Your insurance company will appreciate your cooperation and there is no reason for you not to be fair with your company.

Notify your insurance agent or the office as listed by your insurance company and tell them the pertinent details about the accident. Obviously, they are more concerned with details about personal injuries than property damage because serious injuries can result in a large claim whereas property damage is limited.

Notify some member of your family if the accident is a fairly serious one. Your husband, wife, son or daughter can be of help once they are notified.

If the accident is a fairly minor one, your state law may still require that you notify your police department within 24 or 48 hours and fill out an accident report form. If there is doubt, telephone your local police authorities and find out their requirements.

You don't have to be impolite or rude to the other driver. BUT, DON'T BE A BIG TALKER. Your policy provides that you do not have the right to admit liability, so don't say to the other driver, "I am sorry but it was all my fault because I was not watching and my insurance company will pay your claim for damages." If you do, you may find yourself fighting your own insurance company in court when they claim they are not responsible because of your violating the terms of the insurance contract. You do have the right to give the other driver the name and address of your insurance company and obtain the same information from him. You can be more efficient and helpful if you are quiet than if you are a gabby indidivual.

If you are served with any summons or other legal papers in connection with the accident, it is important that they be turned over to your insurance company or their agent promptly, so that they can refer them to the lawyers for the insurance company. If you are negligent and ignore or forget them, the other side can take a judgment against you by default.

### Who Controls The Lawsuit?

Most motor vehicle liability insurance policies give the insurance company the right to investigate, negotiate, and settle any claim or lawsuit as it deems expedient. In other words, the insurance company runs the show and you have no voice in the matter. You must cooperate with your own insurance company if you expect them to pay the claim or lawsuit against you. The thinking behind this provision is to prevent collusion between the parties. All insurance policies say that your company agrees to pay any judgment awarded against you up to the limits of the policy.

Peculiarly, if there is a lawsuit, the name of your insurance company becomes a big mystery and the fact that you are insured may not be mentioned in the courtroom before a jury. I will agree that this rule is archaic and unnecessary, but the insurance companies feel that the juries will bring in larger verdicts if the fact of insurance was featured in the trial. Yet, in this modern day and age, all jurors know that motor vehicles operated by companies are always covered by insurance. The law is old-fashioned and slow to make changes.

There is one important exception to the rule that the insurance company controls the pending lawsuit against you. For example, you are covered for $25,000 and the other side is willing to settle their claim for serious personal injuries for $26,000. You want to get rid of the pesky and dangerous lawsuit, and you are willing to pay the additional $1,000 out of your own pocket. You can now put your insurance company on notice that if they fail to settle and the jury brings in a much larger verdict than the $26,000, that the total judgment will fall on your insurance company. The reasoning behind this rule is that some insurance companies are "chincy" and they are only concerned with the legal limits of their liability. This rule enables the insured to bring pressure on his own insurance company to be fair or else suffer the consequences. I have seen cases where there is no question about the liability of the insurance company, however, they will take advantage of their legal limit of liability and offer less on the theory that the limit is all they can be forced to pay. Chisel! Chisel!

If there is a lawsuit against you as a result of the accident, your insurance company will hire their lawyers to defend you. Your insurance policy so provides and they are interested in your lawsuit only to the extent of their limit of liability. If you are sued for $50,000 and your coverage is only for $10,000, the insurance company lawyers will ask if you want to hire them for the $40,000 overage or do you want to hire your own lawyer? This is what happens when you are not adequately covered by your policy. You could say that you were under-insured which is worse than being over-insured. If you are over-insured, you pay a higher premium but will not be reimbursed by your insurance company for the higher loss. A good example would be if you insure your home for fire insurance for $30,000 and your home is only worth $20,000. If it burns to the ground, your insurance company will only pay $20,000.

## Subrogation Of Insurer

The insurance company has the right to be subrogated to the rights of the insured against the wrongdoer in the amount they have paid. For example you carry $100 deductible collision insurance and the other car wrongfully caused $500 damage to your car. Your insurance company pays $400 and you pay $100 and your insurance company becomes subrogated to your rights against the wrongdoer to the extent of $400 and you still have your $100 claim for your loss. Your contract of insurance gives your company this right to become subrogated for the amount they pay.

Sometimes, the same insurance company is covering both cars, in which case they cannot collect from their own customer. In this case they would not take any right of subrogation but you still have your $100 claim that can be enforced.

### "Family Purpose" Doctrine

The legal principle of "family purpose" holds that when parents permit junior to drive the family car, junior is the agent for the parents and they are responsible for his negligence in driving the car. A number of states have laws that provide for this liability on the part of parents. In order to protect yourself, make sure that your car insurance policy protects you in the event your youngster has an accident and it is determined that he was at fault.

The family purpose doctrine is not a new one which has arisen since the use of the automobile became general. I cannot resist citing the Kentucky case decided in 1864, where the court held a father responsible for his minor son's negligent act while driving his two sisters to a picnic in his father's carriage, drawn by his father's horses with his approval, saying that the son must be regarded as in the father's employment, discharging a duty usually performed by a slave and therefore must, for the purposes of this action, be regarded as his father's servant.

In order for the family purpose doctrine to be applicable, it must be shown that at the time of the accident the car was being used for the pleasure and convenience of the user, with the permission, either express or implied, of the owner. If the title to the car is in the name of the minor child who has paid for it out of his earnings, the parents cannot be held liable for its negligent operation under the family purpose doctrine. But even if the child paid for the car, if the title is in the parent's name, then the family purpose doctrine does apply.

Actually, the entire problem of protecting yourself when your car is being driven by someone else with your knowledge and approval, can be solved by your car insurance policy provision that covers your car and you and any authorized driver.

### Collecting Twice Legally!

This may sound like a gimmick but it can happen and it is honest and legal. It may help to set forth a set of facts to explain the point. Your car is involved in an accident and you are injured and the other driver is at fault. As a result of your injuries, you are hospitalized and wind up incurring medical and hospital expenses totaling $1,500. Fortunately, your own insurance policy protects you for all of your $1,500 medical expenses and these bills are paid by your insurance company.

You now assert your claim against the other driver and his insurance company. Whether you collect the $1,500 medical and hospital expense or more due to your pain and suffering is aside from the point. You are legally entitled to collect the $1,500 medical and hospital expense from the other side, even though these bills were paid by your own insurance company. The law says that your medical insurance was paid for by you and was for your personal benefit and does not give the other driver the right to benefit from your coverage.

Normally, people who suffer any type of loss are fortunate if they wind up breaking even, let alone make a profit. Under this unusual situation, it is a rare example of a person being able to honestly and legally collect a claim twice.

# DEATH AND FUNERALS

*A Good Death*

EUTHANASIA is derived from the Greek, meaning "good death." Death control, like birth control, is a matter of human dignity. "To everything there is a season...A time to be born and a time to die."

The following form was prepared and is reproduced by the courtesy of Euthanasia Educational Fund 250 West 57th Street, New York 10019.

## A LIVING WILL

### TO MY FAMILY, MY PHYSICIAN, MY CLERGYMAN, MY LAWYER

If the time comes when I can no longer take part in decisions for my own future, let this statement stand as the testament of my wishes:

If there is no reasonable expectation of my recovery from physical or mental disability, I, _____
request that I be allowed to die and not be kept alive by artificial means or heroic measures. Death is as much a reality as birth, growth maturity and old age — it is the one certainty. I do not fear death as much as I fear the indignity of deterioration, dependence and hopeless pain. I ask that drugs be mercifully administered to me for terminal suffering even if they hasten the moment of death.

This request is made after careful consideration. Although this document is not legally binding, you who care for me will, I hope, feel morally bound to follow its mandates. I recognize that it places a heavy burden of responsibility upon you, and it is with the intention of sharing that responsibility and of mitigating any feelings of guilt that this statement is made.

Signed _____

Date_____

Witnessed by:

_____

_____

This worthwhile non-profit organization believes that at times the prolongation of living may be a prolongation of dying. The right to die is as valid as the right to live. When the body is maintained after the person is gone, this basic right is denied. Medication should be given the dying patient in whatever quantity is needed to relieve pain, even if tending to shorten life. Supportive measures should be removed in cases of terminal illness with intractable pain or irreversible brain damage. Society should support the medical profession in permitting "a good death."

In view of the modern trend of the transplant of various organs of the human body, sometimes with and without the consent of the donor, the following professional statements are pertinent:

"The old argument still runs that only God has the right to decide the termination of any life. Man himself is determining that, with his scientific medicine prolonging the average span of life from the thirties in early colonial days to nearly seventy now, and in individual cases extending the hopeless suffering of those whom nature, left to herself, would release. Man must shoulder the responsibility thus thrust upon him, and must devise some way of mercifully liberating the hopelessly ill from needless agony."

— Henry Emerson Fosdick, D.D.

"The removal of pain and consciousness by means of drugs when medical reasons suggest it, is permitted by religion and morality to both doctor and patient; even if the use of drugs will shorten life."

— Pope Pius XII

"We must get civilized, kind-hearted and thinking persons to acknowledge the right of a suffering person with an incurable disease to demand an end to his suffering."

— Walter C. Alvarez, M.D.

"Death is both a friend and an enemy...We have a basic human right in certain circumstances to decide for ourselves when it is one more than the other."

— A.B. Downing

Some people think that "mercy killing" is the same as euthanasia but this is not so. Jerome Nathanson, chairman of the board of directors of the New York Society for Ethical Culture, and a strong proponent of euthanasia says that the question is not one of killing people, it's a question of letting one die. Mr. Nathanson is quoted as saying that he knew of a doctor who, if a patient is suffering from a terminal illness, leaves three pills on the bedside table and tells the patient, "Take one every four hours. If you take them all at once, they will kill you."

I agree with the philosophy of euthanasia and believe that the medical profession should leave the decision to the patient in cases where the illness is terminal instead of prolonging life under conditions that are horrible for the patient and his family. With all due respect to the medical profession and modern advanced techniques that prolong life, it is desirable to "pull all of the plugs" when the patient is suffering from a terminal illness and life is unbearable. One doctor referred to this procedure as "minicare."

## Economics Of Euthanasia

The cost of hospital and medical care has reached astronomical figures and the average person is not wealthy enough to pay the bills. Even with health insurance and similar coverage, the cost is prohibitive. With the continuance of inflation, there is little if anything that a person can do about it.

Avoid the emotional impact that occurs when a member of your family becomes seriously ill or is hospitalized or institutionalized with a serious terminal ailment. The time to think about the cost of keeping a terminal patient alive is before you are faced with this rough decision. Some doctors tell the family of the terminal patient, "We are working on the cancer problem and hope to solve it in the near future" or "we are obligated to keep a patient alive as long as we can." Keeping your loved one alive after he is terminal or reached the vegetable stage is costly and is no good for the patient or anyone else.

If you are faced with this unpleasant decision, sit down with your doctor and discuss the matter in great detail. A patient in the vegetative stage is not enjoying life and the realistic fact is that the patient and his family are better off if life is not prolonged by artificial means.

## Dead Bodies

The legislature of each state has the power to exercise complete control of the care of dead bodies and the disposition of them by burial or otherwise, for the protection of public health. The local board of health may require a certificate as to the cause of death as a condition to the issuance of a burial permit. It has been said that decent burial or cremation is a part of a person's rights, and these rights are well guarded by the law.

On the death of a husband or a wife, the right to control the funeral disposition is in the surviving spouse, and not in the next of kin. A New York court ruled: "A wife from whom the decedent was separated does not have the rights of a widow concerning his remains." If there is no surviving spouse or if they have waived their rights, then the next of kin are in control of the funeral services. The chain of command of next of kin would normally be: children of proper age; parents; brothers or sisters; or more distant relatives.

The courts agree that a person's wish or direction as to the disposal of his body after death, whether expressed orally or in writing, is entitled to respectful consideration. The late Billy Rose was not that fortunate and his body was kept by a mortuary in New York for more than two years, while his family fought each other in the courts.

Urgent need may require the burial of a body at sea, and where such is the case, the relatives of the dead have no recourse in the matter. The only requirement of the law is that the disposition of the dead body be sanitary and decent. Hundreds of years ago, an English ecclesiastical court ruled: "No mode of burial could be permitted which would prolong the natural decay of the body; that the dead have no legal right to crowd the living; each buried generation must give away to its successor; and that therefore an iron coffin, which would unduly prolong matters, was ecclesiastically inadmissible unless an extra fee was paid to the church."

The rights of relatives of a deceased person to have his corpse remain undisturbed after his burial must yield to the public interest. In a prosecution for homicide, the court may order the body exhumed and an autopsy performed, where it is absolutely necessary to determine the guilt or innocence of a suspect. In an unusual Florida case, a probate judge held: "In ascertaining heirship, the issue can be disproved in this case by an examination of the body of the decedent for the purpose of proving that she had never given birth to a child, and that such issue is material and can be refuted by no other evidence."

The transportation of dead bodies is regulated by proper authorities. An Indiana court held: "A regulation of a state board of health providing that every dead body must be accompanied by a person in charge; who must present a transit permit from the proper health authority giving permission for the removal and showing the name and age of the deceased; the place and cause of death; the point to which the body is to be shipped; and the names of the medical attendant and undertaker; is a reasonable regulation."

## Autopsies

Conditions for inquests or autopsies by coroners are prescribed by the laws of each state. Some states permit the delivering of dead bodies to medical schools for purposes of study and dissection. A private physician must receive the consent of the proper person, in order to perform an autopsy. For the inexperienced, an "autopsy" is an examination of a dead body usually to determine the cause of death.

## Death And Lawsuits

The old common law rule used to be "an action for damages dies with the person." This caused great hardship in cases of personal injuries resulting in death and Lord Campbell's Act, passed in England in 1846, changed this rule of law. It provided that if the injured person had remained alive, whatever rights he possessed during his life-time, may be maintained for 12 months after his death by his executor or administrator for the benefit of his family. Now all of the states have "wrongful death statutes" that protect the survivors in an accident causing death.

The laws of each state provide a statute of limitations; that is the period of time during which a lawsuit must be filed for an alleged wrongful death. This time period will vary from one to three years in different states. In addition to the laws of each individual state, claims filed under federal jurisdiction are covered by the Federal Tort Claims Act, which sets forth time limits.

### Death In Common Disaster

By the Roman law there was no presumption that all who perished in the same disaster died at once. Some of the countries of Northern Europe, notably Holland and Germany, have declared by statute that two persons perishing in a common disaster are presumed to have died at the same moment. This problem becomes very important in cases where property rights depend on priority of death.

Many states have adopted the Uniform Simultaneous Death Act. It provides if there is no clear evidence that the persons involved died otherwise than simultaneously, the property of each person shall be disposed of as if he had survived. In the case of husband and wife, the families of each side would each inherit one-half. A Missouri case held: "Proof of survivorship for only one second would permit the survivor to act as a conduit of title to his or her heirs under the Uniform Simultaneous Death Act."

### Death Certificate

A death certificate is just the opposite of a birth certificate. In most states, the bureau of vital statistics maintain detailed records of persons born in and die in that state. Most mortuaries obtain a number of death certificates for their customers, knowing that they are always needed for insurance companies, social security and many other purposes.

### 7 Years Absence And Death

Most of the states have laws that provide a presumption of death if a person is absent from his residence for 7 years without any information about his whereabouts. The period of absence must be a continuous one. There is no presumption as to the precise time of death.

## When Are You Dead?

In past years a doctor certified when a person was dead. With the advent of transplant of various organs of the human body, the question of life or death has become complicated. The medical profession is not in accord and there is considerable doubt among the legal profession. Death seems to involve more than the heart beat of the patient and artificial stimulants have complicated the answer to "when are you dead?"

## Funeral Directors

The care of dead human bodies, their burial or other disposition, together with the conduct of the funeral services is a function of the undertaker. Some use the name of undertaker and embalmer; funeral director; mortician; or funeral home; but they all mean the same thing. The public health does not require that an undertaker also be an embalmer. An embalmer prepares human remains for burial and also provides the supplies, equipment, and accommodations necessary to accomplish that end. The work of the undertaker begins when the work of the doctor ends and continues until the final disposition of the body. The undertaker is classified as a business man and not a professional man. His business is subject to regulation under the police power of the state, including licensing.

## Funerals

The dictionary defines funerals as the ceremonies held for dead persons, usually before burial. Each individual has to decide how much or little ceremony is desired for the funeral of his loved one. Just as some people try to "keep up with the Jones" during their life-time, they maintain the same philosophy when ordering the funeral arrangements. Basically, they fear what others might say, plus the fact that the survivor is invariably under an emotional strain. The funeral director is a business man and he has things to sell, ranging from a casket to clothes and flowers.

The usual result is that the surviving members of the family, already grief-stricken, wind up by incurring a bill way beyond their financial ability to pay. You hear this type of person say, "Wasn't it a lovely funeral and that is the way Mom or Dad or Uncle Joe would have wanted it." I am not so sure that statement expresses the true desires of the departed relative.

## Mausoleums

Whether the deceased is buried in a gravesite; cremated; the ashes strewn over his favorite spot; or the remains placed in a mausoleum, is a matter of personal preference. A mausoleum is a large tomb usually with a number of places for entombment of the dead, above ground.

Some people object to the body being buried in the ground, even though the body has first been placed in a casket made of varied materials. They prefer the mausoleum tomb which is similar to a filing cabinet and for all practical purposes the casket is filed away, however, it is above the ground.

## Cremation

A crematory is a furnace which reduces the dead body to ashes with fire. The quantity of ashes will vary but usually are limited and will fit into an average size mason jar. This might offend some people, so the funeral director suggests and sells a fancy urn, used as a container for the ashes. The urn can be kept anywhere. Most people seem to prefer to have the urn kept in a building located on the cemetery grounds. Thus, they can pay their respects to their departed loved one at any occasion.

Some years ago, a lady client had a small grocery store located on an Indian reservation in New Mexico. She observed that when an Indian died and was buried in a gravesite, the family would place various food items on top of the grave. During the night, roving bands of dogs would eat all of the food. My client asked an Indian friend, "Why do you place food on your relative's grave when you know the dogs will eat the food?" The Indian replied, "For the same reason that you place flowers on your graves when you know that the person cannot smell them."

## Ashes To Ashes

Some people prefer to keep the ashes of their cremated loved one in an urn, while others prefer to scatter the ashes over some favorite place. Some human ashes have been scattered over the mountains; the ocean; and many other sites. The laws of your state should be checked to find out what limitations, if any, exist as regards scattering of human ashes.

## Veteran Benefits

Important burial benefits are available to men and women who served in the armed forces of the United States. Some of these benefits pass along to the wife and children of the service veteran.

The Veterans Administration, a federal agency, handles all affairs pertaining to veterans. In order to make sure of your rights and benefits, you are urged to contact your closest Veterans Administration in person and find out what they are. The Congress of the United States frequently changes the benefits.

One of the many benefits pertain to burial of veterans and their dependents in national cemetaries that are located throughout the country. Some of the national cemetaries have been filled, in which case similar privileges become available in the closest cemetary that has space. In addition, a coffin draped by an American flag is furnished by the government at no charge and the entire burial service is without charges. For those veterans that prefer to be buried in their private family cemetaries, the government will furnish the coffin draped with an American flag and will pay a cash allowance to apply on the private mortuary bill.

## What To Do With My Body?

When preparing your will, it is a simple matter to direct the executor of your estate to dispose of your body in accordance with your wishes. In addition, it is recommended that your wishes be made known to the immediate members of your family, so that there will be no doubt as to the method of disposal.

People used to be squeamish about discussing death and funerals. The modern trend is the other way which is more practical. If you want to be cremated or have your remains placed in a mausoleum, let your wishes be known to your family as well as by the more formal means of a provision in your last will and testament.

## The High Cost Of Dying

To the high cost of living can be added the high cost of dying.

Most people visit t' ə mortuary of their choice only when they are faced with making funeral arrangements for some member of their family. They are already under an emotional strain and the loss of their relative is equally upsetting. At this sad moment, they are faced with decisions that have to be made in connection with the funeral arrangements.

Even though many mortuaries are fair and reputable, the fact remains that their business is selling coffins and clothes for the dead person, as well as arranging for music and the clergyman to preside and the time for the funeral services. There is a tendency for some people to go overboard and order a funeral that is beyond their financial pocketbook.

In addition to the normal costs of a funeral service, the largest items of expense are the coffin; the burial plot of land at the cemetery; and the cost of perpetual care for the plot. It is impossible to estimate the entire cost because it can vary from one extreme to the other.

Cremation is the most inexpensive means of disposing of the human body. Unlike normal burials, there is no plot of land to buy and there is no perennial care bill to pay. Even the coffin selected can be less expensive for purposes of cremation than for regular burial.

For those that prefer to keep the urn containing the ashes in the cemetary area, there is usually a building known as a crematorium and it contains rows of niches that hold the urn. There is usually a one-time charge for the use of a niche to hold your urn.

### Is A Coffin Necessary For Cremation?

A recent ruling of the California Supreme Court that a coffin is not required in cases of cremation, is sound law. Memorial services for your loved one can be held without the presence of the body, thus savi⁻ɔ ɪe cost of a casket. If regular funeral services are held in the funeral parlor or church, there would be need for a casket to hold the body. I interested, check the law in your state.

# WILLS AND
# PROBATE COURT

The chief object of a will is to enable a person to make provisions for the distribution of his property after death. Some people make wills in satisfaction of moral obligations. It is a very important legal document and the law books are filled with cases of disappointed relatives trying to break a will, usually where large sums of money are involved. If Uncle Joe died a "poor boy" his family is unhappy about his poverty but there is no need for a lawsuit.

## Definitions

It will help to understand "A Last Will And Testament" better with the following definitions:

**Testator or Testatrix:** A male or female maker of a will

**Testate:** Death with a will

**Intestate:** Death without a will

**To Probate:** The process of proving a will in court

**Executor or Executrix:** A man or woman named in the will to handle the assets of the estate

**Administrator or Administratrix:** A man or woman appointed by the court to handle the assets of the estate

**Bequest:** A gift of personal property under a will

**Devise:** A gift of real property under a will

**Legatee:** The person to whom a legacy or bequest is given

## Who Can Make A Will?

Every sane person can make a will. The laws of each state grant this right and they vary from state to state. The laws of the state of your residence are your only concern. Because a person is old and forgetful does not preclude them from making a valid will. A mere use of drugs or intoxicants is not in itself sufficient to prove that a person does not have the mental capacity to make a will. A child over 14 years old can make a will disposing of personal property.

### Can A Will Be Changed?

Yes, during the lifetime of the testator, a will is a meaningless piece of paper. A will takes effect only when the person who made it dies. When you talk about wills, you must talk about death. A will can be destroyed or changed at anytime. This can be accomplished by making a new will or by a codicil. A codicil is a separate document, changing a provision of the original will. The latest will is the only effective instrument. Earlier wills should be destroyed but if not, they are of no legal value. There is no limit to the number of times a person can change their will.

### Must A Will Give Property Away?

Whether or not a will is testamentary in character depends upon the intention of the maker. If there is no testamentary intent, there can be no will. An old Pennsylvania case held: "The words "if enny thing happens" in a paper making provisional disposition of property is valid upon the death of the writer."

### Form Of A Will

No particular form of words or expressions is necessary to constitute a legal disposition of property by will. A Kentucky court ruled that a letter written to his daughters by a man sentenced to death, stating that he made them a deed to the house and lot, may be probated as a will sufficient to pass title to the property.

### Must A Lawyer Be Hired To Prepare A Will?

No, any person can prepare his own will if that be his desire. Forms are available at most stationery stores at a nominal cost. If you think you are knowledgeable, fill in the blank spaces.

There is no law that makes it mandatory to hire a lawyer to prepare your will, however, it is strongly recommended. The legal fee charged is nominal as compared with expensive problems that can develop when a will is prepared by an untrained person. If you prepare your own will and name your executor and fail to add the magic words, "to serve without bond" your legal fee saving is down the drain. Your named executor is required by law to provide a surety bond to indemnify the estate against any loss and the cost of this bond comes out of your estate. You did not want your executor bonded because of your faith in him, yet your lack of knowledge caused this unnecessary expense. You may be pleasantly surprised when you ask your lawyer what his charges are to prepare your will. If you need or want a will, hire your legal expert and don't be penny wise and pound foolish. Don't emulate a business man who tried to save $25 and made out his own will. He wanted his entire estate to be divided equally between his adult son from his first marriage and his second wife who was active in the family business. His home-made will was not clear and the dispute landed in probate court. I agreed with his widow who compromised and settled the lawsuit even though we were confident of a favorable trial result. The lady said: "The last thing my husband would have wanted would be for his son and I to fight each other in a courtroom."

## What Happens If Part Of A Will Is Invalid?

The failure of the validity of one part of a will does not effect the portions of it which are valid. A South Carolina court held that a bequest to a man's mistress which exceeded one fourth of his estate, in violation of the law, is void only as to the extent of such excess and does not defeat the rest of the will.

## Immoral Persons

Morality is not a test of testamentary power. Social outcasts and underworld characters are competent to bequeath to and to receive bequests from another.

## What About Murder Of The Testator By A Beneficiary?

An exception to the right of persons to take property by will is made in the case of a beneficiary who murders the testator. It is based on public policy and applies to cases of manslaughter as well as murder. The law says a man shall not profit by his own wrong and in depriving the testator of the right to change his will, is not permitted to receive benefits under the will.

In cases where the testator has been murdered, provisions other than those involving the murderer, are fully operative.

### Who May Inherit?

In ancient times, corporations and bodies politic were not authorized to inherit any property. The laws of the various states now permit corporations or the state or federal government to be named as beneficiaries. Some people who have no families, leave their entire estate to the United States of America, a church of their choice or some charitable organizations. The Smithsonian Institute at Washington was created by the bequest of an Englishman.

### Formal Requirements Of A Will

The right to dispose of property by will is a creature of statute and subject to legislative control. The laws of each state vary and it is important to understand the requirements of your particular state. Not all documents which are testamentary in content constitute valid wills. No other legal instrument requires such solemnity in the manner of its execution. The reason for all of the formalities are to prevent fraud and to insure that the testator's property will go as he wills it.

Some states require that a will be signed in the presence of two witnesses, while others require three witnesses.

It is the policy of the courts to sustain a will as legally executed, if it is possible to do so consistently with the requirements of the statutes.

### Will Witnesses And Appearance In Probate Court

Usually, one of the witnesses to a will is required to appear in probate court at the time the will is admitted to probate. Attorneys and others who have moved or are not available are permitted to sign an affidavit form that answers pertinent questions. Examples might be: "Did you see John Jones, the testator, sign his will on such and such a date?" "Did he appear to be mentally competent?" "Was Mary Smith, the other witness to the signing of the will, present at the same time?" The affidavit form and the questions are purely routine and inasmuch as most wills are uncontested, the probate judge leans over backward to approve the will and admit it to probate.

Most attorneys use their legal secretaries to witness the signing of will by clients. If the attorney is named in the will to be the executor, he prefers not to be a witness. If the witnesses died or can not be found, the attorney could testify as to his preparation of the will and the pertinent facts as to the presence of the witnesses and the important fact that he observed each witness sign his name.

## Must A Will Be In Writing?

Years ago, many people were unable to read or write and oral wills were valid. This was accomplished by words or signs. Later the law provided that real property could pass only by a will in writing, while personal property could be bequested orally, without any formality whatever.

Currently a will must be in writing to be valid whether it disposes of personal or real property. The two exceptions will be discussed later in this chapter.

## Must A Will Be Typewritten?

No, it may be written by hand or typewritten, or printed from plates or type. So long as a will is written, it does not matter on what material, whether on paper or parchment. It can be written in pencil or ink or a combination of both. It may be written on one or more sheets of paper. It is advisable for the testator to sign his name or initials to each page so that no claim can later be made that there was a substitution of pages.

A will is valid even if written in a foreign language and the judge can appoint an interpreter to translate it into English.

One case held that it was not a desecration of the Sabbath for a will to be executed on Sunday.

## Must The Testator Sign The Will?

Yes, a will must be signed by the testator in order to be entitled to probate, whether it disposes of real or personal property.

In an unusual case, a testator started to write his name, but, after making one stroke of the pen, laid the pen down saying, "I can't sign it now." The judge held there was not a sufficient signature.

Some judges hold that an illegible signature may be regarded as the testator's mark within the rule that permits a will to be executed by mark. A will may be signed by mark affixed by another in the presence and at the direction of the testator, where the statute permits a valid signature to be affixed for the testator. Under some statutes a testator signing by mark must expressly declare his inability to sign his name.

### Do You Need A Seal On A Will?

No, although seals are frequently attached to wills, they are unnecessary and do not take the place of the signature. A seal is strictly window-dressing because it can easily be counterfeited.

### Where Do You Sign A Will?

The statutes of most states fix the location of the signature and require that it must be at the foot or end of the will. Otherwise, the door might be opened to fraud in adding new provisions to the will that were not authorized by the testator.

### What Is Attestation?

Attestation consists in witnessing the signing of the will by the testator. It included the manual act of signing afterwards as a witness as well as the visual act of observing the testator.

Attestation is required in order that evidence will be forthcoming after the testator's death of the circumstances surrounding the signing of the will. The witnesses are neutral and are able to observe the mental capacity of the testator.

### Can A Relative Or Beneficiary Be A Witness?

No, the laws of most states provide that the witness to a will must be disinterested. If a witness will gain or loose as the direct result of a proceeding to probate a will, he is barred. A husband or wife may not act as a witness to the other's will.

### Can My Lawyer Be A Witness?

Yes. Lawyers are competent to attest to wills which they have drafted in accordance with instructions received from their clients.

### Can A Will Be Broken Or Set Aside?

Yes. Undue influence, fraud, and mistakes are recognized grounds for contesting the probate of a will or setting aside probate. A sane testator has the right to dispose of his property as he chooses. Undue influence overcomes the free volition of the testator and substitutes the desires of another. The undue influence in the execution of a will which will invalidate it may be that of a third person, as well as of a beneficiary. A husband or wife may be guilty of undue influence invalidating the will of his or her spouse.

As a practical matter in cases where large sums of money are involved, a lawsuit to contest the will becomes a matter of economics. Beneficiaries who inherited a lot of money decide they are better off to settle the disputed claim, rather than have the estate tied up in litigation for years.

Undue influence and fraud are very closely associated in reference to the contest of a will. The words "fraud," "duress," and "undue influence" are frequently used interchangeably in contests.

A mistake whereby the wrong instrument is executed by the testator is sufficient to invalidate a will, if the intent of the testator is thereby frustrated.

## Can You Revoke A Will?

Yes, the easiest way to revoke an existing will is to make a new one. The old will should be destroyed, however, if it is not destroyed, the latest will is the only one that counts.

## Does Divorce Affect A Will?

As between the spouses, a divorce in and of itself would have no bearing on either of them. If either of the parties permitted an existing will to continue without change, the terms of the will would be valid in spite of the divorce.

Immediately upon completion of the divorce as well as property settlement agreement, the parties should prepare a new will if they desire to delete their former spouse from being a beneficiary under the old will.

## Does The Birth Of A Child Revoke The Will Of The Father?

The after-born children takes his share as an heir of the testator. Technically, the will is revoked to accomplish this desirable result. The birth of a posthumous child is within the same rule. A posthumous child is born after the death of the father. The legal reasoning is that marriage and the birth of a child effect such a change in the circumstances of the testator that it is presumed that he intended to alter the disposition of his property.

In many states the effect of the birth of a child on a will previously made is controlled by statute.

### What About The Rights Of An Illegitimate Child?

The answer to the question depends upon the law of each state as to whether the illegitimate child would share in the estate as an heir in the absence of a will.

The birth of a child which, although illegitimate upon birth, is later legitimatized by the marriage of its parents has been held to revoke a will executed by one of its parents before the marriage.

### Can A Child Be Disinherited With A $1 Bequest?

A child can be disinherited but the old theory that he must be left $1 is groundless. In order to avoid any claim by the disinherited child that he was "overlooked" the will can state that he is not being overlooked but he is being disinherited and left nothing.

### Holographic Will

A holographic will is one that is entirely written and signed by the testator in his own handwriting. If a date is required, as it is in some jurisdictions by statute, the date must also be in the handwriting of the testator. An instrument prepared by filling blanks in a stationer's form, and adding specific provisions, does not create a valid holographic will. A holographic will need not be acknowledged in the presence of witnesses.

### Nuncupative Wills

A nuncupative will is a will that is not in writing, and exists only when the testator, declares his will orally before witnesses.

### Can A Husband Disinherit His Wife?

No, it does not matter whether a wife is a good wife or a bad wife.

Unfortunately, there is no answer to the question, "What is the American law on wills or probate court proceedings?" because each state has its own laws. Although the laws of the 50 states are frequently similar, they still differ to an important extent and one must look to the state of his residence to learn the applicable law.

The wife has certain rights in her husband's estate and he is not permitted to cut his wife off entirely. In many states, a wife is entitled to 50 percent of her husband's estate and he controls the remaining half. The husband can will his one half to his parents, family, mistress, or anyone of his choice.

If the husband does not leave a will, then the laws of the particular state apply. As an average guess, the widow would inherit about 5/8ths and the remaining 3/8ths would go to the child or children.

In some jurisdictions, the privilege of making a will by nuncupation is denied absolutely. The general rule followed by most authorities is that an oral or nuncupative will can be made only when the testator is in his last illness. The testator must practically be on his death-bed so that a nuncupative will is exercised as a matter of necessity and not of choice. Where a testator lived for nine days after the nuncupation, the judge ruled he had the time, opportunity and means to have reduced the will to writing but failed to do so.

## Soldiers' And Sailors' Wills

The oral wills of soldiers or sailors are to be regarded as informal wills rather than nuncupative wills. The privilege of making a soldier's or sailor's will is limited by state law which confers it to the disposition of personal property only. A statement made by a soldier when embarking with his regiment for overseas service that a certain person should have everything he possessed if anything should happen to him, has been held to be testamentary declaration.

## Conditional Wills

An example of a conditional will is where the testator refers in the will to his possible death upon a trip contemplated by him, from dangers involving military service, from a surgical operation. etc. The will becomes unconditional upon the testator's death under the circumstances stated in the condition. A statement made in a soldier's will, written in the form of a letter, "If I never get back to you I want all I have to be yours," was held to make the will conditional. If death does not occur from the feared event, the will never becomes operative.

## Joint Wills

A joint will is a single testamentary document which contains the wills of two or more persons, is executed jointly by them, and disposes of property owned jointly, or in common by them.

"Reciprocal" wills are those in which the testators name each other as beneficiaries under similar testamentary plans.

### Where To Keep Your Will

The only important will is the signed original. The unsigned copy is kept by your attorney for future reference but is not a valid will. The signed original will can be kept in your safety deposit box with this information passed along to your family. Many banks will keep your will in their vault as a customer service with no charge. The will is only of value as of the time of death of the testator. Many testators deem it advisable to inform members of the family involved in their will as to the main provisions and also the name and address of the attorney and executor. Sometimes the attorney and executor are one and the same person.

### Should The Executor Be Bonded?

The only reason for requiring an executor to be bonded is to indemnify the estate in the event the executor "dipped into the till." Most testators name their spouse, adult child, or some other person held in high esteem, as their executor and feel no need for requiring a bond. If a bond is required, the cost of the bond premium is billed to the estate.

If the testator does not desire that his named executor be bonded, his will states: "I hereby name and appoint John Jones, my beloved son to act as executor of my estate and to serve without bond." If those magic words "to serve without bond" are not included, even a son will have to order a bond and the estate has to pay for it.

Many states have exempted banks and trust companies from being bonded. The reasoning is that they are financial institutions and are financially responsible in the event of any claim against them.

### Husband And Wife Die Simultaneously

Death in a common disaster occurs more often today due to modern automobiles and aircraft. Unusual situations have developed in cases where it became financially important to ascertain whether the husband and wife died at the same moment or one survived the other by seconds. To solve this problem in a fair manner, many states have adopted a "Simultaneous Death Act" which presumes that husband and wife died at the identical moment unless there is clear proof to the contrary. If the couple left children there is no problem. If no children are involved, then one half of the couple's estate goes to the husband's family and the remaining one half to the wife's family.

*Should I Have A Will?*

Yes, it is recommended that you have a will if you have accumulated a reasonable amount of assets. Obviously, if you are a pauper there is no need for a will. The main reason for having a will is the orderly disposition of your estate in a manner that you prefer. The cost of a simple, uncomplicated will is nominal and should be drawn by your attorney. During my years of law practice, there were certain situations where I recommended the preparation of a will, even though I was able to help my clients in preserving their estate in such a manner that their will would not be used. This may sould like "double talk" but the facts will be explained in detail in following subtitles.

*What Happens If I Don't Have A Will?*

Every state has enacted laws to cover the estates of persons who die intestate, meaning without a will. Things that you could have covered in a will are now done in your behalf by the probate judge. You could have selected an executor in your will, and now the probate judge will appoint an administrator or administratrix to handle your estate, however, they will have to furnish a bond and the cost is charged against your estate. If a husband dies and his wife is appointed the administratrix of her husband's estate, the law says a bond is mandatory. This expenditure is needless and wasteful but is one of the penalties for not having a will.

In a will, after a wife's interest is deducted, the husband controls the disposition of the rest of his estate. When the husband dies without a will, the laws of his state control. The widow is entitled to her legal share and the same applies to a child or children. Children share equally, regardless of need, age, health, or other factors.

Not having a will is not a complete disaster but it is preferable to have a will. It is cheap insurance in case of need.

*Can Costly Probate Court Proceedings Be Eliminated?*

Yes, under certain circumstances. Under the subtitle, "Should I

Have A Will?" reference was made to a will that might never be used. If you are scratching your head in wonderment as to why a will would be prepared if it was not going to be used, there is a reasonable explanation. The preparation of the will is cheap insurance in the event the estate planning did not work out to avoid probate proceedings. in which case the will would be used and proven in probate court.

## Why Avoid Probate Court?

There are two important reasons for doing everything possible to avoid probate court in connection with proving a will. Probate court proceedings are expensive and take a long period of time. The procedural rules for probating a will in many states are archaic and should be streamlined and changed. The cost and time factor are the subjects of complaints, not only from the dead person's family who pay the bill but also certain members of the legal profession. As a member of the bar, I agree with those lawyers who are more concerned with the welfare of the testator's survivors, than earning bigger fees by keeping estates in probate court for long periods of time.

## Is The Size Of The Estate Important?

Yes, when talking about ways and means of avoiding probate court proceedings. Under present federal law, each person is exempted from federal/inheritance tax for the first $60,000. For a married couple, this exemption means $120,000.

For those whose estates are much larger or who are involved in complicated trust agreements, probate court proceedings would probably be required. The reasoning being that federal inheritance tax starts after $60,000 for one person or $120,000 for a married couple.

The recommended plan that follows to avoid probate court proceedings is designed for the average American family where the total value of the family estate is less than $120,000. Those that own larger estates should seek the advice of their lawyer, certified public accountant and or estate planner.

## Probate Court - How Much Does It Cost?

The main expense of probate court proceedings is not the minimum court costs and expenses of about $200 but the fees for the attorney and sometimes the executor, which are usually regulated by the laws of each state. Usually, the fee schedule for the executor and the attorney is the same and is based on a percentage of the value of the estate. The percentage is scaled downward as the amount of the value of the estate increases. For the average sized estate, a rough rule of thumb is five percent of the appraised value of the estate for attorney's fees and if there is an outside executor, his fee would be the same.

## Who Should Be Named As Executor?

There are a number of recommended choices and they vary with each family situation and the complexity of the estate. If the estate is a large one and the various holdings and equities and assets are complex, some people prefer to name their bank as executor. The advantage of naming a financial institution is that no bond is required which means a saving for the estate. Also, death of any named individual is eliminated because banks do not go out of business and the present trust officer will always be replaced by a successor.

Others have explicit faith in their attorney and name him as executor of the decedent's estate. Like banks, the laws of many states exempt attorneys from posting any bond, while acting in the capacity of executor. Most attorneys charge no additional amount for acting as executor where they are retained as attorney for probate purposes.

Most married couples prefer to name their surviving spouse as executor in the case of the husband and executrix in the case of the wife. There is no reason to have your spouse bonded, so your attorney who prepares your will, will use the magic words "AND TO SERVE WITHOUT BOND." Although a spouse who serves as executor or executrix is legally entitled to the same fee as earned by the lawyer, it is usually waived in order to avoid income tax liability.

## How Long Do Probate Court Proceedings Take?

The time factor is shocking and no one can explain any valid reason for long delays that are provided in the archaic laws of most states. In one state, the minimum period of time to conclude a simple probate proceedings is nine months, if every step is accomplished on its due date with no delays. As a practical manner, one year would be a more reasonable estimate for the completion of a simple probate proceeding. If the estate involves a large sum of money or there are disputes between members of the family, the one year estimate can stretch out to a number of years.

*Why Does It Take So Long?*

The laws of many states give creditors of the decedent six months in which to file their claim against the estate. No distinction is made in cases where the testator operated on a cash basis and there are no creditors. So the estate probate file lies dormant and all concerned twiddle their thumbs waiting for the six months silly law to pass.

If a will is contested or any other litigation develops, be prepared for a long delay until the dispute is settled by a ruling of the judge. The longer it drags and the more appearances in court, the higher the attorney's fees.

As one judge said to the eight lawyers present in the courtroom, where a litigated estate involving millions of dollars was at stake, "Gentlemen, if a reasonable compromise is not affected soon, the attorney's fees will eat up the assets of this estate."

Oldtimers in the legal profession tell the story about the father attorney and his young son who just became an attorney. While the father was away he received the following telegram from his son, "Just completed the Jones Estate that you have been working on for twenty years." The father's reply read: "Sorry about that. Now, we will both have to go to work."

*The Plan For Married Couples*

The plan refers to legal methods of avoiding probate court proceedings. The plan is simple and involves a married couple who get along reasonably well and have faith in each other. *ALL OF THEIR ASSETS ARE KEPT IN JOINT OWNERSHIP.* This means that the survivor gets all. If the couple are suspicious of each other or are headed for divorce court, forget about the plan.

Title to everything that the couple own, real or personal property, is in the name of husband and wife, jointly. Upon the occasion of death, the survivor gets all without any necessity for going into probate court.

Real property is usually the deed to the family home or could be other real estate. The most common items of personal property involved, are checking accounts; savings accounts; safety deposit boxes; title certificates to all motor vehicles; certificates of stocks or bonds; etc.

*Why Joint Ownership?*

Between husband and wife, whichever dies first, the surviving spouse has access to all of the family estate assets immediately. If either or both had previously prepared wills, the wills can be ignored and probate court proceedings eliminated.

## What About The Children?

Remember the primary requirement for the plan for married couples was those that get along reasonably well and have faith in each other. Faith means that the surviving spouse will do the right thing by the children that the couple brought into the world. If the wife who is now a new widow, runs off with a travelling salesman and leaves the children to fend for themselves, the plan would be a failure. The same if the husband, who is now a new widower, remarries and fails to provide for the children of his first marriage.

## Is Real Estate Handled The Same As Personal Property?

No, title to real estate is manifested by a deed. In the case of joint ownership, the deed to the family home or other land is made out: "John Jones and Mary Jones, his wife, as joint tenants with rights of survivorship."

A joint bank account is accomplished by both parties signing an appropriate card furnished by your bank.

For all title certificates to a motor vehicle, it would read: "John Jones and/or Mary Jones, his wife." Ditto for stock certificates.

## How Does Title To Real Estate Pass To The Surviving Spouse?

The name of the game is how to avoid expensive probate court proceedings. Personal property passes to the surviving spouse under joint ownership with no problems. It is immediate and certain.

There is one requirement necessary to complete the passage of title to real estate to the surviving spouse. Many states have a simplified procedure known as "Waiver of Administration" and it involves a simple form filled out by the new widow, with the help of her attorney. In a matter of a few weeks, a waiver is issued in the new widow's name and she is now free to sell, borrow on or give away the family home or other real estate. The cost is minimal in comparison to probate court proceedings.

## What Happens If A Husband Buys Real Estate In His Own Name?

If the deed for a land purchase is made out to "John Jones" or to

"John Jones, a married man" or to "John Jones and Mary Jones, his wife" with no other designation, the death of the party results in bad news, meaning probate court proceedings. When you buy a home, you are buying land along with the improvements on the land. The example above of the deed made out to "John Jones and Mary Jones, his wife" failed because it did not specify that title was being taken as joint tenants with rights of survivorship. The laws of the fifty states do vary and the reader is urged to consult with his attorney to learn the law in your particular state.

## Can The Plan For A Married Couple Be Used By A Widow And Her Children?

Yes. Joint ownership of personal or real property can be accomplished by any two or more persons. They do not have to be husband and wife and they are not required to be related.

On numerous occasions, a widow would ask if probate court proceedings could be avoided where she had $60,000 in cash or equities and three adult children. Children who are minors present legal problems in that they can legally receive property but cannot sell without a guardian and court approval. My answer to such a widow was yes, under the following plan. If you have faith in your three adult children and all get along well, take your $60,000 and open a joint account with each child for $20,000. All of your children understand that even though legally they have access to their $20,000 joint account with Mother, that Mother controls the funds during her lifetime. Upon the occasion of Mother's death, each child has access to their particular account. If Mother needed $6,000 during her lifetime for medical or other expenses, she should take $2,000 out of each of the three joint accounts, so that each adult child receives equal and fair treatment.

## Why Do We Need Probate Courts?

As modern politicos might say, "That is a good question and I am glad that you asked it." The fact of the matter is that there is no real need for a separate court to handle wills and the estates of dead persons. We are prone to continue with customs established by our forefathers, even though times have changed and the need no longer exists. Years ago, there probably was a need for Justices of the Peace for every small area. Today, that need no longer exists.

Most state courts handle any number of civil and criminal

matters. Federal courts handle any number of civil and criminal matters involving federal jurisdiction.

The jurisdiction of Probate courts is restricted to proving the validity of wills and any and all other disputes pertaining to the estate of a deceased person.

## What About A Dead Person Who Owned Property In More Than One State?

If the decedent owned property in more than one state, his state of residence would handle the main probate court proceedings and the other state or states would handle ancillary probate proceedings. Ancillary can be compared with a branch office that reports back to the main office for completion of the estate. The more branch offices involved, the longer it takes and the higher the court expenses and attorney's fees.

## American Citizens Living Abroad And Their Wills

It is estimated that more than one half million Americans live outside of the continental limits of the United States. Most American citizens living abroad are residents of some state in the United States. Residence is a matter of intent and does not require physical presence.

Under normal conditions, a will would be probated in the state of residence of the decedent. If an American living abroad decided to become a resident of some foreign country and then died, his will would be probated in the country of his residence.

# MARRIAGE

"Love and marriage; love and marriage;-...you can't have one without the other;" is part of the lyrics of an old song. But the statement is no longer true. A number of young people have decided that life in a commune is more desirable than the old-fashioned concept of marriage. Others seem to prefer living together as a married couple, without benefit of marriage. Some even claim that marriage is going out of fashion. The former concept is that marriage is a wonderful institution — *IF* you want to live in an institution.

Marriage is the status of a man and a woman who have been legally united as husband and wife. Marriage is a legal state of wedlock or union of two persons of opposite sex associated together as husband and wife for the prime purpose of establishing a family. Because of the importance of marriage as a social relationship, it is favored by public policy and the law. The state has a vital interest in the marriage and particularly in the children that are born the issue of the marriage. Thus, the state may enact rules regulating requirements of the parties entering into the marriage contract.

Under American law, all valid marriages continue during the joint lives of the parties or until divorce or annulment. There are three parties to a marriage and mothers-in-law are not one of them. The three involved are the man; the woman; and the state. Some courts are now holding that marriage is more than a contract; that it is a status. But the final result of rights and obligations of parties to a marriage contract are fixed, changed, or dissolved by law.

A Colorado judge ruled as follows: "That a written agreement entered into after marriage by a husband and wife that provided for the dissolution of their marriage on the consent of either party, with release by the wife of all her rights upon the payment by the husband of $100 for each year they lived together, was nothing more than an attempt to legalize prostitution under the name of marriage, at the price of $100 per year." This man could hardly be called "a big spender." When his death occurs, the cause will probably not be "enlargement of the heart."

*Proxy Marriage*

A proxy marriage occurs when one or both of the parties is absent and is represented by an agent who has authority to act for the principal in the marriage ceremony. Sometimes soldiers are ordered overseas on such short notice that they cannot get married before leaving the country; in other cases soldiers whose service abroad will be extended desire to marry before they return to their girl back home. The purpose of such marriage may be to legitimatize a child born or conceived before the marriage, to afford financial assistance to the party back home, to merely satisfy a desire to be married, or to fulfill any other legal purpose. Some states recognize proxy marriages, however, most states do not.

*Minimum Age*

It is within the legislative power of each state to determine the age at which persons can marry. While there are variations of as much as 2 or 3 years among the various states, the laws of most states provide that males may marry at 21 without parental consent and at 18 years with such consent. That females may marry at 18 without parental consent and at 16 with such consent. Marriage of even younger girls is authorized where pregnancy or birth of an illegitimate child is established.

*Physical Requirements*

While physical health is not a requirement for a valid marriage, the laws of some states prohibit the marriage of persons with specific diseases or other physical disabilities. A Delaware statute prohibits marriage of persons who are epileptics, venerally diseased, habitual drunkards, or confirmed users of narcotics. A Pennsylvania court, noting that the discovery of new drugs had dramatically reduced the ill effects of epilepsy, said that enlightened medical opinion now regards the absolute bar to marriage of epileptics as harsh, unjust, and unnecessary.

Impotency, which is the inability to have sexual intercourse, is frequently held to render the marriage voidable. A West Virginia judge said: "Pre-existing incurable impotency of one of the parties to a marriage renders impossible the procreation of children, and such defeats one of the chief purposes of marriage."

Sterility, however, which is the inability to bear children, is not a disqualification for marriage. If the parties can have sexual intercourse, the requirements of the law are fulfilled. The marriage of a person who is sterile may be annulled for fraud, if representations to the contrary were made before marriage.

## Formal Requirements

It is within the legislative power of each state to regulate and require certain procedures in order to obtain a marriage license. The usual requirements include a blood test or other physical examination; the issuance of a license; persons who shall perform the ceremony; witnesses required; and that a certificate of marriage be signed, returned, and recorded with the county clerk. Some states further provide for a waiting period before the marriage license may be issued. This waiting period is supposed to prevent hasty or ill-advised marriages, and vary from 3 to 30 days.

Some states have enacted laws providing that unmarried persons who have been living together as husband and wife may be married by a clergyman without a license. The public policy behind such laws is to shield the parties and their children, if any, from the publicity of a marriage recorded in the regular way. The law thinks it will encourage unmarried persons who have been living together as man and wife to legalize their relationship.

## Common-Law Marriage

A common-law marriage is an informal arrangement whereby a man and woman live together as husband and wife without benefit of marriage. Marriage by consent is another name for common-law marriages. This relationship is recognized by some states and is not recognized by others. Unfortunately, for those states that do not recognize common-law marriages as being valid, the woman receives no protection. Sometimes, when the couple have lived together for many years, it is very unfair to the woman who does not receive the usual benefits that belong to a legal wife. In a normal marriage, if the husband died and left no will, his widow would inherit his estate. If there were no children, she would inherit all and with children, her share would vary starting at one-half. In a common law marriage in a state that does not recognize them, under identical facts, the wife would lose out entirely and inherit nothing. The moral is obvious, wives should protect themselves by entering into a legal marriage contract.

In those states that recognize common-law marriages, cohabitation or public recognition is essential to establish such a marriage. A Florida judge ruled: "Something more than a secret or undisclosed private agreement between the parties must be shown in order to establish a common-law marriage, because the state is a party to every such agreement, and it must necessarily be of a public nature."

*Incest*

A legal marriage cannot be formed if the parties are already related to each other, within certain degrees, that are prohibited by law. Religious dogma has played a large part in the history of incest regulations. The science of eugenics preserves and strengthens the racial and physical quality of the population by preventing inbreeding. A New Jersey court noted "medical opinion that the only effect upon offspring of a marriage between an uncle and his niece would be an increased chance of transmitting any disease or weakness which already existed in the bloodline, and that such relationship might be treated not as biologically harmful but only as sociologically improper," but nevertheless concluded that the public policy of New Jersey was opposed to such marriages and that they should not be recognized as valid.

No state or country permits the marriage of brother and sister or parent and child. Even the marriage of first cousins is prohibited by some states.

The chief fear of inbreeding is that children born of the union will be defective physically or mentally. Royalty of years gone by are good examples of the dangers of inbreeding.

*One Color And Another*

At one time many of the states enacted laws prohibiting marriages between persons of different races. Many of these same states enacted laws prohibiting a white person from marrying a black. Finally, the United States Supreme Court ruled that state laws prohibiting a person of one color from marrying a person of another color, violated the equal protection and due process clauses of the Fourteenth Amendment of the constitution. At the time of the United States Supreme Court opinion, 16 states still had miscegenation laws on their books. Miscegenation laws used to prohibit the marriage of one color to another. Now the universal law provides that a person of one color may marry a person of another color.

# ADOPTION

## Background Information

The most pleasurable experiences in my twenty-five years of law practice came from handling adoption matters. It did my heart good to know that I was contributing to the happiness of some unfortunate youngster, even though I rarely saw the baby or child to be adopted. I cannot ignore my Goddaughter Nancy, whose adoption resulted in the honor bestowed upon me by her adoptive Parents. Being the natural Father of two young adult Sons, I was delighted to acquire my first Goddaughter.

It is sad that the law says that a child born out of wedlock or to an unwed mother is an illegitimate child. I have always contended that the parents are illegitimate inasmuch as the child is an innocent victim.

I shall never forget the Navy couple who had adopted a Japanese boy while stationed in that country; a Korean girl while stationed there and a Spanish-American boy in New Mexico. When I told them that the world would have fewer problems if more people were as liberal, kind and broadminded as they were and what a blessing for the three children involved; they replied that the adoption of the three children was a blessing for them, rather than the children.

In the United States the right of adoption is governed by the laws of each state. Although the laws of individual states will vary, generally speaking, the basic requirements are similar for most of the states. A good example of an exception occurs when the laws of a particular state permit an adoption to be completed by a single person rather than a married couple.

Each state has the power to provide for the adoption of a child or children after notice to, and with the consent of the natural parents. In the case of an unwed mother, her consent alone is sufficient. An unusual situation arises when a couple are divorced and the custody of the minor children are awarded to the wife and the husband is under court order to pay child support and he fails to comply with the court's order. Under these facts, it has been held that upon remarriage of the wife, she and her incoming husband may adopt the children without obtaining the consent of their natural father. If the father had complied with the court's order and supported his children, it is mandatory that his consent be given, otherwise no adoption can be completed against his will.

## How To Adopt A Child

The procedure for filing a petition in court to adopt a child is quite simple. Many states have printed or mimeographed forms that merely require the filling in of routine information. One question calls for the new name of the child being adopted, if the adoptive parents desire to change its first name. Some couples have decided that they are capable of filing their own adoption petition without hiring an attorney. This is possible if they are knowledgeable because the law does not require that an attorney be retained.

After the adoption petition has been filed in duplicate, one copy is referred to an investigative agency of the state, usually the Child Welfare Department or comparable. In due course of time, the adoptive parents will be notified of the welfare worker assigned to investigate the home conditions and certain requirements, preliminary to the home visit. The adoptive parents are usually required to complete a physical examination by their personal doctor; proof of their marriage or divorce and similar necessary "red-tape." Remember, when the welfare worker assigned calls at the adopting home, her chief function is not to be personal or nosey but to verify that the adoptive child will be raised in a loving home. There is no requirement that the adoptive parents must be wealthy or anything of the sort. The law is more concerned with the welfare of the child to be adopted than with any other factor.

Many states have a waiting period before the adoption petition may be completed. Frequently, the waiting period is six months from the filing date or in the case of a new-born infant, on its first birthday. You may wonder why there is a waiting period or why it takes so long. One reason is to enable the state's agency to investigate the home of the adoptive parents and insure that it will be raised in surroundings that are clean, wholesome and loving.

There is a serious pitfall in connection with adopting a newborn infant from an unwed mother. Frequently, the unwed mother leaves her own community and goes elsewhere to complete her pregnancy and await the birth of her baby. The identity of the father is either unknown or his name is shielded and in view of the fact that he refused to marry the girl, he plays no part in the adoption proceedings. Usually, the unwed mother winds up in a strange community with limited funds. She may be forced to live in a home for unwed mothers, while waiting for the birth of the child. The unwed mother's obstetrician is the first to learn that she is unable or unwilling to provide for her unborn infant and that she is desirous of having her baby adopted by a married couple. Many doctors have a list of married couples who are anxious to adopt a child and this information is relayed to one of them.

Now we come to the important part where employing an attorney is strongly recommended. Someone has to meet the unwed mother before the baby is born and act as intermediary between the parties and explain the legal situation to the unwed mother. It is desirable that the unwed mother and the adoptive parents not meet each other or even know each others identity. Yet, each side wants background information about the other. The adoptive parents are vitally interested in the occupation and educational background of the unwed mother and as much inforamtion as she is willing to furnish about the father's background. On the other hand, the unwed mother is interested in learning about the type of home her baby will be raised in and most of all, that it will be loved.

The important part played by the attorney involved is to explain in great detail to the unwed mother about the seriousness of the entire adoption proceedings and the gravity of not changing her mind later. The law books are filled with heartrending cases where the unwed mother consented in writing to the adoption of her unborn baby. Then the adoptive parents paid the hospital, doctor and attorney's bills and made all the necessary preparations for the baby's clothes, toys and room. No one can fall as madly in love with a child as can adoptive parents. Now comes the tragedy in the case of the unwed mother who says, "I am sorry but I have changed my mind and I now want my baby back." As you can well imagine, this heartbreaking situation is not pleasant and the lawsuit that follows leads to varied results. Of the hundreds of adoptions that I handled over a period of many years, I was never faced with this problem.

In a happier vien, the adoption petition has been completed and approved by the court and the baby has its new name as selected by the adoptive parents. One important final step remains, namely a birth certificate that will not disclose any adoption proceedings. Most states issue a corrected birth certificate, even though the word "corrected" obviously does not appear. On the corrected birth certificate, the date and place of birth of the adopted child cannot be changed but the names of the adoptive mother and father are filled in, the same as if they were the natural parents. Thus, as the years go by, anyone examining the adopted child's birth certificate would have no way of knowing about any adoption.

## Are Adoptions Secret?

In the average American city, the local newspaper publishes a daily vital statistics page listing who married yesterday; who died; who had a baby; who filed for divorce or legal separation; and who sued someone else for many and varied causes of complaint.

However, adoption petitions are treated differently than other legal cases. They are not available for newspaper publication and are filed separate and apart under lock and key. In order to maintain the required secrecy of an adoption petition and keep the information away from nosey newspaper reporters and even outside attorneys, they are kept in closed files controlled by the clerk of the court. The actual adoption petition is thus available only to the judge and the attorney who filed it.

## Where Do We Find Our Baby To Adopt?

Case workers for Child Welfare Department and comparable state agencies will advise you to get your adopted baby by complying with their red-tape forms containing gobbledygook and join a waiting list that may take years. Sometimes, the case worker is a young single girl who will tell you that she is trying to match the baby available for adoption with perfect parents. This is nonsense and I have successfully fought the Child Welfare Department on numerous occasions.

The only important factor involved is the welfare of the child to be adopted and the important requirement is not perfection of the adopting parents but love. In one unusual situation, my clients were black and wanted to adopt a baby from an unwed mother who was white and the father was black. The Child Welfare Department objected to the proposed adoption but we argued and the Judge agreed that it was a perfect solution to a difficult situation.

Many of my adoption clients were successful in obtaining their baby from their family doctor or particularly from an obstetrician, regardless of whether he is a MD or an Osteopath because they usually have the first contact with the unwed mother-to-be. Most of these doctors agree that there is no need for any silly attempt to match a newborn infant with so-called perfect parents. If the unwed mother or adopting parents have any qualms about religion or anything else, the doctor can bear that in mind when selecting a couple from his waiting list. Even though the adopting parents dealing with an unwed mother, agree to pay her hospital, doctor and attorney's bills, this does not mean that they are buying a baby. The illegal practice of "selling babies" or "black market" results when some outsider like a doctor or lawyer or private hospital receives money in connection with the adoption of a child by merely furnishing said child.

Other adoption clients found their adopted child in an orphanage. This usually means that the child is not a new-born baby but that really does not matter. In the case of a new-born infant, the adopting parents are gambling on the condition of health whereas in the case of the orphanage child, a physical examination of the child by a pediatrician can be agreed to as a condition before proceeding with the adoption. Some clients went to special homes in Chicago and other large cities in search of their baby. One military client even arranged for the adoption of two new-born infants, each from different mothers and fathers, from a home for unwed mothers in Dublin, Ireland.

Whenever I heard prospective adopting parents relate the many conditions that had to be fulfilled, such as race, religion, education of the parents, etc., I could not help but think of the very wonderful couple who deliberately adopted two physically handicapped children. Fortunately, they were financially able to provide the best of medical care for their two handicapped youngsters.

Find your baby wherever you can and don't take the advice of the Child Welfare Department too seriously. You probably know more about raising children than the case worker who is single and recently received her university degree. Book knowledge is beneficial but there is no substitute for horsesense and love.

## Should The Adopting Parents Meet And Know The Natural Mother?

Again, the Child Welfare Department and their case workers will advise that the two parties should never meet each other under any conditions. The main objection to the parties meeting, is the possibility that the natural mother will want to maintain some type of contact with her baby that she placed for adoption.

There is always an exception to the rule and I will never forget a favorite client, who was attractive, fat and jolly, and enjoyed parties that somehow or another resulted in her frequent pregnancy. Our client will be called Mary Jones and on various occasions she would come to my office with a couple who wanted to adopt her most recent new-born baby. Mary would state in the presence of the couple, "I met these people and they are very nice and they want to adopt my baby and I want them to have her." Even though the Child Welfare Department case worker might shudder, this informal arrangement worked out perfectly with no problems.

### Is Permanent Residence Required To File An Adoption Petition?

In most states, the answer would be no. Residence is not a vital requirement for the completion of an adoption. In the event the adopting parents have to leave the state by virtue of transfer or otherwise, the state of origin will send the required forms to a comparable investigative agency in the new state and the case worker there will complete the mission. If the residence requirement were otherwise, military personnel and many others who are forced to move by virtue of their employment would be needlessly handicapped.

### Is Consent Of The Adopted Child Necessary?

In practically all states, the adoption laws require the consent of a child who has reached a designated minimum age. An average minimum age requiring the child's written consent would be about 14.

### Is The Age Of The Prospective Adopting Parents A Factor?

The laws of each individual state must be examined to determine an official and correct answer. In many cases, the courts have granted the petitions of grandparents for the adoption of a grandchild, without discussing the age factor. The adoption case of Jimmy Durante, the famous entertainer and his wife was approved by the California court. The judge ruled that the mere fact that Mr. Durante was in his sixties at the time of the adoption, did not preclude the approval of his adoption petition. The main concern of the courts is the welfare of the child.

*Should An Adopted Child Be Told About The Adoption And If So, When?*

Opinion varies, however, I have had the benefit of talking to many adoptive parents years later. We all know that children can be very cruel in their relations with another child. When the adopted child later attends school, other children frequently seem to have acquired knowledge of the adoption. If the adopted child has not been told about his adoption, you can imagine the shock of learning about his status from a strange child in a derogatory manner.

It is my considered opinion, shared by other experts, that the adopted child should be told about its adoption at an age to be decided by the adoptive parents. The exact words are not important but it is very important that the adopted child understand that he or she was "selected" by the adoptive parents because "We loved *you* and wanted *you*."

*Legal Status Of Adopted -vs- Natural Child*

Once the adoption has been completed and approved by the judge, the legal status of the adopted child is identical to that of the natural born child. There are no differences between the two categories.

# ANNULMENT

## General Information

There is a very important difference between obtaining an annulment of a marriage and a divorce. It may help to start off with the fact that a marriage is a civil contract usually between a female and a male. The reason that I stated "usually between a female and a male" is that new concepts and philosophies are being developed wherein two lesbians or two homosexuals are currently demanding their right to enter into a legal and binding marriage contract.

A divorce action takes place to sever a marriage relation, admitted to exist, for causes arising after the marriage. An annulment proceeding is for the purpose of obtaining a court order decreeing that no valid marriage took place between the parties because of some disability or defect or fraudulent representation. Some of the more common grounds for obtaining an annulment of a marriage are where the female is already pregnant by another and withholds the information; where one of the parties is legally married to another with no valid divorce; refusal on the part of the female to bear children after representing otherwise; the male withholds information regarding prior criminal activity and prison time; refusal on the part of either party to have sexual relations without any justification; and any other type of misrepresentation amounting to fraud.

There have been situations where one or both of the contracting parties to a marriage ceremony were under the influence of alcohol or dope to the extent that they did not know or realize they were entering into a marriage contract. Obviously, this would be a proper ground to annul the marriage.

After discovery of the defect constituting grounds for an annulment, the victim must act promptly in filing an action in court. Usually, the time of discovery of the fraud starts the running of the statute of limitations, which means the time alloted in which to file an action for annulment. If the innocent party waits for an unreasonable period of time, the law says he is guilty of laches for his negligence in not filing an action within a reasonable period of time and his petition is thrown out of court. Each state prescribes its own period of time within which a lawsuit must be filed for different situations and the reader who is concerned with this problem must learn the statute of limitation laws of his particular state.

### What Are The Advantages Of An Annulment Over A Divorce?

There are a number of advantages to obtaining an annulment of a marriage in preference to a divorce. The main one is that a marriage that is annulled is legally the same as no marriage having ever occurred. Frequently, on employment applications and elsewhere, the question is asked "have you ever been married" or "what is your marital status." In the case of a divorce you are obligated to classify your status as divorced. If the same marriage had been annulled, you could legally and truthfully state, "my status is single or unmarried."

Many states require one year or similar periods of residence before one is eligible to file for a divorce. There is usually no residence requirement in connection with filing for an annulment.

Another advantage of an annulment over a divorce is that many states have a waiting period in connection with the granting of a divorce decree before the parties are permitted to remarry. This prohibition does not occur in an annulment.

### Can Cousins Or Other Blood Relatives Marry?

The laws of each state vary in regard to so-called incestuous marriages. In some states, first cousins are permitted to enter into a marriage contract while in other states it is prohibited.

An incestuous marriage can be annulled by a court of competent jurisdiction at the request of either party, even if the applicant knew that it was in violation of law. The legal reasoning is that this type of marriage is contrary to good morals and public policy. Incest is sexual relations between a male and female who are related to each other to a degree prohibited by law. For those closely related, like father and daughter, it is a very serious criminal offense.

The laws of the state where the marriage took place would control the situation. An unusual case involved a marriage between first cousins in Massachusetts, one being a resident of Massachusetts and the other of Ohio. Their marriage in Massachusetts was legal and they later moved to Ohio. The Ohio law is silent as to marriage of first cousins, that is it does not approve or prohibit this type of marriage.

The Ohio resident filed for an annulment in Ohio on the grounds that their marriage was not valid from the beginning and the court ruled against that contention.

Many southern states enacted laws to prohibit the marriage of a white person and persons of other colors. The United States Supreme Court has ruled this type of law unconstitutional and today a person may marry another, regardless of differences in color.

## Fraud As Grounds For An Annulment Petition

Whatever the grounds for an annulment may be, basically it involves some type of fraud or misrepresentation. The result of such fraud or misrepresentation being that the victim legally says: "I would not have entered into the marriage contract but for the fraudulent representations of the other party" or "had I known the truth, I would not have married the person."

Public policy demands that the integrity of the marriage contract be preserved whenever possible. Therefore, the charge of fraud must be such as is deemed vital to the marriage relationship. The fraud must be perpetrated before the marriage, and be calculated to induce it. A Florida case held: "Where a 64 year old woman married a 46 year old man and, although she could not be said to be actually insane, her mental condition made her an easy prey to his machinations, the fraud practiced by him and her incapacity justified an order of annulment." In another type of fraud, a man married a woman to get out of trouble with the immigration authorities but refrained from telling her because he was afraid she might refuse to marry him if she knew it, and the parties never cohabited, and the judge granted the annulment. In another example of fraud: "A representation by a Filipino to a white girl that he was a Spaniard was said to be fraud that touches a vital spot in the marriage relation and constitutes a cause of action for annulment."

Exceptions to the general rule pertaining to fraud, involve misrepresentations or concealment concerning identity, birth, rank, reputation, family, fortune, health, character, morality, habits, temper, party married for money, or false age. Each case depends on its own facts and there can be a variance. There is no hard and fast rule that applies to all situations. It is important that you realize that the laws of your state is the main factor in your case.

In a case where a man and his relatives assured a woman he enjoyed good health and no bad habits when in fact he was a tubercular and a drug addict, the judge approved the annulment. A wife unsuccessfully sought an annulment on the ground of fraud when her husband had represented to her before their marriage, that he drank only beer and no hard liquor and after marriage he drank hard liquor and got drunk a number of times. The case didn't state if she drove him to drink.

Nondisclosed intent on the part of one of the parties to a marriage not to have children is fraud warranting annulment. A refusal on the part of either spouse to have sexual intercourse without justification, goes to the essence of the marriage relation and of course is ground for annulment. Concealment of sterility may be such type of fraud as to invalidate the marriage contract and justify an annulment.

Free consent and agreement of the parties is essential to a valid marriage contract. If the marriage resulted from the use of force, restraint, or threats, then the duress would be the inducing cause of the marriage. If the duress dominated the marriage transaction to the extent that the party did not act as a free agent because of violence or threats, then annulment is proper. Threatening suicide has been held not to be such a threat as to give a right to an annulment of a marriage.

What is the legal consequence of the famous "shotgun" variety of marriage? As a general rule a marriage will not be annulled on the ground that the man entered into the marriage because of threats of prosecution, arrest, or imprisonment. Some judges rule that it is not duress to insist that an unmarried man marry an unmarried woman whom he has caused to bear a child.

The legal definition of impotency implies some malformation or organic defect that prevents the couple from successfully completing sexual intercourse. One of my former clients, a 68 year old new bride complained that her new 72 year old bridgroom was impotent. The husband testified in court that what his wife thought was impotency was actually lack of interest on his part. The judge denied the annulment and my client later divorced her disinterested lover. Impotency occurring after marriage is not of itself ground for annulment.

Chastity, it is said, is a mere personal quality. Prenuptial unchastity does not prevent the woman from being a faithful wife or from bearing children. Similarly, prenuptial sexual activity of a husband, concealed from his wife, is not ground for annulment. You may not agree with the ruling of law that provides there is no difference in degree of unchasteness or promiscuity, whether it is for hire or not, but that is the law. You may prefer the court's ruling in granting an annulment to an aged and crippled man where the woman before marriage had falsely represented that she was virtuous, whereas she had worked in a house of prostitution for some years. Another court ruled there was no fraud where a woman falsely represented that a child which the man knew of, was hers by a former marriage, when in fact it was illegitimate. Ditto result where the man failed to disclose that he had fathered an illegitimate child.

Some states have laws providing that a prenuptial pregnancy by a third person is a ground for divorce or annulment. Then there are cases where the man wants an annulment on the ground that his wife's claim that she was pregnant by him proved to be false and she was not pregnant at all and he would not have entered into the marriage contract if he had known the truth. The court ruled that he was not entitled to an annulment because having engaged in illicit intercourse, he does not come into court with "clean hands." For the uninitiated, "washing of the hands" before entering the courtroom will not solve the problem.

The equitable doctrine of "dirty hands" says that if a person has done something wrong the court will refuse to help him. An example could be an agreement entered into by two men to rob a bank and after the robbery, one refuses to divide the loot and the other sues him for his share of the money. Obviously, the judge would rule that the subject matter of the agreement was illegal and throw them both out of court. Their criminal liability is something else again.

Logic and legal authorities deny annulments when the complaining party, though innocent at the outset, continues to cohabit with the wrongdoer, after learning of the illegality of their relationship. This point of law is emphasized in the case of an invalid Mexican divorce, where the parties lived together for 15 years, after knowledge of the illegal divorce.

## Marriage Under Age Of Consent

Each state has enacted laws stating the minimum age required before a marriage license may be issued. Usually, the minimum age limit is lower for girls than it is for boys. These requirements apply when the two young people go to the county courthouse on their own to obtain their marriage license.

In addition, most states have laws that permit young people to marry at a tender age if they have the written consent of their parents.

In order to determine the age limits of your state, contact the County Clerk or comparable public official.

Many states have special laws permitting a young female who is pregnant, to marry at a lower age than specified by law, by obtaining approval from a District Court Judge or one who has jurisdiction over the matter.

A marriage entered into by a person under the legal age of consent may be ratified by the parties living together as husband and wife after reaching the age of consent.

Ordinarily, lying as to age at the time of getting the marriage license does not prevent the guilty party from getting the marriage annulled. This is an exception to the doctrine of "dirty hands."

*Bigamy — One Spouse Too Many*

Bigamy is the act of marrying one party while still legally married to another. This problem frequently occurs in those states that have a waiting period before a divorce decree becomes final or operative. I am reminded of the young lady who employed me to obtain a divorce. Under New Mexico judge-made law, a cooling off period of 30 days was required before a divorce could be completed. My Client wanted to leave the state during the waiting period and I asked the Judge to hear her testimony early, to allow her to leave for new employment in California. The Judge heard the brief testimony and signed the divorce decree, however, he instructed me not to file it until the 30 day waiting period was up and instructed my Client not to remarry until her divorce decree was filed. In spite of the cooperation and clear instructions of the Judge, my Client saw fit to remarry in California before her divorce was entered. She then returned to New Mexico with her new and illegal bridegroom and advised of her tangled marital affairs. She confessed her sins to the original Judge and he threatened to send her to jail for contempt of court but she cried and he relented. We then completed the annulment of her new marriage with the cooperation of another Judge. The punchline of this true story is that after the annulment and completion of her divorce, the fickle lady decided not to remarry husband number two.

When a bigamous marriage does occur, it may be annuled by the guilty as well as the innocent party.

If you are wondering about pregnancy in connection with a marriage that is annuled, there is no serious problem. In spite of the annulment the man is legally responsible for the support of his child until it reaches his or her majority.

## May A Wife Collect Alimony In An Annulment?

Alimony is the money award to the wife and has nothing to do with child support, which is a money award for the sole benefit of the child. Divorce and alimony go together like ham and eggs but annulment and alimony is not possible. The legal reasoning is that alimony is based on the duty of the husband to support his wife. If the annulment succeeds, there is no valid marriage to begin with and no duty for the husband to support his ex-wife.

## What Happens When An Annulment Action Fails?

If for any reason the annulment petition should be denied by the court, the remedy of a divorce action is always open to the same parties. There may be and usually are reasons why one of the parties prefers to terminate the marriage by way of an annulment but divorce is always available as a substitute. In a borderline situation, the annulment petition can ask that if denied, the court grant a divorce in the same case. This is called alternative relief.

## Catholicism And Annulments

There are approximately 48 million members of the Catholic faith in the United States. Catholic lawyers advise that there is nothing in the canons of catholicism that prohibits a member from obtaining a divorce, however, they are prohibited from remarrying in the church.

Some of my Catholic clients had domestic problems and desired to terminate their marriages. In cases where reasonably proper grounds were available, they preferred an annulment to a divorce. If both husband and wife were agreeable, some judges were inclined to be liberal in interpreting the law.

The law says that the legal status of a husband and wife whose marriage is annulled is the same as if they had never married.

# DIVORCE

An absolute divorce dissolves an existing marriage and terminates the bonds of matrimony. A limited divorce does not dissolve the marriage but terminates the obligation and right of cohabitation. In many states the only form of divorce authorized by state law is an absolute divorce. If a limited divorce and a legal separation sound the same to you, then you are right because there is no difference between them.

Other than for extremely wealthy couples who are trying to arrange a settlement of their property rights, I have never been able to understand any benefits from a legal separation. Over a period of 25 years, I have had hundreds of wives and husbands ask about filing a court proceeding for a legal separation. If a couple are not getting along and want to separate, I know of no benefits to be gained by appearing before a Judge and hearing the Judge say, "I now declare you legally separated." Most attorneys charge the identical fee to file a petition for a legal separation as they do for a divorce. I have always felt that it was poor policy for an attorney to permit his client to file for a legal separation.

Some states have laws providing for an action for separate maintenance, usually filed by the wife. A separate maintenance decree recognizes the continuation of the marriage relationship, the continuing right of the wife to participate in her husband's estate on his death, as well as the possibility of a reconciliation that will end the necessity for the separate maintenance award. Meanwhile, the husband has the obligation of supporting his wife and children just the same as if they were living together as a family unit.

Divorce is a creature of statute in the United States, and the legislature of each state has the power over the subject of marriage and divorce. For example, the legislature of the state of Nevada had the power to provide for 6 weeks residence in connection with filing for a divorce. Most states require one year's residence. A phony situation occurs when the wife from New York flies to Reno and lives at a dude ranch for the required 6 weeks and then testifies in court that she is a bona fide resident of the state of Nevada. As fast as she is granted her divorce, she takes the next plane back to New York. That is why I was delighted recently to learn that the Mexican government has taken steps to prevent this type of phony divorce by Americans flying in to El Paso, Texas and obtaining a "quickie" Mexican divorce by falsely claiming that they were bona fide residents of the Republic of Mexico. For many years, the only grounds for divorce in the state of New York was adultery and this resulted in the sham of hiring a private detective to supposedly catch the husband in a hotel room with a female and the taking of a phony picture and this perjured testimony resulted in a divorce being granted. The husband probably had a girl friend or mistress on the side anyway, however, I think the law ought to encourage people to be honest instead of encouraging people to cheat and lie. Now the state of New York through its legislature has modernized its divorce laws and the former sham and perjured testimony has been eliminated. For many years, the state of South Carolina was the only state in the union that had no provisions for a divorce. The constitution of the State of South Carolina was amended in 1949 and now divorces are available under reasonable grounds, just as in most other states. As you can well imagine, residents of South Carolina found ways and means of circumventing their no-divorce period. The country of Spain has no provisions for any couple to obtain a divorce. In spite of the bonds of Catholicism, those that are interested go elsewhere to obtain their divorce and then return to Spain. Many married men in Spain seem to approve the existing law and enjoy the company of their mistress as well as their wife. The divorce situation in Italy is quite interesting since divorces have been permitted for only a short period of time. Instead of hundreds of thousands of Italians rushing into divorce court, many are content to keep the status quo. One Italian dentist who had been separated from his wife for 15 years said he was very happy to keep the present arrangement of his mistress and wife and family and he was really not interested in obtaining a divorce. Sort of like eating your cake and having it too!

### Are You Ready For A Divorce?

After listening to domestic problems over a period of years that number into the thousands, I have arrived at the following conclusions. If there are no children involved, the divorce problem is greatly simplified. If children are involved, they are better off living with their Mother alone than to be subjected to constant bickering and name-calling that takes place in unhappy households. I used to think that a child needed its father to such an extent that it was imperative that divorce be avoided at all costs. With the passing of time and years of experience in dealing with divorces in wholesale quantities, I have changed my mind. Even though some mothers will attempt to poison the child's mind as to their "bad daddy" the child will make up its own mind in due course of time as to whether their father was a "good daddy" or a "bad daddy".

Whenever I listened to a wife tell the story about her husband Joe, it sounded like a phonograph record because I heard the same story hundreds of times. "My Joe is a wonderful guy when he is sober but unfortunately he drinks too much and then he is mean and nasty." This lady has endured Joe's drinking for a number of years and she cannot make up her mind whether or not to terminate the marriage. I recommend to these wives that they do nothing other than go home and live with their problem until they have made up their mind.

For the unhappy wife who is unable to make up her mind about filing for a divorce I recommend a voluntary separation. This does not require any ballyhoo or lawyers or judges or publicity. By mutual agreement, both husband and wife have the opportunity to find out how it is to live without each other. If they wish, they can even agree that each may date during the voluntary separation. The wife will soon learn that most dates will suggest sexual intercourse immediately on the theory that she is a married woman and "knows all about it." If their marriage really has the spark that reasonable marriages require, they can discuss their marital problems in a reasonable and frank manner and work out their differences by compromise and cooperation and terms of endearment instead of profanity. They can even become reconciled. If they are looking for perfection, the reconciliation is doomed.

The drinking problem, usually on the part of the husband rates number one for domestic unhappiness. Chasing other women and financial problems follow in that order. I ran into one of my lady Clients for whom I had obtained a divorce from her Joe because of his excessive drinking. She had remarried and I inquired as to her current marital bliss. Her answer was classic: "Mr. Colby, I divorced Joe because of his excessive drinking and when I remarried Bill I was determined not to be faced with another drinking problem. Bill brought some brand new problems into our marriage and I am very unhappy. If I had it to do all over again, I would take my Joe back with his drinking problems."

## Three Dont's

Whenever I hear about a couple who have been married for many years and claim that they have never had a fuss, or cross words or a family argument, I think they are lying or are at least exaggerating. How dull a marriage would be if the wife and husband didn't have an occasional difference of opinion or disagreement. Kissing and making up is a normal and desirable part of married life.

1. After a family spat don't rush home to your parents. They have their own problems and mean well but cannot live your life and solve your marital disagreements. Your parents will be biased in your favor and are unable to judge the problem fairly.

2. After a family argument, neither spouse should talk to friends about the problems at home and seek advice. Your friends have their own problems and prefer to be neutral in your family disagreement. They should not take sides and they cannot solve your personal problems. Friends do spread gossipy rumors that can hurt your marriage.

3. After a family row, do nothing immediately. Think out the problem and best of all, allow for a "cooling off" period. Whatever the problem may be, it will not seem as horrible the following day. Don't rush to a lawyer to even talk about a divorce. It is very easy to get a divorce but that should be the last resort to solving the problem. Ask yourself "is this problem really earth-shaking?" If you are looking for perfection in your spouse, how perfect are you? If you are honest with yourself, you will agree that marriage is a give and take arrangement and you may have failed in making your contribution.

## How To File For A Divorce

There is no law that says you have to retain a lawyer to file your complaint for a divorce. If you think you are knowledgeable and can do the job, you can act as your own attorney. However, it is recommended that you be represented by a lawyer of your choice. You do not need any papers; no marriage license; no birth certificate; or anything else. You merely furnish the vital statistics of your marriage; names in full; date and place of marriage; length of your residence in the state where the divorce complaint is being filed; names and ages of children born the issue of the marriage; what property has been accumulated during the marriage as a result of your joint efforts; what bills are owed and to whom, incurred during the marriage; how much the husband and wife earn in their respective jobs; the figures on the family home and mortgage payments and balances; the amount of child support available and needed to raise the child or children; the possibility of alimony for benefit of the wife; who is to have custody of the children; rights of visitation for their father; when the husband is going to move out of the family home and find a place to live elsewhere; and similar jolly information.

Your lawyer will either dictate the divorce complaint to his secretary or sometimes, the legal secretary has prepared so many divorce complaints that her employer gives her the bare information and she fills in the usual blank spaces. Within a day or so, the complaint is ready for your signature and is then filed in the local courthouse. The following day your divorce case is listed in the vital statistics column of the local paper and no one seems to get very excited about your divorce case. Just one more happy marriage on the rocks.

If the wife sues the husband for a divorce, she is the Plaintiff or the Petitioner and the husband becomes the Defendant. If the parties have not agreed to the divorce and the husband signed a Waiver, then he must be served with a copy of the divorce papers. A waiver is used where the defendant agrees to the divorce without objection. When he or she signs the waiver, there is no need for any other papers to be served. This is called an uncontested divorce and the plaintiff can proceed to complete the divorce. In rare cases where one of the spouses has disappeared and cannot be located after an honest effort has been made to locate him or her, then service of the divorce papers is permitted by the substitute of publication. This is accomplished by publishing a notice in a local legal newspaper that very few people ever read and the Plaintiff signs an affidavit of how hard she tried to locate her Joe and was not able to and Joe is gone and knows nothing about the publication of the filing of his divorce case. It costs extra money for the publication and takes a bit longer but the completion of the divorce is accomplished.

Now the husband has either agreed to the divorce and signed a waiver or he has been served with a copy of the divorce complaint. Like all other lawsuits, the Defendant is granted a certain period of time to file an Answer to the Complaint. Usually this is 30 days but each state has its own rules on time.

If the husband does not want to fight the divorce, he can agree to terms that are acceptable to both sides. He can do this with or without a lawyer. If the parties are agreeable to the divorce and the terms, one lawyer can handle the transaction. The lawyer selected cannot represent both sides, however, if there is nothing to fight about, there is no real need for a second lawyer. I have seen divorce cases where nothing is involved; no children, no property; and the couple wind up with two lawyers which is slightly ridiculous. Much ado about nothing and usually the husband has the legal obligation of paying all legal expenses in a divorce case.

If the husband wants to delay or fight the divorce, we now have the usual court battle with the airing of the family linen in a public trial. It may take a number of months before the trial is heard but meanwhile the love has turned to hate and each party cannot think of enough insulting names to call our former beloved. Many wives in divorce court would like to "take" their husbands for every penny he has or can earn. Many husbands are equally unfair and when you talk to them about contributing towards the support of children they helped to bring into the world, they ask "how little do I have to pay?" In spite of this unfair attitude on the part of both parties, the Judge by his ruling will effect a compromise which usually makes both sides unhappy. The wife says the child support award is not adequate to raise the children and the husband says he needs some money to live on and possibly remarry later. One lawyer used to brag about the thousands of divorce cases that he won in court. He is really not being truthful because no one wins a divorce case. Both parties are losers as far as I am concerned. The real losers are the young children who start off with equal affection for their Mother and Father and then observe the hatred that permeates their home. I know of cases where junior high school age children will lie to their schoolmates about the whereabouts of their Father, rather than tell the truth about the fact that his parents are divorced.

The happiest cases occurred when I was able to get the couple to reconcile and both try to make a go of their marriage. I was not always successful but I did try to convince couples of the evils of divorce and what life is like after the divorce. One failure occurred with a very nice couple who had two wonderful youngsters. They should have been the happiest couple in the world but they wanted a divorce. I convinced them of the advantages of trying life together again and they agreed. Three months later they returned and said: "Mr. Colby, we did try again and it is just not good for us to be together and we want a divorce." I later ran into both of them and they had each remarried other mates and were getting along famously. In another case, the wife's sole complaint was excessive drinking on the part of her jet pilot husband. She did not want a divorce but wanted to "shock" the husband. We filed a divorce complaint that asked for the moon and left the poor pilot with hardly enough money to buy a coke and a package of cigarettes. When the husband was served with a copy of the divorce papers he was "shocked" and came to my office. We both agreed that the complaint of his wife was justified and he offered to "go on the wagon" and said he, too, did not want a divorce. Whenever both parties are in accord in not wanting a divorce there is no serious problem. I later ran into the pilot and his lovely wife and was happy to hear that all was well with their marriage.

## Divorce — How Much Money — How Much Time?

The cost of a divorce will vary in different sections of the country and the wealth of the client will affect the legal charges. The figures I will quote are mere guidelines and are not official fees. Usually, the minimum fee for handling a simple default divorce case (this means there is no contest or trial) is $250, plus court costs of about $25. Legal fees seem to be higher in larger cities than in smaller communities.

Most legal fees are based on the time factor and it is for this reason that contested divorce cases would result in higher legal fees. When there are extensive property holdings and other assets, there is more to bicker about and as the time factor increases, the fees go up. In other words, the "meter is running." There is no maximum on legal fees and in most states, the Judge will award the wife's attorney a fee for his services. Sometimes, the court award is adequate and on other occasions it is up to the attorney and his client to have a definite understanding on the fee arrangement.

The laws of most states provide that the husband is responsible for and is supposed to pay the wife's attorney fee. It is frequently impossible to collect from the husband for various reasons (he is unfriendly and lives out of state and does not want the divorce) in which case the wife is obligated to pay her own attorney.

It takes anywhere from one day to more than one year to complete a divorce action. Each state has its own laws and the time factor will vary greatly depending on the local ground rules. Most states have a prescribed residence period, usually one year that tends to force residents to file for divorce in their own home state. You can't file in a nearby state because it is easier or quicker to get a divorce there.

In New Mexico it is still possible to obtain a one day divorce. There is supposed to be a 30 day "cooling off" or waiting period but if both parties assure the court that it is not possible to reconcile and one of the parties wants to leave New Mexico, the judge will oblige by granting an immediate divorce. Divorces when granted in New Mexico are final and there is no waiting period for remarriage. I handled many divorces where my client completed his divorce on the third floor of the courthouse and immediately went to the marriage license division on the first floor and started all over again with the new bride or bridegroom, as the case may be.

Other states award an interlocutory decree and then there is a waiting period that varies from 6 months to a year before the parties may marry again. Colorado and Arizona have 6 months waiting period, while California has a one year waiting period between the interlocutory and final decree. Apropos of nothing, California has established the dubious honor of roughly 7 out of 10 marriages winding up in divorce court.

The most important factor in the time to complete a divorce is how friendly and cooperative both parties are. If they both want the divorce and agree to all requirements, the mission can be completed in a hurry. However, divorces are frequently one-sided affairs where one party wants it and the other does not want a divorce. Then it becomes a new ball game and the name of the game is delay, stall and hold the lawsuit pending for as long as possible. There are tricks to every trade or profession and divorce cases are no exception to the rule. The more money involved, the greater the fight and more lawyers are available to join in the legal battle of wits. Eleanor Holm, the former Olympic swimming champion and the late Billy Rose fought their divorce case through the New York courts for years and years. It was very bitterly contested and a sizeable sum of money was involved. Winthrop Rockefeller, former Governor of Arkansas, had an easier time when he divorced Bobo Rockefeller and she reputedly received six million dollars as a property settlement. These are cases of "wine, women and song" whereas some of the poorer cases refer to "beer, the old lady and TV."

## May I Date While My Divorce Is Pending?

In spite of the "Women's Liberation Movement" this still seems to be a man's world or at least the man is favored. While the divorce is pending, husbands did not ask whether they should date other females, they obviously went ahead and did it on their own. If the wife complained in the courtroom and accused the husband of infidelity or adultery, the judge didn't seem to be very excited or interested in this type of testimony. Wives are naturally concerned about their rights and privileges, particularly in cases where the husband has threatened them with taking the children away from them, supposedly because of some immoral conduct on their part. My advice to wives whose divorce case is pending, yes, you can date but use good judgment. Don't permit your conduct to place you in an embarrassing position. Instead of having dinner with your gentleman friend alone, have another couple join you. Don't jeopardize your pending divorce by engaging in extracurricular sexual activities. If you do, don't get caught. The law does not require the married woman involved in a divorce case to stay home every night and twiddle her thumbs. If she uses horse sense and conducts herself as a lady should, there will be no problems.

## Grounds For Divorce

Each state has its own laws that provide for the various grounds for divorce. Most states have just about the same general grounds with different names and then comes the catch-all called incompatibility. The more common grounds are: adultery; conviction of a crime; cruelty; impotency; insanity; habitual drunkenness or use of narcotics; desertion; nonsupport; and incompatibility.

Incompatibility translated into ordinary English means "the couple do not get along." It does not place the blame on the wife nor does it place the blame on the husband. It does away with stupid newspaper items of prominent couples in divorce court where the article says "the wife didn't make good toast" or "the husband watched pro football on TV every Sunday" as a ground for divorce. Many judges prefer to grant a divorce on the grounds of incompatibility even though the testimony clearly indicates the husband guilty of adulterous conduct because of the harm it can do to their children. Even if their Father or Mother did commit adultery, there is nothing to be gained by making this conduct a matter of public information.

It really does not matter why a couple wind up in divorce court as long as the marriage is dissolved by a court order. This is called a final decree of divorce and not degree.

In some states where the grounds of divorce might benefit an innocent wife whose husband is guilty of adultery, she would be justified to use adultery rather than incompatibility. Your lawyer is the best authority on the proper grounds to use in your divorce complaint.

Some people who are involved in divorce cases are shocked when they appear in the courtroom. Their lawyer has already told them that the contested divorce trial is open to the public and any nosey person interested can sit in and listen to the airing of the family linen in court. Actually, the only persons present in the courtroom, other than the litigants and their lawyers and witnesses, are the judge and the court reporter who takes down all of the "juicy" testimony that may later be transcribed. Outsiders and other lawyers could care less because divorce trials are not very interesting. Even the judges get bored with testimony that they hear practically on a daily basis in divorce cases. In spite of the recent flurry of sex books and movies, there is really very little new under the sun and adultery is not one of them.

In spite of the many problems, he or she say that married life is unbearable and is determined to obtain a divorce. If one party is not interested in maintaining the marital status, there is little that the other party can do about it. In many states, one spouse cannot prevent the other from obtaining a divorce. Under the general rule of incompatibility, if one party says the couple are incompatible, that makes it so and there is nothing the other party can do to prove otherwise. No doctor, lawyer, clergyman or even judge has the ability or the right to define the requirements for a so-called happy marriage. Happiness is a state of mind and varies with each married couple. What makes one married couple happy may not hold true for the next couple. The marital relationship between a husband and wife is so personal and intimate that only the couple themselves know the truth about their married life. Experts have said that all divorces start in the bedroom and I am inclined to agree with that statement.

*Alimony — How Much — How Little — Is It Fair?*

The same women who think "diamonds are a girl's best friend" are likely to think that an alimony award is grand. The word alimony comes from the Latin "alimonia," and means the sustenance or support of the wife by her divorced husband. There are many alimony-paying husbands who would like to give "alimonia" back to the Latins.

Temporary alimony is also known by its legal name, alimony "pendente lite," which means while the divorce case is pending in court. It does not matter whether the wife filed for the divorce or is being sued by the husband for divorce, in order for her to collect temporary alimony.

Permanent alimony is sometimes agreed upon between the parties or may be ordered by the Court. When the divorce case is brought to its final conclusion and the divorce is awarded, the alimony award may be for a given period of time or may continue until the wife remarries or dies, whichever occurs first.

The laws pertaining to the granting and grounds for a divorce are statutory and thus vary from state to state. The identical situation applies to the granting of alimony, temporary or permanent. One has to look to the laws of his own state to learn the ground rules about the granting of alimony.

Any lawyer who handles divorces in wholesale quantities is going to represent the wife in a given number and is also going to represent the husband in a given percentage of divorce cases. Thus, the lawyer gets a birdseye perspective that is different from a husband who is unhappy about an alimony award in his own case. I have heard dozens of husbands complain bitterly about the treatment they receive in divorce court, concerning property settlements, child support awards and particularly the alimony award. Some states have laws that are very liberal in favor of the wife receiving alimony, while other states are very conservative in the granting of alimony to a wife.

Based upon my years of experience and a desire to see both parties receive fair treatment I think there is a happy medium. Many judges are opposed to a young wife who has been married for only a reasonably short period of years receiving alimony that goes on for years and years. There are certain situations where a young wife is forced to learn some type of work to provide her own living, such as going to business school for 6 months or so and there is nothing unfair about the young husband helping out with a reasonable alimony award to help his ex-wife reestablish herself.

We have all heard the lament of women who have been married for many years saying: "I have given you the best years of my life and now that I am old and gray, you want to get rid of me." In cases where the couple have been married for a "reasonable" period of time, something within the 25 year range or longer, I agree with the predicament of the wife and she is entitled to a percentage of the husbands earnings. I agreed with the judges ruling in a divorce case that I handled in which the wife was awarded 50% of the husband's take home pay from the railroad. The couple had been married for over 30 years and the wife did need the financial help from the husband.

Some wives get the wrong idea about alimony from reading about some young movie starlet who married an old wealthy man and received a goodsized endowment for the rest of her life in the form of alimony. I think we would all agree that there is no justice or fairplay in that result.

In the state of Illinois, some husbands refused to pay the alimony award that was granted to their ex-wife by Illinois judges and wound up in jail for contempt of court. They were trying to prove their point of injustice even though they were financially able to pay the alimony award.

The laws of each state vary materially in this regard and I liked the New Mexico law which gave the judge discretionary power to award or deny alimony based on the facts of each case. The net result was fairness in that young brides could forget about hoping for an alimony award. The new freedom of women and working wives have also changed the overall thinking in connection with alimony awards.

### Why The $1 Alimony Award?

We read about divorces in some states involving prominent or theatrical people with an award of alimony to the wife in the sum of $1. The reason for the $1 alimony award is to give the ex-wife protection for the future in the event there should be a change of circumstances in the financial status of the parties. At the time of the divorce, the wife is in good financial shape and there is no need for any help at that time. If the final divorce decree contained no provision for any alimony award, then the wife could not legally make any claim for alimony in the future. Under the $1 alimony award, the award has already been decreed by court order and there is only the question of increasing that amount in the future. The amount of any alimony award is always based on the financial ability of the husband to pay the money. Obviously, a man who earns $400 per month cannot be ordered to pay $400 per month alimony because that would be a physical impossibility.

Some husbands encourage their ex-wives to marry another for

their own selfish motive of terminating the alimony award. If the ex-wife's second marriage proves to be unsuccessful, she may not come back into court and ask for a renewal of the alimony award. She gambled on her second marriage and lost. Marriage is said to be a gamble at best and some people are born losers.

## May A Husband Collect Alimony?

In rare and exceptional circumstances, a court has awarded alimony to the husband. This could only happen in cases where the wife was independently wealthy in her own right and the husband became ill and was not able to support himself. Barbara Hutton, the wealthy Woolworth heiress, has been known to make pre-nuptial property settlement arrangements with her various husbands. In this manner they were not able to claim alimony or any part of Miss Hutton's personal fortune upon the dissolution of their marriage.

If any man marries a wealthy woman in the hopes of collecting alimony in the event of a future divorce, he has my sympathy but not my respect.

## How Does A Judge Determine The Amount Of Alimony?

The important criteria would be the wife's need and the husband's ability to pay. Some judges go along with the theory that the wife is entitled to live in her accustomed style of living according to her station in life. Most judges, however, are more conservative and base the alimony award on the income of the husband and the needs of the wife. There has to be a tightening of belts when the parties wind up in divorce court. In the famous divorce case of the Reynolds of tobacco fame in Georgia, the court held an alimony award of $1,042 per month inadequate but listen to the facts. Mrs. Reynolds said her net worth was $400,000 and her husband had been spending about $250,000 a year on her during their marriage; that Mr. Reynolds had assets worth $25 million; he had income of $6-1/2 million the previous year, on which he paid income taxes of $1-1/2 million.

## Can A Wife Guilty of Misconduct Collect Alimony?

Generally speaking, yes for temporary alimony and no for permanent alimony. Most state laws provide that the wife is entitled to be maintained during the pendency of the divorce and she needs temporary alimony and attorneys fees in order to properly conduct her defense of the lawsuit. If the husband is able to prove the misconduct at the time of the final divorce hearing, usually the temporary alimony award will then cease and terminate.

In every divorce case involving the charge of adultery on the part of either spouse, the courtroom testimony invariably follows the same pattern. The husband who is caught redhanded making a cross-country trip with his female friend always claims that he slept on the couch while the young lady occupied the motel or hotel bed. The husband is perspiring while giving his testimony and the judge and attorneys involved smile to themselves. It is presumed there was sexual activity under these circumstances and it is too bad if the parties did not get together because no one believes the husband's story in court. The same would hold true if the facts applied to his wife. The moral involved is "don't go around with your neighbor's wife unless you can go 10 rounds with your neighbor." Under modern air travel, people seem to run into others that they know in remote parts of the world. If you are trying to hide your illicit romance, it may be better at home than a thousand miles away.

### Who Pays Suit Money; Travel Expenses; And Attorney's Fees?

"Suit money" is the money necessary for the wife who is being sued for divorce by the husband living elsewhere, to properly defend herself and hire an attorney of her choice. The judges of most states will award the wife living away from the state where the divorce was filed by the husband, suit money to pay for her travel and living expenses as well as money needed to retain an attorney to represent her in the divorce lawsuit. An award of suit money to the wife does not automatically mean that she will also receive an alimony award because the two matters are entirely separate.

In a California divorce case, the court held that the husband had to pay accountants' fees of $750 for services in examining the books of three corporations where the husband had title to all of the common stock, but the wife alleged the stock was community property and the husband contended that payments which the court had ordered were beyond his ability to pay. In an unusual Rhode Island case with international implications, the husband, having a wife in Sicily, established a home in America. He sent her $4,000 to enable her to come to America with her child, but she remained in Sicily and invested the money in property. The husband sued for divorce and the wife applied for travel expenses. The judge refused her travel expenses but allowed her the cost of taking a deposition. (a deposition is sworn testimony given in question and answer form outside of the courtroom) Usually, the husband is responsible for the payment of services rendered by a detective hired by the wife to check up on the husband. In a unique New York case, the husband told the wife he was in love with another woman and lived with his mistress but supported his wife. Then the wife hired a private detective and the judge said the husband was not obligated to pay the detective because the wife already knew everything there was to know about the other woman.

## Death And Alimony

In the case of the divorced wife, either death or her remarriage will end the alimony award. In the event of the husband's death, the alimony award terminates. I have always advised my female divorce clients not to "kill the golden goose" because that is the source of the money that she is seeking. Even though the wife tells the husband to "drop dead" she would suffer financially from his early demise. The love has turned to hate and each party would like to kill the other but for the penalty of the law for the crime of murder.

## Bankruptcy And Alimony

The bankruptcy of the husband does not solve any of his problems because the wife's alimony award is not dischargeable in the bankruptcy proceedings. The same rule for child support and all forms of taxes, federal and state.

## How About Husband's Remarriage And Alimony?

Sympathy but no relief for a husband who marries again but is obligated to pay alimony to a former wife. He may get a break when he receives an increase in pay and his former wife wants the alimony increased and he now has another wife to support. People like Mickey Rooney, the actor, who go through life entering into many marriages and divorces and many alimony awards are gluttons for punishment but under the law are obligated to support former wives as well as children they helped bring into the world. A change in financial circumstances or a nationwide increase in the cost of living may be a factor in modifying a decree for alimony. As a result of changes, it can be increased or decreased, depending on the facts involved. An Illinois case held that an increase of a wife's alimony from $175 per month in

1931 to $415 per month many years later was proper due to inflation; the increased needs of the wife after the divorce and the financial ability of the former husband to pay such increase.

### How To Collect Alimony From A Non-Paying Ex-Husband?

Many husbands are of the opinion that paying alimony is comparable to paying for a dead horse and they are unhappy and unwilling debtors. In most states, the laws provide for the wife to petition the court to find the non-paying husband guilty of contempt of court for his failure to comply with the court's order. There must be a demand for payment and notice to the husband before he can be cited into court. Technically, the judge can send the non-paying husband to jail for contempt but that would not get the money to the wife and besides, we don't have enough jails to handle the non-paying husbands. So, the judge tries to be practical about the problem and does everything in his power to persuade the husband to meet his legal obligation and he gives him more time to purge himself of contempt and then, if that fails, he cajoles and pleads and finally threatens the husband with a jail sentence.

In spite of all efforts of the wife's lawyer and the judge, it is not always easy or possible to catch up with the non-paying culprit. Frequently, the non-paying husband has moved to another state or is unemployed and the only good thing about his disappearance is that he won't be able to heckle his ex-wife or bother her. Some wives are delighted that they will not see the ex-husband again and are willing to forego the money involved.

### When Can Alimony Be Increased Or Decreased?

Any order of alimony that is issued by a Judge is subject to later hearings on petitions for increase or decrease due to change in circumstances. Even in cases where the two attorneys involved worked out a property settlement agreement between the husband and wife that provided for an agreed sum of alimony, the judge has the power to later change that amount.

Like all other types of litigation, it is easy for a divorced wife or husband to file a petition asking for a change in the existing alimony award. Proving your case in court to the satisfaction of the judge is another story. The mere fact that the wife says she needs more money is not the controlling factor. The husband's ability to pay is also an important factor.

There is no set formula and each case goes on its own factual situation and the laws of the particular state involved and the mood of the judge who controls the particular case. The judge who heard the matter originally, usually continues with the same case all the way through. Otherwise, many lawyers would try to juggle their divorce cases to be heard by a judge who is receptive to the desires of a husband or a wife, as regards alimony, child support, property settlement and other divorce facets.

## Custody — Who Gets The Children?

Under normal conditions, custody of minor children are awarded to their mother and daddy has the obligation of contributing to their support and he has the right of reasonable visitation. Frequently, couples who wind up in divorce court are not emotionally normal; their marriage that started out with love has now turned to hate; they are each trying to get even with the other and will use the children as pawns to carry out their hatred and revenge. Small wonder that so many children of divorced households are unhappy with their parents and will lie to their schoolmates to withhold the fact that their mother and father are divorced.

The only time a judge will take minor children away from their mother is when the father can make out a strong case in court to prove to the satisfaction of the judge that the mother is an unfit person to be permitted to care for her own children. This is quite a brand to place on the mother for the rest of her life and some judges refuse to do so, even where the conduct of the mother leaves much to be desired. Part of the problem is who will care for the children if they are taken away from their mother? The average father has to go to his job and hiring a housekeeper is a poor substitute for their natural mother. It is a difficult problem at best and sometimes a judge is placed in the position of being a biblical "Solomon."

I have listened to dozens and dozens of husbands whom I represented in divorce cases, say that their wife was unfaithful or kept a dirty house or didn't keep the children clean and therefore they wanted the children taken away from their mother. When I pointed out to them that strong proof was required by law, they then agreed that their information was only a suspicion and the children remained where they belonged with their mother. Many women clients advised me of threats on the part of their husbands to take the children away from them on false charges of adultery. Then, when I asked the husband his reasons for threatening his wife, he would usually say: "Oh, I was trying to scare her."

The judge has wide discretionary powers in determining a custody case. Under a given set of facts, one judge can rule in favor of the wife and another judge on identical facts can rule in favor of the husband and the decision of both judges can be upheld. The reason for the appellate courts upholding the ruling of both judges is the legal reasoning that the judge has wide discretionary powers and neither judge exceeded his authority by acting in an arbitrary or capricious manner. This is a good example why it is difficult to predict the result of a lawsuit. Law is different than mathematics and you cannot always come up with a surefire guaranteed result.

Many wives are of the opinion that their ex-husband is obligated to contribute towards the support of their children and has no rights otherwise. This unreasonable attitude is not supported by law. Every father of minor children has certain obligations and he also has certain rights. His primary obligation is that he must support his children by paying a reasonable sum of money. If the parties cannot agree on an amount, then the court sets the amount. In turn, the father of the minor children has the right to visit his children at reasonable times and places. It is sad but true to learn that many divorced couples are so embittered with each other, that they are not able to agree on a time for daddy to visit his children. Daddy has to work during the week and thus the weekend is the only available time for him to spend some time with his children. The working mother complains that she wants to spend some time with the children over the weekend and the battle for rights of visitation goes on and on. If the divorced couple cannot agree on a reasonable time then this momentous problem is presented to the judge and he designates the hours that the father may see his children and the hour that he must return them to their mother.

Legally, there is no obligation on the part of the father to visit his minor children. Sometimes, the visitation rights are made so unpleasant by the mother that daddy decides to pay the child support and ignore the children. The innocent children hear their mother complain bitterly about their father's failure to visit with them.

On numerous occasions, the mother of minor children wants to move to another state and the husband says that he is being deprived of his visitation rights if his children are moved away from his permanent residence. The law does not require that the mother and the children remain in the same community with their father, in spite of the problem of visitation rights of the father. Again, if the parties cannot come to an agreement between themselves, the matter is presented to the judge and usually he will give the wife permission to move to some other city or state. The father still retains his right of visitation and he can either visit the children during his summer vacation or pay for the transportation to have the children visit with him in his own community. The ages of the children is obviously an important factor in arriving at a solution to this problem.

The wishes of a child who is sufficiently mature to express an opinion and desire as to its custody may be considered by the court. The main thought going through the judge's mind is what is best for the child.

The fact that a mother is guilty of adultery does not disqualify her to have the custody of her children. Even though she may have been a bad wife, she may be a good mother. Some judges have ruled that if the mother's misconduct did not take place in the presence of her minor children, they were not affected nor harmed.

The state has an interest in the welfare of all resident children. When a couple conclude their divorce case and the judge grants a divorce, the court's ruling is final and binding on both parties. The law presumes that being adults they know what they are doing. However, any ruling of the court pertaining to minor children is never permanent and it is always subject to change. The mere fact that the care, custody and control of the minor children are awarded to their mother does not automatically mean that upon proper grounds, the custody cannot be changed and the children taken away from her. Even after the divorce is concluded, if the mother's future conduct is such that the welfare of the children is seriously affected, the court has the legal power to change custody of the children. If the judge rules that the mother's misconduct makes her an unfit mother, he can award custody to their father or sometimes to other members of the family or even an outsider.

Similarly, the amount of child support is never permanent and is subject to future orders increasing or decreasing the amount due to a change in circumstances. As children get older, their financial needs increase and if their father is able and has the means, he should pay more.

There have been many disagreements as to when the child support award ends. The laws of the various states vary in this regard and as always, one must turn to the laws of his state to get the answer. The laws of most states provide that the father must pay child support until the child attains his or her majority, usually 18 for the girl and 21 for the boy. Many experienced attorneys solve this problem at the time of the divorce by having the final decree spell out the pertinent details. A popular provision could be "child support in the sum of blank dollars per month shall continue until each child attains his or her majority, marries or enters the armed forces of the United States." If a daughter marries, her husband has the responsibility of supporting her. If a son marries, it is presumed that he is financially able to support a wife as well as himself. Interesting legal questions arise when the young son wants to attend university and his father refuses to pay child support after his son attains his 21st birthday. Morally, the father ought to be fair and encourage the education of his son but legally he has discharged his obligation when the son becomes 21, the magic age of adulthood.

Although the court has the power to divide or alternate the custody of a child between the parents, it usually does not work out well for the child. As a Florida court ruled: "The result of shifting custody is, in most cases, to confuse the child and cause it to doubt where constituted authority lies, and largely to disregard the precepts of both custodians." Some children take advantage of the sad fact that their parents do not speak to each other, and later the parents discover the sharp tricks used by the child for his benefit.

Opinion is divided as to whether a father who fails to comply with the court's order and does not pay his child support obligation, loses his rights of visitation. I agree with the majority that reason that failure to pay the money is proper grounds for the mother denying rights of visitation. The fact that a parent has been cruel to his children may be valid reason for denying visitation rights. A drunken father has no business to visit his children while under the influence of liquor. The wife is not always right in visitation disputes. Some wives can be very ornery and uncooperative without any justification. If the wife refuses the husband his rights of visitation for no valid reason, he is justified in refusing to pay the child support money. I would urge him to set the money aside in a special account until the wife is fair or until the problem can be resolved by the attorneys or the judge.

Mere past delinquency of a parent is not a ground for withholding enjoyment of the right of visitation. For example, even in cases where a child has been taken away from its mother because of her adultery, she is still entitled to rights of visitation. There have been cases holding that a prostitute can be a good mother.

If custody of minor children is granted to their mother and she later dies, the father is next in line. The right of custody automatically passes to the surviving parent. Sometimes the grandparents make claim to their grandchildren when their daughter dies but the claim of the children's father is paramount.

## Child Support

Modern life has become quite complex and the problem of fixing for the father to pay as child support in connection with divorce proceedings is not always simple. In the "good old days," the judge started out with the father's income and then decided what portion ought to be paid as child support. Taxes and other deductions from the father's paycheck have changed the picture and the important figure is "take home pay." Modern mothers are now "working wives" and the take home pay of the wife is nearly as important as the net income of the husband. In some cases, the income of the wife is greater than that of the husband and this fact does affect the amount awarded as child support.

Another new problem is which parent gets to claim the child as a dependent for income tax deduction purposes. If the father does not pay the amount ordered by the court, he obviously is not entitled to claim any income tax deduction. Internal Revenue Service has ruled that the parent that contributes more than 50% of the child's support, is entitled to claim the child as a dependent for income tax deduction purposes. Note that IRS does not mention any specified sum but merely says 50%. Then comes the argument between the parents and if they cannot agree, the judge will have to decide for them. It is much better for all concerned if this matter is agreed upon between the parties at the time the divorce action is concluded. Experienced divorce attorneys will include this information in the final decree of divorce so that no misunderstanding can arise in the future. If the wife is not a working wife, there would be no possible reason for her claiming the child for income tax deduction purposes. If the husband earns considerably more than his divorced working wife, the deduction of his minor children will mean much more money left for the parties to share, than it will if the wife claims the deduction. The parties should be fair with each other and work together for mutual benefit even though their marriage is being terminated by way of a divorce. As disagreeable as divorces generally are, intelligent people agree to disagree in a pleasant manner, which is better for all concerned, including the minor children.

Over a period of years, I suggested to hundreds of my female clients that the children in a divorce case should be told "Your Father is a good man, but we are not able to live together happily so we are going to separate and live apart." Even if the Daddy did not quite live up to that complimentary description, it is still better for the children to hear something nice about their parent in preference to four letter words and comparable. The identical suggestion was made to my male divorce clients.

The fact that a divorced wife has remarried does not relieve the children's father of his obligation to support them. The incoming stepfather is not required to support someone else's children. We all know that as a practical matter, the children are members of the household, and their new stepfather does provide food and shelter for the entire family. The only way a father can get out of his legal obligation of supporting his children would be to agree to an adoption by their mother and stepfather. Upon the completion of the adoption, the stepfather assumes all of the rights and obligations formerly enjoyed by the natural father. It goes without saying that the completion of the adoption terminates any rights of visitation by the natural father.

Child support payments must be made to the mother of the children. Many fathers complain that their child support money is being misused by their ex-wife for purposes other than for benefit of the children. In a proper case, the wife could be ordered to appear before the judge and explain why she is not using the child support money for the children's benefit. In spite of this type of complaint by the father, there is no practical way for a minor child of tender years to handle money. Even when the children are older, money paid directly to the child as support, creates problems in the household. If the father really wants to help out financially, he can purchase extra clothing for the children, with the knowledge and approval of their mother.

In addition to a specified sum of money to be paid as monthly child support, other problems include medical and dental care for the minor children. Most employers provide some type of group insurance for benefit of the father and his dependents. Even though the divorced wife is eliminated from the group insurance coverage, it is very important that the children be covered and protected. This information should also be spelled out in the final decree of divorce. A Tennessee case held that a divorced wife who engaged hospital and medical care for minor children in her custody is entitled in equity to recover the cost from her husband, even though the final decree of divorce was silent in this regard.

A divorce court cannot award any part of the father's property to his children. He is obligated to support them, but not to settle an estate upon them. Ordinarily, the husband cannot be forced to maintain life insurance for the benefit of a child. A Wisconsin case held that a divorce court could order a father to keep life insurance in force for the benefit of his minor children but that the insurance policies could be lapsed when the children reached the age of 21.

Some wives in divorce court are so anxious to rid themselves of their husbands that they will agree to anything to accomplish this mission. The wife now hates her husband and cannot stand the sight of him so they enter into an agreement that if he will stay away from her and the children, she does not want any child support payments from him. The law frowns on this illegal contract because the rights of the children are being ignored. In one unusual case, the child brought a suit against the father for child support and the court properly ruled that the illegal agreement entered into by the father and mother did not preclude the child from benefits that could not be taken away from him. In this case, the father had paid a lump sum amount to the wife in return for the agreement releasing him from paying any child support.

The fact that the father has remarried, thus increasing his expenses, is not a proper ground for reducing child support. He knew about his prior commitment at the time of his second marriage. A California judge ruled that the support of his children takes precedence over the expense of supporting a second wife. A Kentucky judge ruled that a father's first duty is the support of his children. They are to be given preference over new automobiles and new wives. Other judges have ruled that young divorced husbands do remarry and additional children are born to the second marriage whose interest and welfare is of as much concern to the courts as those of the first marriage. Now we are down to the modern "your children and my children and our children" dilemma.

It is advisable that the final decree of divorce itemize the amount of child support per child, rather than list the total amount. If there are four children and the child support is $75 per child per month for a total of $300 per month, it should be detailed in that manner rather than provide for $300 per month as child support. I have run into this situation where the divorced wife wants to argue that the husband is obligated to continue paying $300 per month, even after one child has been eliminated by age or marriage.

Where the father is granted the right to have the children with him for a portion of each year, he is not obligated to pay child support during his allotted time. As a practical matter, the father usually winds up paying considerably more while his children are with him than the customary child support payment. I have run into a high percentage of fathers in divorce court and found that many will do more for providing for their children on a voluntary basis than if placed under a formal court order. In those cases, I recommended to the wife that if he were that type of person, she would be better off placing her faith and trust in him. Besides, if he later failed to do the right thing, she could always cite him into court on a request for an increase in child support.

The father is liable to outsiders for necessaries, including hospital and medical care furnished to the child. Parents are under a legal obligation to support their children, and a divorce does not relieve the parents of liability for the support of the children of the marriage. A Minnesota judge ruled that "The legal duty on the part of the father to support his children is sufficient to raise an implied promise on his part to make payment for the necessaries of life, whether for food, clothing, or care, and whether furnished by their mother or another." A Tennessee judge ruled "If the custody of a child is awarded to the mother, who lives in one state, it is no defense that the father is willing to support the child only in another state where he resides.

*Can You Afford A Divorce?*

We have all heard gag stories about "Two can live as cheap as one" and "It only costs $5 to get a marriage license" and similar. A serious economic problem arises in connection with a couple dissolving their marriage by way of a divorce. Getting a divorce is comparatively simple but what happens afterwards? Between increased taxes, inflation and the high cost of living, it is rough enough for the average household to make ends meet. Brand new economic problems arise with a divorce and the couple should give mature thought to the practical problems involved.

When things reach the stage that the couple are not able to live under one roof, regardless of having normal sexual relations, someone has to move out and obtain separate living quarters. If children are involved, the wife usually remains in the home with the children and the father has to seek other living quarters. I was always able to convince stubborn husbands that it was neither feasible nor practical for him to occupy the family home alone and ask the wife and children to move elsewhere. Besides, if he refused to be fair and reasonable, the judge would order him to leave the family home. So now we have a new and additional item to add to the family budget, namely room rent for dad. He starts to eat out in restaurants and the cost of food increases the budget. The father soon discovers that living alone in a motel room or small bachelor apartment is a lonely life and he needs recreation or companionship of one type or another.

Now let us look at the other side of the coin and the story is even sadder. Mother and the children are trying to adjust to their new life of occupying the family home without their father. It may be quieter with no arguing or name-calling or bickering, however, new problems now develop. Mother discovers that the cost of operating the family household is just about the same as it was before father moved out. The food bill may be a bit less but all other normal household items of overhead remain the same. The cost of daily needs of the children, particularly if they are of school age, now seem more of a problem than ever. The plain truth is that there is not enough money available to make the wheels turn. If mother is not already a working wife, she ponders the possibility of supplementing the family income by going out to work. Her educational background and prior training and experience are most important factors. Mother soon discovers that the cost of hiring a lady to look after the children during working hours is high and would leave very little net out of her take-home pay. Problems, problems, and more problems, all without any practical solution. The family has no choice other than to pull in their belts and make the best of it.

The marriage is already on the rocks and one of the parties has or is considering filing for a divorce. More often than not, the couple can hardly speak to each other, let alone sit down and discuss family finances quietly and fairly. Father says his needs are greater and mother says she needs more money. There is no real solution or answer to this problem because the fact of the matter is that they cannot afford a divorce. There just isn't enough money coming into the household to permit the couple to operate two households. They both knew from past experience that it was rough enough to operate one household when the family unit lived together.

After the divorcing couple have agreed on the amount of child support or had the judge decide the amount for them, new problems continue to plague both of them. The husband thought his new bachelor life would be like seventh heaven if he didn't have to listen to his nagging wife. The wife thought a quiet, serene household without the husband finding fault with everyone and everything would be blissful, but life doesn't seem to work out that way.

The husband now has a girl friend and it does not matter whether he found her before the divorce or afterwards. The children report to mother about the new lady after their weekly visit with their father. Father asks many questions of the children about who came to visit mother and how are things at home. When the children are returned to their home, mother fires similar questions to find out what father is doing and the news of the new girl friend does not make her any happier.

The wife is still complaining about the need for more money to pay household expenses and the husband is talking about the possibility of his second marriage. At first, the husband says he cannot afford to take unto himself another wife but he and the new bride-to-be agree that she will continue working and use the pill and somehow or another they will be able to make a go of their marriage. In spite of the pill, accidents do happen and in due course of time father announces the start of his new family and the expenses that go along with the new baby. Let us not overlook the loss of income because of the pregnancy of the second wife. In due course of time, the baby is born and now things are rougher than ever, financially speaking.

The husband wants to reduce his child support obligation because of the change in his financial needs and his ex-wife says it serves him right because he knew about his child support liability when he married a second time. The wife says she needs more money because the children are older and their needs are greater.

You can now see the final chapter of this happy episode. Husband and wife are back in divorce court, this time on their respective motions; one for a reduction and the other for an increase in the monthly child support payments. The judge listens to the testimony and he knows from years of listening to the identical economic problem of insufficient money, and his decision is a sort of compromise with the result that both husband and wife leave the courtroom completely unhappy.

## Property Settlements — Your House Or Mine?

In every divorce case where the couple have accumulated various items of property, both personal and real, there is a need for a detailed agreement as to the division of the property. Real property is real estate or immovable and personal property is movable like a car, furniture, etc. Included in the property settlement agreement is custody of the children; alimony, if any is involved; child support; life insurance policies; and practically all of the important details of the divorce. Then, when it comes time to complete the divorce, the property settlement agreement is submitted to the judge for his approval and it becomes a part of the final decree of divorce as if it were included. The property settlement agreement also surrenders the rights of inheritance on the death of the other; and agrees that each will execute all documents necessary to carry out the provisions of the agreement.

Usually, a property settlement agreement between husband and wife is made with a divorce or separation in prospect or pending in court. Some wealthy couples decide to enter into a post-nuptial property settlement agreement merely for the purpose of adjusting their property rights and interests, with no divorce or separation in mind. A postnuptial property settlement agreement takes place after the marriage, whereas a prenuptial property settlement agreement takes place before the couple enter into the marriage contract. Barbara Hutton, The Woolworth heiress, is reputed to have given her various husbands one million dollars as a pre-marital property settlement, so that if, as and when the marriage terminated by way of divorce, the husband waived any claim to Miss Hutton's property or estate.

If the couple have accumulated enough property and assets to warrant the preparation of a property settlement agreement, it is recommended that each party be advised by a lawyer of their choice. Even though it means the husband will have two lawyer's bills to pay, the wife is entitled to independent advice and not have to rely on the opinion of the husband's lawyer. One lawyer cannot serve two masters. There have been cases where the husband keeps his business affairs a secret and the wife is truly in the dark. In such a case, if the husband withholds assets and property that are later discovered by the wife, she can ask the court to reopen the matter on the ground that her ex-husband perpetrated a fraud upon her by withholding assets.

In most states, the judge handling the divorce case will automatically approve the property settlement agreement entered into between the parties. First of all, the judge has faith in the lawyers and knows that each of them has looked out fairly for the rights of his Client. Secondly, the judge feels that if the two interested parties are satisfied with the terms of the property settlement agreement, there is no need for the court to spend any time on the matter. An Illinois judge said: "Parties to divorce suits are to be commended for their attempts to settle their property interest amicably. This not only saves the courts from being fraught with detail, and the necessity of repeated, recurrent hearings, but leads to better feeling and peace of mind among the litigants."

The disposition of life insurance policies on the life of the husband are proper subject matter for a property settlement agreement as well as the final decree of divorce. If the insurance policies are of long standing they may have accumulated substantial cash surrender values. In any event the usual divorce hassle results in the husband saying that he is willing to have the children named as beneficiaries under his policies but he does not want to continue paying insurance premiums that might benefit his ex-wife and mother of his children. If the wife is also primarily interested in the future welfare of the children, she should have no objections to the children being named as beneficiaries. This is better than having the policies later lapse because of non-payment.

What happens if the husband and wife are not able to work out their own property settlement agreement? Like all other facets of domestic problems, the judge will decide for them. Because most couples accumulate equities in homes, cars, furniture, etc., it is not always a simple matter. If the couple have two cars, it is easy to award one car to each. However, if they only have one car, it is more important that the car be awarded to the husband who needs it for his work rather than the wife who has need to transport the children from one place to another. The house and furniture usually go to the wife and children and the court tries to work it out 50-50 but sometimes the equities seem to work out closer to 80-20, always in favor of the wife. There is no set pattern or formula and each case goes on its own facts.

Some wives are so anxious to terminate their marriage that they will agree to anything in order to "get rid" of their husband. Sometimes, the husband has another female that he desires to marry and he is so anxious to "get rid" of his wife that he will agree to most anything to accomplish this mission.

## Who Has To Appear In Court?

Someone has to appear in court in order to complete a divorce action. Either the husband or wife must appear in person before the judge handling their divorce case and give testimony as to the reason they are asking for a divorce. The attorney may have heard all of the facts, however, he is not qualified to testify.

Usually, the person who filed for a divorce is the one that testifies as to why their marriage failed and why they are asking the judge to grant them a divorce. However, in certain circumstances, the named defendant can appear and explain to the judge that the other spouse had to leave the state and offer testimony for the granting of the divorce. The judge is really not too concerned whether the wife or husband or both of them appear in his court to testify in an un-contested divorce hearing. If they both want the divorce, the judge is not too fussy about the routine testimony. Some states require the brief testimony of one witness who testifies under oath that they know of their own knowledge that Mary Jones, the Plaintiff in the divorce case has lived in the state for more than one year, before filing for divorce. This is called a witness for purposes of residence only. Lawyers kid among themselves that they have never lost a default divorce case.

The divorce is usually granted to the wife on the grounds of incompatibility or similar catchall. If the husband is a true gentleman, he will permit his wife to be awarded the divorce, regardless of the factual background. The reason being that it is more important for the wife to be able to brag later that she divorced her husband, whereas the average husband does not have to boast to wife number two about being granted a divorce from wife number one.

## Insanity

In the United States, the usual remedy for the dissolution of a marriage, where one of the parties was insane at the time of the ceremony, is by annulment.

More often than not, the problem of mental ailments develop years after the couple have been married and what happens then? The laws of each state must be referred to in order to obtain the correct answer. Mental illness is a sad situation at best and the laws of the various states generally try to protect the ill spouse, even though the sane spouse has the right to a divorce.

Usually, the sane spouse can obtain a divorce, however, it is not easy and the procedure is obviously quite different than under normal circumstances. Most state laws talk about "incurable insanity" and require that the defendant shall have been adjudged insane and been committed to a mental institution for periods ranging from 2 to 10 years. Doctors are appointed by the judge to examine the patient and advise the court as to the condition of the patient.

If the husband is the sane spouse, he is legally obligated to continue supporting his insane wife, even after the divorce.

*Community Property*

Community property is defined as that property acquired by a married couple from the time of their marriage onward, as a result of their joint efforts. It excludes the separate property that each party brought into the marriage, as well as inheritances and gifts because that would constitute separate property.

At present the eight community property states are Arizona, California, Idaho, Louisiana, Nevada, New Mexico, Texas and Washington. Even the laws of the eight community property states vary and no two states are exactly alike. A community property law does not deal with the personal rights or conditions of married couples, only with property, real or personal.

Earnings of a working wife are community property just as are the earnings of the husband. The law makes no distinction between husband and wife in determining whether property is separate or community. A gift from the husband to the wife, is her separate property even though it was purchased with community funds. The basic intent of community property laws is to provide a return to the wife for her labors in the home. In borderline situations, the courts rule in favor of community property because public policy is in favor of maintaining the marital status. Marriage is said to be a partnership and chances for a successful marriage are enhanced when each party owns one-half of the family property.

The community property rights of a so-called "bad" wife are

equal to those of a "good" wife. It has been held that a wife guilty of adultery by her own admission, is still entitled to her community property rights in spite of her transgressions. Misconduct on the part of the husband would work out the same as regards his property rights.

The fact that a husband, for income tax purposes, listed all income as community property, has been held not to prevent him from asserting in a divorce action that the income was in fact his separate property.

A common problem occurs when funds are commingled and one party says they were separate funds and the other claims they were community funds. Where separate and community funds are mingled, the commingled funds are presumed to be community.

Either husband or wife can buy land in his or her name and it really has no legal significance. The important test is the source of the money that was used for the down payment or the full amount paid for the land. The mere fact that the warranty deed is made out in the husband's name only, proves nothing as to its being separate or community property. The same rule would apply if the deed were made out in the wife's name only. A wealthy wife in her own right, buying land with her own funds, should have the deed made out to "Mary Jones, a married woman, dealing as her sole and separate estate."

When it comes time to sell real estate, the signatures of both husband and wife are usually required.

All property owned by either spouse before marriage continues to be his or her separate property after marriage *IF* they do not convert it into community property. A gift or an inheritance is also classified as separate property of the recipient *IF* treated as such. The classic example is where the wife tells her husband she just received a $10,000 check from Uncle Joe's estate. This $10,000 is the separate property of the wife until she announced that she was going to pay off the mortgage on the family home which was community property. By her voluntary act, the wife converted the $10,000 from her separate property to community property. I approve of the wife's actions on the reasoning that it helps to make for a happier marriage. That way, we don't have to talk about "my property" or "your property" because it is all "our property."

To my female readers I regretfully advise that money saved by a wife out of household money given to her by her husband, does not become her separate property, but remains community property.

Divorce dissolves the community. Therefore, there can be no community property after divorce. Death also dissolves the community.

# BANKS;
# FINANCE COMPANIES;
# PAWNBROKERS

Banking is not a profession, it is a business. A banker is a dealer in money, who borrows from one party and lends to another. A borrower is one who rents money and the rental charge is called interest.

## Who To Borrow From

If you have the need to borrow money and have established credit, it is a lot cheaper to borrow from your bank in preference to a finance company or pawnbroker. Good bank credit can be invaluable in times of need. The slogan used by credit bureaus, namely, "Treat your credit as a sacred trust" is sound advice.

## Finance Statements

It is desirable that you deal with your personal banker if that is possible. You become acquainted and he has the opportunity of observing how you handle your financial obligations. The first bank requirement in connection with your borrowing money is that you furnish a current financial statement. This is a detailed list of what you own and what you owe, called assets and liabilities. Be fair and honest with your banker and it will pay dividends in the long run. All banks furnish their own forms for financial statements. If you own real estate don't try to fool your banker by listing the value at a high price because he will reduce your figure by about 50 per cent. Instead, list the value of your land on the basis of your cost price even if it is worth more.

## What To Do If You Can't Pay As Agreed

Just as you should anticipate your financial needs in advance, do the same as regards your payment commitments. Don't wait until the last minute or until you are delinquent and then run to your banker with your problems. He will think more of your business ability if you keep him posted in advance of your delinquency.

Even if you are not able to pay as agreed, your banker will be fair with you if you are fair with him. Sit down with your banker in person and tell him what your problem is and when you will be able to pay your obligation.

### Consult Your Banker But Make Up Your Own Mind

If you are considering a business transaction involving a sizeable sum of money or buying some land that will require borrowed money to swing the deal, consult your banker first. He is your financial advisor and has your interests at heart. After discussing the matter in detail, the final decision is up to you and you will have to make up your mind. Don't ask your banker what value he places on the land you want to buy because he is not an expert in every category. Your stockbroker cannot predict what the stock market will do in the future and your banker is not clairvoyant either. In my years of legal experience I handled thousands of real estate transactions for clients and always refused to express my opinion as to values because I was wrong as often as I was right.

Your banker is experienced in general business and financial matters and serious consideration should be given to his professional advice. The average banker is trained to be conservative and your judgment may be better than his.

### What About Co-Signing For A Friend?

Reference is made in the bible to "Neither a borrower nor lender be." Your banker and your lawyer will back up the biblical statement. Seven out of ten loans made with co-signors result in bad news for the co-signor because the original borrower failed to pay and the co-signor gets stuck.

The quickest and best way to lose a friend is to become involved in money matters and particularly in lending him money or co-signing his note at a bank or finance company. If the borrower does not pay as agreed, the co-signor becomes a guarantor. If your friend needs grocery money and you wish to help him out, don't lend him money, instead make a gift of whatever amount you feel you can afford. Bankers and attorneys know what happens when the co-signing friend gets stuck and the parties soon become enemies. Peculiarly, the borrower is the one who is unhappy with his former friend who he asked to co-sign his note.

Don't compete with your bank. The practical way to turn down your friend's request for a loan of money or your signature on his note is to advise that your bank won't permit it because it will affect your line of credit. Regardless of what words you use, the important thing is to turn your friend down. Even though he may resent the turndown, your actions may save your future friendship. If it doesn't it wasn't much of a friendship.

## Are Joint Accounts Advisable?

A joint bank account involves two or more persons and permits any one of the parties to make withdrawals at any time without notice to the others. It has good and bad features. If the parties are close to each other, such as husband and wife; parent and child; or even business partners; with implicit trust and faith in each other, there is no problem. The possible problem is where one of the joint account holders becomes greedy or dishonest and withdraws all or part of the money in violation of the agreement.

If two people have a joint account and one dies, the survivor has access to all of the money. If more than two people are on the joint account and one persons dies, then all of the survivors have the same rights of ownership that they held before death occurred.

In cases of a married couple where their marriage is normal and the wife and husband have faith in each other, I strongly urge and recommend joint ownership of all of their assets including bank accounts. This has a definite tendency to help the marriage relationship. There is a certain type of husband who maintains bank accounts in his own name and his wife is kept in the dark as to his finances. One of the factors that contributes toward the high divorce rate is the husband or wife who continually says: "My children; My car; My home; My money, etc."

An actual example may be of help to the reader. Mother is a widow with two adult children both of whom are married. Mother is getting up in years and is in poor health. All members of the family get along extremely well without problems. Mother has accummulated $20,000 that she wishes to divide equally between her two children. She can open one joint account with the name of Mother and adult child number one for $10,000. Mother can duplicate this procedure for joint account number two with child number two. Mother has access to the money in both joint accounts during her lifetime if there is need. Upon the occasion of Mother's death, each child has access to the money in one of the joint accounts. The ownership of stocks can be handled in the same manner. Even real estate can be divided between more than one surviving child.

The one advantage of having money or other property in joint accounts or joint ownership is that the survivor has access to the money or property without need for probate court proceedings. This saves time and sometimes a lot of money. A joint account may not always act as a substitute for a will, but in many cases, it can result in avoiding probate court proceedings and the designated parties receive the money promptly.

### Should A Safety Deposit Box Be Held Jointly?

The same reasoning that applies to joint bank accounts applies to joint safety deposit boxes. If some member of the family wishes secrecy or privacy, he or she can open a safety deposit box in one name only. No other person would have access to the contents until death occurs. Then the laws of the individual state would control. Some states are anxious to collect inheritance taxes that may be due and the safety deposit box is sealed under court order. It can only be opened later for the sole purpose of making an inventory of the contents in connection with probate court proceedings.

Even if you don't want the safety deposit box to be in joint names of two or more persons, banks will permit you to sign a card authorizing your representative to have access to the contents of your box. You would either give them a key during your lifetime or advise the location of your safety deposit box key upon your death. If not prohibited by state law, they would then have access to the contents of your box.

### How To Keep A Running Balance

Many people with limited business experience dread looking at their monthly bank statement. They feel that they are not good at arithmetic and would prefer to play ostrich and file it in some drawer. It is really not that difficult and it is important that the bank's figures be checked with your own. Most banks now use computers but mistakes will occur. If you ever discover an error in your favor, be just as prompt in notifying your bank as if the error were not in your favor. "Honesty is the best policy" and the computer will later pick up the error and you could be embarrassed and will not have gained anything.

The secret to keeping a running balance is very simple. Each time you write out a check, deduct the amount of the check from your previous balance. Each time you make a deposit, add the amount to your previous balance. Now that counter type of checks are no longer accepted by banks, you have to use your own check that has the number of your account perforated on it. It only takes a jiffy to write out your check and less time to deduct the figure from your previous balance. This simple task is habit forming and the time to do it is when you are making out your check. Then, when the monthly bank statement arrives it is an interesting game to check all of your deposits and withdrawals and see if the bank's records tally with your own. When they do there is a good feeling of being efficient and of accomplishment. If it doesn't jibe, time must be spent going over each item to find the error.

Where husband and wife each use a separate check book for the same joint account, it is mandatory to pass along the information about checks written to whoever is keeping the running balance.

## Is A "Hot" Check Bad?

Yes, a check returned because of insufficient funds is very bad. Your bank makes a service charge, sometimes as high as $1; the recipient of your check is unhappy with you; and nothing could be worse for your credit record. There is no good reason for writing out a check when you do not have sufficient funds in your account to cover the check. You know that a check is an order on your bank to pay the amount named in your check and charge same against your account. If your account does not have the money, your bank will bounce it back to the recipient. Even your own bank is not pleased about returning your check and your credit is being hurt in many different directions.

All of the time-worn alibis are passe. Some of the old-timers are: "I thought I had enough money in my account to cover your check. My bank must have made a mistake because I just made a deposit. I thought my husband was going to deposit some money in my account. I thought I was going to receive a check to cover your check; etc., etc."

Unless your credit is established at your own bank, the mere deposit of an outsider's check to your account does not mean that the money is available to you immediately. Some banks insist on having your deposited check cleared before the funds are available to you. There are two cardinal rules: (1) Never issue a check unless you have the funds available in your account to cover it. (2) As soon as you issue a check, charge the amount against your running balance. Don't gamble on when your issued check might be cleared and get back to your bank.

## Bank Service Charges

In the good old days, the only requirement for a checking account was to open an account with $100 and you were free to write as many checks as you wished. All at no charge. Those days are gone forever and now the bank computer determines whether your small checking account balance is adequate for the number of checks you issue during an average month. If your average balance is not profitable to your bank, a service charge is made automatically against your account balance. This charge would seem to be a fair one if the bank gave credit to customers who maintain a very substantial balance. However, banks are "funny that way" and they pay nothing for the use of substantial sums of money that is kept in checking accounts.

Some banks have set up a charge for each check written, so that the customer knows in advance how much it costs to issue a check.

The practical way of keeping your cost down on the issuance of checks is to refrain from writing out checks for trivial amounts. Some people have a bad habit of writing checks for small amounts for pocket money and this habit is now an expensive one. If your checking account is being charged with a service charge, you should either keep more money in your account or cut down on the number of checks you issue during each month.

## How Are Checks Cleared?

Under the Federal Reserve System, most large cities have a clearing house for all banks located within their immediate area. Years ago, checks were sent from one part of the country to a clearing house located in another section and mail took a number of days. With the advent of modern aircraft, things have changed and most checks arrive at their local clearing house in a hurry.

For example, a check is mailed in Los Angeles to a magazine publisher in New York and the check is drawn on a Los Angeles bank. The New York publishing firm deposits the check in their New York bank account and it goes from the New York clearing house to the Los Angeles clearing house, who in turn pass it along to the bank of origin.

The amount designated is charged against the account of the check's issuer. If this procedure sounds complicated, it really is not and the time factor has been shortened.

## Bank Savings Accounts

All banks want customers to open savings account with them. The rate of interest is not as high as other financial institutions but banks advertise that they render a greater variety of services for benefit of their customers. Generally speaking, federal savings and loan associations pay a higher rate of interest than the banks. Both groups have their accounts federally insured so the safety factor is the same. Banks have their customers accounts insured through the Federal Deposit Insurance Corporation (FDIC) whereas federal savings and loan associations have their customers accounts insured through the Federal Savings and Loan Insurance Corporation (FSLIC). Both organizations are agencies of the United States government and for all practical purposes there are no differences from the customer's viewpoint. The claim of some bankers that a defunct bank would pay off quicker than a defunct federal savings and loan association is not true.

## Escheat - What Is It?

Escheat has nothing to do with the art of cheating. It is the process whereby each state claims ownership of property, including bank accounts that lie dormant for a number of years and the owner cannot be found. Banks and other financial institutions have found over a period of years that persons will open an account, savings or checking, and after many years the account indicates no activity and the customer cannot be located.

In the case of a checking account, the bank has had free use of the money in this account for years which is good for the bank. In the case of savings accounts, the banks or other financial institutions add the interest earned to the account but no one knows the whereabouts of the mysterious customer. All mail is returned and he cannot be located.

What happens to the money?. It does not belong to the bank who has already enjoyed use of the deposited money for a given number of years. The individual states discovered another source of revenue and each state enacted comparable escheat laws providing that the money involved goes to the state after a prescribed number of years. This will vary from five to twenty years of account inactivity and inability to locate the owner of the account. The laws of most states further provide that should and if the true owner of the money or his legal heirs later claim the money that upon satisfactory proof the state will pay them the money.

## Finance Companies

The extensive growth of credit and installment buying has helped to increase finance companies. Most states have enacted laws regulating finance companies from their charges to their right to open new offices or branches. The finance business is a legitimate operation, in spite of their high charges and unpopular and aggressive tactics. Most finance companies know that most of their customers prefer to deal with a bank but do not have sufficient assets or established credit to satisfy the requirements of a bank. The charges made by a bank are lower than those made by a finance company.

Finance companies cater to two different types of customers. One is making direct loans to the customer under what the laws of many states call "The Small Loan Act." The second is a involuntary type of customer who buys furniture from a credit furniture store on the installment plan. The furniture store needs money and they sell the paper to a finance company. The customer did not know when he purchased furniture from the X furniture store on the installment plan, that his conditional sales contract would be sold or assigned to some finance outfit.

The second category of customer has not been harmed if the finance company charges are the same that the agreed to pay under his contract with the furniture store. The fact that the finance company may have private arrangements with the furniture store to charge the purchase price back if the customer does not pay, is of no concern to the customer. It does not matter to him whether he owes the money to the X furniture store or to the Y finance company.

## Finance Company Borrowers

Some people who borrow money are not concerned with interest or any other charges that they have to pay in return for the use of the borrowed money.

Even though most finance companies are subject to the laws of the state where they operate, the finance charges are still high when compared to bank charges. The finance company know that their customer does not qualify for a bank loan because of his poor credit or lack of collateral. The risk of the finance company is greater than that of the bank, even though the finance company takes a chattel mortgage on the borrower's furniture, car, radio, television set, washing machine and just about everything else other than the borrower's children.

A chattel mortgage is to personal property what a real estate mortgage is to land, namely security for an obligation. If the borrower fails to make his monthly payments on the mortgage on his home, the holder of the mortgage is privileged to foreclose against the borrower, to take the home away from him. The same procedure is followed on a chattel mortgage, where the borrower fails to pay his agreed obligation and the creditor sues to take the mortgaged items to apply on the obligation.

Automobiles are frequently sold on a conditional sales contract, with title remaining in the seller, until fully paid. If the buyer fails to pay as agreed, the finance company is able to repossess the car because they hold the legal title. The laws of certain states provide that the finance company must first file a lawsuit in court and obtain a court order before they are privileged to get possession of the automobile. This eliminates the undesirable procedure of the finance company collector from grabbing the car wherever he is able to find it.

Collateral is the security given to the creditor as a guaranty for payment if the borrower defaults. Some banks require collateral for personal loans and the collateral could be stocks; jewelry; cars; or any other items of value.

The Congress of the United States in an effort to protect the gullible public, enacted legislation known as "The Truth In Lending Act." Sellers of cars, appliances, etc., as well as money lenders are required to make a full disclosure as to all of their charges. Many people are only concerned with the amount of the monthly payment and ignore the interest and carrying charges. When a car dealer advertises that you can buy car X for your old car plus $83 per month that is only part of the story. The important information that is being ignored is: "What is the total price of the car and how many months does the buyer have to pay $83 per month?" The Truth In Lending Act was aimed at stopping sharp practices on the part of the money lender or credit grantor but is only effective for those that want to be protected. If the buyer doesn't care how many months he is agreeing to pay $83 per month, it is unfortunate but that is his problem.

The saddest cases of all occur when the borrower has a champagne taste and a beer pocketbook. This is the type of individual who has a limited earning capacity but buys a large and expensive colored television set or car when a smaller substitute would be more appropriate. He knows that his income won't permit him to make his payments. In rare cases, I have known of situations where the income of the borrower was actually less than all of his installment and finance company payments. The borrower says he did not realize that the outgo was greater than his income. Meanwhile, he is being hounded by his creditors, all of whom want their money.

## Pawnbrokers

A pawnbroker has been defined as a person who makes a business of lending money for interest, and receives personal property as security for the repayment of the money. Some people swear by their pawnbroker as another might praise his dentist or stockbroker.

In the world of credit and money borrowing, banks rate the highest, followed by finance companies and pawnbrokers bring up the rear. The pawnbroker and his customer both know that the doors of banks or finance companies are not open to the borrower who is down to his last hope for raising quick money. This borrower has no credit or bank type of collateral other than some item of personal property available as security for a quick loan.

The business of pawnbroking is subject to police regulation because of opportumities it offers to criminals to dispose of stolen goods. Pawnbrokers are also controlled by various state laws and municipal ordinances as regards the rate of interest they may charge; the length of time they must hold on to the pledged article before it may be offered for sale; records to be kept for inspection by the police department and similar regulations. Some pawnbrokers used to be depicted as "shylocks" but many of the modern version are performing a useful and beneficial purpose in helping people in distress to raise money in a hurry. In spite of the high charges and the low sum of money advanced on the value of the pawned articles, many borrowers know that their redemption rights will not be exercised and the pawnbroker adds the item in due course of time to his stock of saleable merchandise.

# GIFTS AND TAXES

Nothing is as certain as "Death and taxes." The subject matter of taxation has become so complex that a growing number of lawyers and accountants limit their practice to this field. Unfortunately, some attorneys and accountants are not knowledgeable in this highly technical and rapidly changing specialty and their clients may suffer as a result. If your tax problem is not a simple one, I would urge you to consult with an attorney or accountant who specializes in tax matters. A license to practice law or accountancy does not automatically make a person an expert in the field of tax problems.

It seems to be the history of taxes that certain prominent wealthy persons are able to hire tax experts and successfully avoid paying taxes. The law says it is perfectly legal to avoid paying taxes but it is illegal to evade the payment of taxes. The result is that certain wealthy persons with incomes of a million dollars annually, or more, are able to legally avoid taxes and pay little or nothing. Yet, many whose income is in the lower or middle tax bracket pay a substantial percentage of their taxable income.

It was hoped that the Tax Reform Act of 1969 would cure these ills, however, life does not seem to work out that way. In spite of the efforts of the Congress of the United States, the rich will become richer and the poor will probably pay more taxes. The purpose of the new law was to produce a more equitable means of income taxation in addition to certain specific goals. If you do not own any oil wells, you may have been unhappy with the oil depletion percentage allowance which permitted those fortunate oil owners to keep the first 27-1/2 percent of each oil dollar received, and pay taxes on the remainder. On the other hand, the oil people are not happy that the federal congress reduced the oil depletion percentage allowance from 27-1/2 percent to 22 percent. With human nature being what it is, it all depends on "whose ox is being gored." The main tax law before the 1969 Tax Reform Act was the Internal Revenue Code of 1954.

*Federal Estate Tax*

In addition to the federal estate tax, most states have estate tax laws that vary from state to state. The one good thing about the federal estate tax is that it provides for an exemption of the first $60,000. Therefore, if you die tomorrow and the value of your estate is less than $60,000, there is no federal estate tax due the United States. The $60,000 exemption is per person and if a married couple die simultaneously, then their joint estates would be entitled to $120,000 exemption. Most families do not have estates valued at more than $120,000 and as a result, there is no liability for federal estate taxes. The reader will have to learn the amount of exemption that prevails under the laws of his particular state. It is usually not nearly as liberal as the federal exemption.

There are federal and state estate taxes as well as inheritance taxes. An inheritance tax is one imposed upon the right to receive while an estate tax is one levied upon the privilege of transfer at death.

An estate tax is imposed upon the net taxable estate of the decedent and has nothing to do with the relationship of the recipient or the amount he takes. It is a tax upon the transfer of property by a deceased person for the privilege of transferring property. It is a tax upon what is left by the decedent and not on what passes to the heirs or beneficiaries. The estate tax is an expense of administration and is an obligation of the estate to be paid by the executor or administrator. If the decedent left a will, he named his executor. If he left no will, the court will appoint an administrator.

The inheritance or succession tax is not new. It was first adopted in Egypt in the seventh century before Christ. An inheritance tax is a succession tax, or, you could say, a succession tax is an inheritance tax. Thus, three separate taxes may be imposed at death; the federal estate tax; the state succession tax; and the state estate tax.

*State Taxes*

The first state to adopt the inheritance tax was Pennsylvania in 1826. New York followed suit in 1885 and since that time it has extended to almost every state. The various state inheritance tax laws are similar.

Death duties or taxes are excise taxes, being levied upon the privilege of transferring property at death. A Connecticut court held: "So-called inheritance or succession taxes are not taxes laid upon persons or property, or strictly speaking, taxes at all. They are death duties, levied as exactions of the state, incidental to the devolution of title by force of its laws."

The power of a state to tax is an incident of sovereignty. The levy of inheritance taxes is within the discretionary power of the state legislature to select the subjects of taxation. If different rates are assessed on inheritance according to the degree of relationship of the heir, the tax is called a graduated or progressive tax.

Just as the federal laws provide for an exemption for the first $60,000 of an estate, each state provides for exemptions in varies amounts. A Kansas court held: "An inheritance tax law which exempts estates below a certain amount when the beneficiaries are related to the deceased within certain degrees does not violate the Bill of Rights, declaring that free governments are instituted for the equal protection and benefit of the people."

Most state inheritance tax laws favor lineal heirs over those of collateral relationship. Lineal heirs are those falling in a direct line of ancestry, such as grandfather, son, grandson, brother, sister, etc. A state cannot grant an exemption from an inheritance tax to a resident of the state, and deny it to persons of like relationship to the deceased, who are residents of other states. The reason being that the Constitution of the United States declares that the citizens of each state shall be entitled to all the privileges and immunities in the several states.

## Contemplation Of Death

The laws of most states provide for a tax on transfers of property made "in contemplation of death." The law presumes that if the transfer is made within 3 years of the death of the donor, it was made in contemplation of death and is subject to the same tax as if made after death. A "gift tax" is much less than the estate tax and it is therefore important taxwise, if the gift was not made in contemplation of death. A Wisconsin court ruled: "A gift by one who desires to retire from active life, and makes the gift because it affords him pleasure and not because he anticipates death, is not "made in contemplation of death" although he was at the time 86 years of age, it appearing that he was in good health."

A transfer of policies of insurance upon the life of the transferor is not in and of itself in contemplation of death. The beneficiaries cannot receive any part of the proceeds while the settlor is living. Every man making a gift knows that what he gives away today will not be included in his estate when he dies. The bodily and mental condition of a transferor at the time of transfer is an important element in determining whether the transfer was made in contemplation of death.

### Are United States Bonds Taxable?

Yes, the statutes and regulations governing United States savings bonds recognize that they may be subjected to both federal and state death taxes.

### Are Life Insurance Proceeds Taxable?

Life insurance proceeds on the life of a decedent which are payable to his family or his estate are subject to estate or inheritance tax. It could be to your advantage to talk to your insurance expert about who owns your life insurance policy. Many husbands and wives think that ownership of a life insurance policy is not important as long as the man's family is protected in the event of his untimely death. That is only a part of the problem and in cases where the couple have done well financially and their joint estates exceed $120,000, a new problem crops up, namely federal estate taxes. One way of reducing the federal estate tax is to keep assets out of the husband's name, so that if he meets with an untimely death, the assets of his estate are not increased. One way of solving this problem is to not only name the wife as beneficiary of her husband's life insurance policy, but also have her named as the owner. Then, if the husband dies first, the life insurance money goes directly to the wife and does not become a part of the husband's estate. If there is any doubt in your mind, consult your life insurance advisor. There can be a very substantial savings in federal estate taxes in given situations. There are certain complications that have to be checked into, such as the source of the money used for the payment of the premiums on the husband's life where the wife is the beneficiary and owner of his life insurance policy. This can be accomplished by the husband making a gift to the wife of his one-half community interest in the money used to pay the life insurance policy premiums.

### Can A Person Be Taxed Twice?

A famous case involved a member of the Campbell Soup Company family who lived in Pennsylvania as well as New Jersey.

When he died and his estate was probated, each state ruled that he was a resident of their state and the final result was that his estate was taxed by both states. The legal problems always center around the problem of residence. Residence is a matter of intent.

Taxation of land in only one state, the state of the land's location, has always been the rule. Two or more states could assess death taxes on a decedent's intangibles or personal property upon a court determination by each state that he was living there. The United States Supreme Court has said, "Even though it believed that a different system should be designed to protect against multiple taxation it is not our province to provide it." Apropos of unusual results, the rulings of our courts are sometimes hard to understand. Many years ago, Secretary of the Interior Albert B. Fall was found guilty of accepting a bribe from oilman Edward L. Doheny but Mr. Doheny was found not guilty of offering a bribe to Mr. Fall.

## Assessment And Computation Of Tax

The state has the power to impose an inheritance tax and to say when and how the amount shall be ascertained and paid. An inheritance or succession tax, as contrasted with an estate tax, is a tax upon the right to receive. It is levied against each recipient and is measured by the amount passing to each heir.

## Gift Taxes

The federal government and about a dozen states have enacted gift tax laws. This is a tax in the year of transfer by living persons that is imposed on the donor. The obvious purpose is to compensate for the withdrawal of property by gifts between the living from the operation of the estate tax. In 1932 the Congress passed a gift tax law and some state laws have been modelled after it. The United States Supreme Court held: "The purpose of the gift tax is to complement the estate tax by preventing taxfree depletion of the transferor's estate during his lifetime."

Those who make gifts are required to fill out and file a gift tax return with Internal Revenue Service, the same procedure as in filing an income tax return. Just as is the case with an income tax return, a gift tax return must be filed annually, regardless of whether any money is owed.

Each donor is entitled to various exemptions. To start with each donor is granted a $30,000 lifetime exemption by the federal government. This means that the first $30,000 that is given away is tax-exempt. In addition, the donor may give away up to $3,000 per person to an unlimited number of people during any calendar year. Any gift in excess of $3,000 per year is subject to a gift tax. The main reason or advantage of gifts during a person's lifetime, rather than waiting for death and the will to pass title, is that the gift tax is much less than the inheritance tax. The amount of each tax will vary, depending upon the amount involved. It is therefore recommended that when parents are up in years and are financially able, that they start their give away program in favor of their loved ones and reduce the tax liability. If they do nothing and wait for death, their children will inherit their estate but the tax liability will be much greater.

An earlier subtitle discussed gifts made in contemplation of death. In a situation where a gift is made and a gift tax return is filed and a gift tax paid by the donor, it is still a worthwhile gamble even if the attempted gift is later ruled to have been made in contemplation of death. The amount of gift tax paid is not lost but is applied against the higher tax rate of the estate tax.

The gift can be money, stock in any corporation, life insurance contract, business interests, or anything else of value.

Under specific provisions of the Internal Revenue Code charitable and similar gifts are allowed as a deduction in computing taxable gifts. Charitable gifts are favorites of the law. This would normally include gifts to institutions for benevolent, charitable, educational, or religious purposes. This kindness on the part of the taxing authorities is contrary to the prevailing result in close cases where the courts say: "Taxation is the rule and the exemption the exception."

*Gift Of Money Or Bank Accounts*

Over a period of years, many people have asked how they can leave money to a child or close friend and still maintain some reasonable control during their lifetime. If the parties have implicit faith in one another and are not worried about the recipient doublecrossing the donor, there is a simple answer. Change your bank account from your name alone to a joint account and add as many names as you wish. For example, a parent can add the names of one or more children to the account if he or she so desires. Another possibility is for the parent who wants to leave $10,000 to two children, is to arrange for two joint accounts, one with each child for $5,000. In this manner, each child receives the same treatment and the parent controls the bank account during his or her lifetime. This procedure is perfectly legal and does avoid probate court proceedings to the extent of the money involved.

The above procedure is recommended only in those cases where the parties get along well and there are no family problems. If there is any jealousy or distrust, don't have a joint account. The one big element of danger is that the "outsider" as regards ownership of the money, has equal control and can withdraw the money at any time.

In normal situations, it works out perfectly and the parent controls the money during his or her lifetime and upon occasion of death, the child has access to the money without any fuss or court proceedings.

## Testamentary Gifts

When a person leaves a will and gives something of value to another, it is called a "testamentary gift." However, when a person provides for a gift during his lifetime, it is called "gifts inter vivos" which is between living persons. "Gifts causa mortis" is in contemplation of death. Legally, a gift is a voluntary transfer of property by one to another without any consideration or compensation for it.

## Can You Be An "Indian Giver?"

Yes, in cases of gifts causa mortis and no in cases of gifts inter vivos. Gifts causa mortis only apply to personal property and not to real estate. If the donor does not die, he can change his mind and cancel the gift. This happens frequently when a person is about to have a dangerous surgical operation and is fearful of dying, but survives and revokes the gift. A gift made in contemplation of suicide is not a gift causa mortis because the person may change their mind and also because such a gift is against public policy. In some states, it is against the law to attempt to take your own life.

## Uniform Gift To Minors Act

Nearly every state has adopted the Uniform Gift to Minors Act. It provides that an adult person may transfer to a custodian for benefit of a minor, a gift of a security, money or a life insurance policy or annuity contract. Any gift thus made may be given to any number of minors. A gift made in the manner prescribed by the act is irrevocable, and gives to the minor a vested legal title. It has tax advantages for people of means.

### Can Fraud Or Undue Influence Affect A Gift?

A court has the power to invalidate a gift where the facts indicate that fraud or undue influence involved. A gift between persons having confidential relations such as attorney and client is carefully scrutinized by a court. A Florida court held: "Gifts of land and money to the donor's attorney from a disoriented and mentally unbalanced aged client was invalid where the attorney failed to establish rectitude of his conduct in accepting gratuitous transfers; the attorney's years of faithful, uncompensated services to the donor were not full justification for the disputed gifts." A New York court held: "The presumption of undue influence arising from the fact that an 82-year old woman conveyed property to her attorney and his wife for a nominal consideration was not overcome."

### Who Owns The Wedding Gifts?

Gifts to the wife from her friends and relatives belong to her, and gifts from the relatives and friends of the husband belong to him. Wedding gifts appropriate only for the personal use of one of the spouses belong to that spouse. Wedding gifts from one spouse to the other have been held to be the property of the donee. A New Jersey court ruled that a gift from the husband to his wife of an automobile bearing her initials was a valid gift for her sole benefit. If a wedding present is given expressly to the married couple they become joint owners.

### Who Gets The Engagement Ring, Jewelry And Gifts?

Many judges rule that where the engagement is broken without legal justification by the donee, recovery of such gifts or their value may be had. It has been generally held that where the engagement is unjustifiably broken by the donor, there can be no recovery of gifts made in contemplation of marriage. Yet, a New Jersey court held: "The engagement ring must be returned to the donor on termination of betrothal, irrespective of which party, if either, is to blame." Some states have solved this problem by having laws that spell out who gets what under given circumstances.

# ANIMALS

*History*

Dictionaries define animals as any animate being, not human, and endowed with the power of voluntary motion. Although the oyster cannot voluntarily transport itself from one place to another, it has a limited power of movement within itself and, in law, is regarded as an animal.

There are basically two kinds of animals, wild and domestic or tamed. In the United States the ownership of wild animals is in the people of each state. Each state holds the title to wild animals in trust for all of its residents. Each state has the right and power to prohibit or regulate the taking of wild animals. This matter is usually handled by the Fish and Game Commission or similar agency. When we talk about state ownership, we mean land that is owned or controlled by the state. By way of contrast, the owner of private land has the right to take any and all wild animals that are found on his land.

Any person has a right to have a wild animal but he can be held liable for resulting injuries if he has not exercised reasonable and proper care in restraining or securing it. An Oklahoma case held: "The owner or keeper of a dangerous animal, classed as ferae naturae, such as a bear, takes the risk of so keeping it that it will not injure persons invited on the premises who are exercising care."

Animals have been classified as ferocious, dangerous, mischievous, and harmless. The first three are of wild nature and the last of tame and gentle disposition, either naturally so or because they have been trained. If that sounds technical, a federal law says the word cattle is defined as one or more bulls, steers, oxen, cows, heifers, or calves, or carcass or carcasses thereof. This type of jargon always reminds me of the typical technical legaleze contract that starts off with party of the first part and party of the second part and then after much legaleze language, concludes with "everything to the contrary notwithstanding."

In an old Maine case, the Judge said: "At common law dogs were not generally the subject of taxation, neither were they regarded as property in such a sense as to make them assets of the estate of a deceased person." Now, the law says that all tame animals are personal property.

Not only are dogs now considered to be personal property, but they are an important feature of divorce cases. In the so-called "good old days" the big fight in divorce court was the ruling pertaining to child custody, division of community property and the amount that the husband was ordered to pay for child support and possibly alimony. However, in today's modern Hollywood type of divorce, sometimes the primary dispute between the childless couple, is which one gets custody of the family pet. A recent divorce case in Illinois is really "one for the books." The husband was sued for divorce and granted the right to visit his dog. The Judge, who had earlier awarded custody of the dog and the childless couple's home to the wife, later relented and gave the husband permission to walk the pooch on Mondays, Wednesdays and Fridays while his wife was at work. Dogs and many other family pets are now considered to be extremely valuable property.

We are primarily concerned with domestic animals who are tamed and accustomed to live in or near the homes of people. The most common group of domestic animals are dogs, cats, birds, monkeys, horses, cattle, sheep, goats, pigs, poultry, and all other animals that by habit or training live with humans.

*Dogs*

DOG spelled backwards becomes GOD. Dogs differ among themselves more widely than any other class of animals. Most of us have seen television pictures taken at fashionable showings of pedigreed dogs and noticed the striking similarity in appearance of the dog and his master. Some people prefer the higher breeds of dogs because of their intelligence. Others like a 57 variety breed for their loyalty and ability to become "man's best friend."

The old legal adage, "Every dog is entitled to his first bite" is now being disputed by some judges. Every dog owner is concerned about the possibility of his or her Fido biting someone and then being sued for $50,000 or some other ridiculous sum of money. The first and main basic legal principle is that the dog owner is not liable for injuries caused by his dog biting some person *UNLESS* he has knowledge that his dog is vicious or dangerous. The law books are filled with exceptions to the established rule. The following unusual facts proved to be an exception to the rule. An owner of an overlyfriendly Great Dane, who jumped on a 74 year old lady who weighed 105 pounds and knocked her down, breaking her arm and leg, was held responsible for the ladies' injuries.

Each of the fifty states have laws pertaining to dogs, cats and other animals and they vary considerably. In addition, each city or county has its own ordinances pertaining to dogs and their requirements. The variance is so great that it is impossible to quote other than general legal principles. Every city publishes a booklet containing local ordinances that are the law of that community. I would urge every animal owner who is concerned, to purchase a copy of his city's ordinances and acquaint himself with the local law pertaining to his dog or cat or other animal. You need not be a lawyer to read and understand local law. Speaking of lawyers, there is no law that requires a person to hire a lawyer to represent him in any legal proceeding. If you think you are capable and knowledgeable about the matter in dispute, you can act as your own lawyer. Members of the legal profession like to use the old phrase, "An attorney who defends himself has a fool for a client."

## Licensing and Registration of Dogs

City ordinances have been passed to regulate and control dogs to a greater extent than for any other class of domestic animals. Reasonable ordinances providing for license fees on dogs are constitutional as a valid exercise of the police power of the municipality. By necessity, the keeping of dogs in thickly settled areas like a city is subject to rigid police regulations. In addition to the usual licensing and tagging of dogs, Santa Monica, California has a law prohibiting dogs from being walked in parks that are so marked. A first offender named Colby received a $20 suspended fine for that horrible offense. Other cities require that dogs be kept on a leash while on the streets or in some cases even muzzled.

In many cities, ordinances are in force providing for the impounding and destruction of all dogs that are caught roaming the streets who are not properly tagged and licensed.

Although I consider myself to be as much of a dog lover as the average person, I think we would all agree that ordinances based on health requirements, prohibiting dogs from entering restaurants or food establishments are reasonable restrictions. A modern Madrid, Spain supermarket has a special bar to which the leashed dog is tied while his master completes the food shopping. Shades of the old wild west, hitching your horse while strolling into the bar for a drink.

### When Is A Dog A Public Nuisance?

As a rule, dogs and other animals are not considered to be nuisances per se. The disposition and conduct of the dog and the manner in which it is kept usually determines the answer as to a dog becoming a public nuisance. For example, it has been held that the keeping of a vicious dog that is not properly restrained may be enjoined. To enjoin is to forbid or prohibit. In given cases, the owner of a vicious dog may be prosecuted criminally for maintaining a public nuisance. It has also been held that a dog accustomed to bite or attack people, may be killed as a public nuisance if permitted to run at large or to escape from his owner's premises.

An old legal maxim is still the law of the land, namely, "One must so use his own property so as not to injure that of another." The barking, howling, and whinning of dogs may constitute a public nuisance and be enjoined, where it results in serious annoyance to neighborhood residents and interfere with the reasonable use and enjoyment of their property. A Colorado case held: "The keeping of 40 to 80 dogs whose kennels emit offensive odors, and whose barking in the nightime when aroused by the passing of automobiles on a much-travelled highway breaks the rest of persons living on adjoining premises, is a private nuisance and may be enjoined." The mere fact that a dog does not like or get along with other dogs or animals, is not binding notice to his owner that he might attack people. Each case has to be determined under its own facts.

Many people are in doubt as to who is liable when a dog is in his own backyard and he bites a person who has no legal right to be on the premises and is classified as a trespasser by law. We start off with the premise that the dog is a watchdog and has been trained to bite or attack people. Most judges have ruled that the owner of a vicious dog who is apt to attack people, is legally bound to restrain the dog even as against a trespasser on his own property. The fact that a person is a trespasser does not make him an outlaw. The owner has no right to cause his being bitten. This reasoning may bother you but the legal principle involved is that the safety of human life may not unnecessarily be endangered in the protection of property. One is not justified in keeping a vicious dog untied on his premises in the daytime. On the other hand, most cases hold that the owner is not liable at night, when his watchdog bites a trespasser, because it is deemed necessary and proper for protective purposes.

Usually, those that tease, torment or abuse a dog are responsible for bites or injuries that follow. People say it serves them right and the law agrees with that reasoning. These uncalled for acts are called contributory negligence on the part of the victim or claimant. By the term "contributory negligence" is meant that even though the dog owner may have been guilty of being negligent, that the wrongful actions of the victim in teasing or tormenting the dog, prevents him from recovering any damages because the law says he was guilty of contributing towards his own plight.

## Cruelty And Kindness To Animals

Saint Francis of Assisi is known as the patron saint of all animals. His kindness and love for all forms of animals is universally respected by all who are fond of animals. In the United States in recent years, many states have passed laws protecting animals from cruel and inhuman treatment by man. It is a sad commentary but there is a dire need for such laws because of the small percentage of humans who seem to hate animals and delight in torturing them in one form or another.

In addition to criminal liability for cruelty to animals, a wonderful non-profit organization known as "Society For The Prevention Of Cruelty To Animals" has been established in most communities. If you observe a cruel or inhuman act or form of punishment being inflicted on any animal, notify this organization and their trained and concerned officials will handle the matter efficiently. If criminal complaints are advisable, they will file the criminal complaint in the name of their organization. Usually, the local animal shelter operated by the municipality is mainly concerned with stray animals that are not properly licensed and not with cruelty performed against animals.

Rabies is an acute deadly virus disease transmitted by the bite of a rabid animal. Should and if you ever become involved by being the owner of a suspected rabid dog or other animal or know of a victim being bitten, the following precautionary measures are terribly important. The rabid animal, even though he is only a suspected rabid animal must be kept alive for a period of time designated by your doctor or if he is not immediately available, by the opinion of your veterinarian. If the rabid animal is not found and confined, the victim of his bite must take a series of horribly painful shots in order to survive. This can be a matter of life or death and the medical advice should definitely not be ignored.

Under its police power, a state may establish reasonable inspection and quarantine regulations for the purpose of protection against the spread of contagious diseases among animals. Various countries are enforcing restrictions against the entry of dogs and cats for reasons of preservation of health. If you plan to move to a new country with your dog or cat, it may be advisable to inquire about their rules and regulations for entry of your pet.

Years ago, many men used to laugh about women drivers and jokes were made about a lady driver getting panicky when a dog suddenly appeared in her path, and taking her hands off the steering wheel and wrecking her car. With the passing of time, statistics have proven that the female of the species are better drivers than their male counterpart. The current "Womens Liberation Movement" is not involved in this matter.

Who is responsible for a dog roaming the streets and directly or indirectly causing an accident? Usually the driver of the motor vehicle is charged with the duty of driving the car in such a manner as to have control at all times. If possible, the driver should try to avoid striking the animal, however, if that opportunity does not present itself, he should strike the animal rather than have a serious accident. If the dog's sudden appearance does cause an accident, it is the responsibility of the car operator. The only possible remote exception to this rule could occur if the driving victim of the car accident can prove that the dog's owner knew that his dog was constantly chasing cars in which case the dog's owner would be liable.

*Cats*

Some people prefer dogs as household pets, while others prefer cats. The author is neutral and no partiality is intended. Basically, the same regulations that apply to dogs would also apply to cats.

Somehow or another, most legal problems involving cats, seem to involve their female owners. Many law cases include the keeping of cats in large numbers. Ordinances regulating or forbidding the keeping of more than a certain number of animals in the municipality are valid. The best way to beat the law on the usual prohibitions against animals generally, is to move to the country and then you can keep as many dogs or cats as you wish, plus hogs, horses or chickens. An Oklahoma judge ruled that forty cats in one house was a public nuisance but he authorized the lady owner to keep four of her pets.

Because the cat is a tame animal, legally its owner may safely keep it without liability for injuries caused by it. As in the case with dogs, in the absence of knowledge on the part of the cat's owner of any vicious tendencies, there is no liability on the owner's part. If the cat's owner knows it likes to bite and scratch people than the owner is responsible for any and all injuries caused by the vicious cat. In an unusual case in New York, the cat owner was held liable where he kept a cat with kittens in his store with knowledge that his cat had previously attacked dogs that were brought into his store by customers. Sure enough, the owner of a dog came into the store and was injured by the cat when the cat attempted to attack her dog and she intervened to save her dog.

## Horses And Cattle

The Restatement of Torts is an attempt by prominent members of the legal profession to rewrite the law to make it more uniform. A tort is a civil wrong other than a crime. One of the Restatement of Torts definitions is "A wild animal is an animal which is not, and a domestic animal is an animal which is, by custom devoted to the service of mankind at the time and place in which it is kept."

If you go to a riding academy and tell the attendant in charge that you are an experienced rider and want a spirited horse, then you are pretty well on your own. If you are thrown and injured, you are guilty of contributory negligence by virtue of your request for a spirited horse. If you state that you are a novice and want a quiet, slow horse, then the burden is on the academy cowboy to protect you. We all know that standing close to the rear of a mule could result in being kicked. If you are kicked and injured, your conduct contributed to your downfall and you cannot collect from the animal's owner.

The right to allow horses and cattle to roam at large was established by custom but is now regulated in most states by law. A colt which is running along by the side of its dam, which is being led through the streets of a city, is not regarded as running at large.

Livestock on public highways has become a serious problem for motorists, particularly if they are in a strange country. If you have never had the unpleasant experience of running into, or being run into, by a horse, cow, razorback hog, etc., keep your fingers crossed. When it does happen, usually at night, it happens within a split second and the results can be quite serious. It is not only property damage to your car but more important, personal injuries to the occupants of your car. The question of who is liable for the damages will vary but most of the western states place the responsibility on the driver because of the importance of protection for the livestock industry. Even in those states where the owner of the animal is responsible for his animal being on the open highway in violation of the law, finding the animal or his owner after the accident is something else again. If you are the victim of this type of accident, you soon learn about home-town loyalty against the visiting motorist, who is looked upon as an arch enemy of the local population.

# PARENT AND CHILD
# — JUVENILE COURT

Laws concerning parent and child are governed by each state individually and not the federal government. The law of parent and child overlaps that of guardianship, since the father or the mother, are the natural guardians of their minor children. The word "parent" means the lawful father or mother by blood or adoption. "Loco parentis" is one who stands in the place of a parent. Thus, a step-parent is not classified as a parent but a "loco parentis."

The term "family" includes those who live in one house and under one head or management. A California judge held: "A man may establish a family consisting of himself, a woman with whom he is living without marriage, and their illegitimate child, so as to effect the adoption of the child by caring for it in such family."

Parents have the right and duty to control, protect, and guide or educate the child. The duty of the child is to serve and obey the parents. The religion of a minor child is governed by that of the parent.

## Rights Of Parents

The paramount right of the parents is to the custody of their child. The law recognizes the natural decrease in parental control as the child becomes older. A South Carolina court held that the parents of a 17 year old daughter were not entitled to open and read her letters before she had an opportunity to do so herself. A Louisiana court ruled that a girl of 17 who has entered a convent without her parent's consent, with the purpose of becoming a nun, may be reclaimed by the father by writ of habeas corpus. A writ of habeas corpus is a court order to bring a person before the judge.

The father may select the place of residence of the child and until the child attains its majority or emancipation, has no rights in this regard. Many states have a law that permits minors of a certain age to file a petition for emancipation. When granted, the minor is legally permitted to enter into contracts as an adult. I handled this situation for a 19 year old married man who wanted to purchase a home and issue a note and mortgage. Most state laws do not permit this until he is granted a decree of emancipation.

In the olden days the father was recognized as the head of the family and all rights flowed to him. The modern laws of many states now provide that the rights of the mother are equal to those of the father.

### Who Gets The Illegitimate Child?

The laws calls a child who is born out of wedlock, "bastard" or "illegitimate." In truth and in fact, the child is an innocent victim and it is the parents who are illegitimate. The rights of the father and mother in the custody of illegitimate children are just the opposite of their rights with respect to legitimate children. The mother is entitled to the care, custody and control of the so-called illegitimate child and may keep the child or place it out for adoption. The father has no choice in the matter, unless he marries the girl and that would automatically change the child's status to legitimate.

### How Much Punishment May A Parent Inflict?

A parent, being charged with the training and education of his child, has the right to discipline the child. This includes the right to punish stubborn and disobedient children. The laws says that in chastising a child, the parent may not inflict cruel and excessive type of punishment. The welfare of the child and not the liberty of action of the parent, is the controlling factor. A good spanking never hurt any child and is still recommended as being necessary to maintain reasonable discipline. In some of the larger cities, it would appear that the teachers need protection from punishment inflicted by the students, where discipline is impossible to be maintained.

### Can A Parent Kidnap His Own Child?

The FBI says no. Even though we have very tough federal kidnapping laws, the FBI refuses to prefer any federal charges against the father or mother, who in violation of a court order, grab their own child and return to their home state.

This situation usually occurs when the divorce court has awarded custody of minor children to the wife and the husband is unhappy with the court's ruling and decides to take the law into his own hands. He goes to their school and on some false pretext obtains possession of his children and runs back into his own backyard. His actions clearly place him in contempt of court but usually do not result in any criminal action. I have always advised against this illegal procedure because it solves no problem. The children are being made pawns and each parent is hurting them by their selfish actions. If there is proper reason for changing custody of the children, the matter should be submitted to the judge and the court room is the best place to solve the problem. The best interests and welfare of the child are matters of chief importance. The judge has wide, discretionary powers in a child custody dispute, but he may not act in an arbitrary or capricious manner. A Utah judge ruled that the best interest of the child meant moral welfare, rather than comforts, benefits and advantages that wealth can give.

## Parental Obligations

The legal duty of a parent to support his minor children is affected by many considerations. His health; his means; his station in life; have a bearing upon it. The duty of the parent is only to do the best he can to support his child in the manner suitable to his station and circumstances. The relative size of the income of the parent must be considered, as well as the number of persons dependent on the father for support. The duty of support falls equally on the father and the mother.

Parents are ordinarily bound to provide a minor child with necessaries and the duty of support, extends only to the furnishing of such items. They will vary with each case.

## What Are Necessaries?

Necessaries must supply the personal needs of the infant. Suitable shelter, food, clothing, and medical attention are always classified as necessaries. Means of education are also vital. The financial background of the parents are an important factor. Piano or ballet lessons could be necessaries in a given situation and be a luxury in another.

The support of a minor child must continue until the child reaches the age of majority, or marries, or is in the armed forces of the United States. In case of physically or mentally defective children, support must continue until the need ceases.

## Must Parents Pay For A Child's Education?

For a public school education; yes. For a college education; a guarded no. The courts have never laid down a hard and fast rule as to the amount of education to be paid for by the parents.

An Oregon case held that at the present time a minor who is unable to secure a college education is generally handicapped in pursuing most of the trades or professions of life and held the parents responsible. A Rhode Island judge ruled that under favorable circumstances a college education may be necessary as respects the parental liability therefor.

Legally and technically, the obligation of parents to support their child terminates at the age of 21 and the child could not force his parents to continue to pay for his education beyond that point. Aside from the technical answer, any child that has the desire and is a good student can manage to obtain a college education by obtaining one of the many scholarships that are available or by obtaining credit from his university and paying the bill later. Parents have no claim for reimbursement from the child for monies paid for a college education.

## Are Parents Responsible For Their Child's Torts?

A tort is a civil wrong other than a crime. Generally speaking parents are not liable for the tortious acts of their child. Parents could be responsible where they are guilty of negligence, such as leaving a loaded gun where the child can easily get his hands on it and then a neighbor child is shot. In the above example, the parent's liability is based on the ordinary rules of negligence, and not upon the relation of parent and child.

In some states, notably Louisiana, the liability of a parent for the torts of his child, is covered by special state law. The variance between states is so great, that the interested reader is urged to learn the law that applies in his home state.

A more common type of state law, imposes liability on the parent owner of an automobile for the negligence of the child operating it with his consent. This is called the "family purpose" doctrine and is discussed in greater detail in the chapter on automobile insurance.

In some states, the common-law rule of nonliability of parents has been given statutory recognition. Under such a state law, a father is not liable for a tort of his minor child with which he was in no way connected, which he did not ratify, and from which he did not derive any benefit.

## What Is The Liability Of A Stepfather?

The universal rule is that a stepfather is under no obligation to support the children of his wife by a former husband. But if he takes the children into his family in such a way that he places himself in loco parentis, he assumes an obligation to support them. The stepfather of an illegitimate child is under no obligation to support it. Neither are stepmothers liable for the support of their stepchildren. However, the voluntary assumption of the obligation of parenthood toward the children of a spouse by another marriage is favored by the law.

### What Are The Rights Of Grandparents?

The general rules governing the custody of children apply to grandchildren. Ordinarily, the parent's right is superior to that of the grandparents. The obligation of a parent to permit a child to visit its grandparents is only a moral, and not a legal duty.

A recent case in Iowa had a shocking result. A father of an 8 year old boy in California, suddenly became a widower. He made arrangements with his wife's parents, the child's grandparents to take care of the boy temporarily, until he could readjust to the tragic loss of his wife. A few years later, he remarried and sent for his son. His former in-laws refused to return their grandchild and the Iowa court ruled that the father's home in California was not as good for the boy as was his grandparent's farm in Iowa. Legally, the court's ruling was incorrect but fortunately, the grandparents bowed to the wishes of their grandson and he was returned to his natural father and step-mother in California.

### Criminal Liability Of Parents

A father who abandons, neglects or fails to support his minor children is guilty of a criminal offense. Under the laws of most states, the mother of the children can sign a criminal complaint against him. As a practical matter, I have never seen any criminal prosecution of a father in such a case, result in any good. A father who requires a judge to urge him to do the right thing by way of supporting his children is just plain no-good. Putting him in jail may bring satisfaction but it will not bring the financial support that is needed by the mother of the children.

The one blessing involved in the irresponsible father is that his wife or former wife and his children will not see him again and that part is good for all concerned.

### Juvenile Court

"Juvenile Court" is a special court that handles problems pertaining to children who are under age and are therefore subject to punishment, different from that given to an adult.

This special court is strictly a "creature of statute" and thus each state has its own laws governing the operation and function of its Juvenile Court. By "creature of statute" is meant that the legislature of a state has enacted laws to cover the subject matter involved. I am an enthusiastic supporter of this special treatment for boys and girls who become involved in some type of criminal or social problem. The average juvenile court judge is a very humane type of person who really tries to help the youthful offender. I am not talking about the 18 year old boy who commits murder or first degree robbery because most state laws provide that he should be transferred to the regular criminal court and be treated as if he were an adult. One judge said that an 18 year old boy who commits rape is committing a man's offense and is subject to adult punishment.

Many young boys and girls dream about learning to drive an automobile and take a course in "driver's training" at the earliest opportunity. Their training is excellent and they have the ability and knowledge to be better than average drivers. In spite of their training, some do receive traffic citations for speeding, running a red light, failure to stop at a boulevard stop sign, and similar violation of local ordinances. If an adult commits this type of driving violation, the adult pays a fine in police court and purges himself of his wrongdoing. A minor does not have that privilege and the minor is cited to appear in person in Juvenile Court and one of the parents must appear in person with their child.

If the traffic citation is the youngster's first offense, one of the juvenile court probation officers will handle this minor matter to relieve the Juvenile Court Judge who is really loaded down with more serious juvenile offenses. The boy or girl receives a courteous but firm reminder of the need to obey traffic rules and regulations and the matter is dropped. No fine is levied because the minor may not be assessed any fine.

If the juvenile appears in juvenile court later for second and third traffic offenses, things get a bit rougher. About the third appearance results in a personal appearance before the Juvenile Court Judge, who is very courteous, kind and lenient and he may suspend the youngster's right to drive a motor vehicle for 15 or 30 days. If this punishment does not end future citations, the child's driver's license can be suspended or revoked for longer periods of time.

Even though some of the offenses committed by juveniles are of a minor nature, there is no other court available to handle their matters, other than Juvenile Court. In addition to motor vehicle traffic violations, other lesser offenses involving minors are truancy from school; curfew violations; neighborhood squabbles; vandalism, etc.

Now we come to the serious offenses committed by juveniles that are referred to Juvenile Court for handling. These offenses can be felonies instead of misdemeanors. A felony is a serious criminal offense, punishable by a penitentiary sentence of at least one year. A misdemeanor is a minor criminal offense, with a maximum sentence of less than one year to be served in the county jail, or a fine or both. The American public has been complaining for years about the undesirable procedure of sending young boys convicted of serious criminal offenses to serve time in the state penitentiary with older, hardened criminals. This resulted in the young, first offender, coming out of penitentiaries with a post-graduate course in how to commit more crimes.

All minors that are found guilty in Juvenile Court of any serious offense, may be given time to serve but the penal institution is not the state penitentiary; it is the state institution for juveniles. Each state has its own institution, which is bound to be an improvement over the older type of penitentiaries. These young offenders attend school and associate with other youngsters who have run afoul of the law. The length of their sentence will vary with the offense of which they are found guilty. The maximum sentence in Juvenile Court is being confined in the state juvenile institution until the person's 21st birthday.

For many years, many state laws prohibited any attorney from appearing in Juvenile Court, in behalf of his young client. The thinking was that the juvenile court judge was humane and interested in getting to the true facts of the incident and he could do a better job if the court was conducted along informal lines. The youngster's parents were not only permitted but were required to be present at all of his court appearances.

Then the United States Supreme Court ruled that a minor charged with a criminal offense, is entitled to the same protection given the adult and specified that attorneys were now permitted to appear in juvenile court with their young clients. Now, some juvenile courts are being subjected to the same type of technicalities and delays that seem to be popular in criminal trials going on all over the country. We all agree that any defendant charged with a criminal offense is entitled to a fair trial but the pendulum of fair play has swung too far in favor of the defendants and against the prosecuting authorities. There should be a happy medium.

*Is Your Child On Drugs?*

In addition to all of the old fashioned problems involving the raising of children, some parents are now faced with the new and serious problem of the use of drugs by youngsters of all ages. The use of acid of various types, LSD; hashish; marihuana and other narcotics has reached a large portion of our youth.

Some of the youngsters are starting to smoke "pot" and use acids at the junior high school level. The authorities are trying to solve the problem but appear not to be very successful. Even the military authorities are becoming alarmed about the use of drugs and strong narcotics in the armed forces.

In those households where there is good communication between the parents and child or children, a frank discussion between them can be quite useful. Unfortunately, in many homes there is no communication and the parents can only worry and wonder if their offspring is using drugs.

It is difficult to offer any solution because there does not seem to be any logical answer. There are persons who are professionally trained in handling young people who are using acids and other drugs. I would contact the family doctor and seek his help; then I would try the family clergyman; next I would contact the school counsellor for his possible help. If all efforts failed, I would plead with my youngster to discuss the matter openly, honestly and in a spirit of cooperation and not threats.

If the child refuses to confide in his parents, then the parents have no choice other than to refer the problem to the juvenile court officials and hope they can help the child to abstain. If that doesn't do any good and the child refuses to seek help in quitting the habit, I would turn my child into the authorities for whatever action they deemed appropriate. This procedure may seem unduly harsh, however, if the youngster is not cured or curbed, the use of acid will later change into stronger narcotics and possible eventually graduate to the use of heroin. By this time they have graduated to the major leagues and all hope is gone. These are sad cases and all the parents can do is use their best efforts to reason with their child.

A good juvenile court can help the average youngster to form a favorable opinion of how "law and order" works. It is usually the first contact that a young person has with court officials and it can be most effective.

# IF ARRESTED, WHAT TO DO AND SAY

"Arrest" is derived from the French "arreter," meaning to stop or stay, as signifying a restraint of the person. An arrest is the taking of a person into custody for the purpose of bringing him before a court. A federal court held: "An arrest is effected by the sheriff stepping upon the running board of an automobile with a warrant for arrest of the person driving it, and announcing to him that he is under arrest." But when one is merely approached by a police officer and questioned about his identity and actions, this is only an accosting, not an arrest.

## Constitutional Rights

The Fourth Amendment to the federal constitution provides: "The right of the people to be secure in their persons, houses, papers, and effects, against unreasonable searches and seizures, shall not be violated, and no Warrants shall issue, but upon probable cause, supported by Oath or affirmation, and particularly describing the place to be searched, and the persons or things to be seized." The United States Supreme Court has said: "The Fourth Amendment teaches that it is better that the guilty sometimes go free than that citizens be subject to easy arrest."

The constitutional requirement of speedy trial has been held to require that a defendant be served with a warrant of arrest within a reasonable time after the filing of the complaint, so that he will get notice of the charge while witnesses in his behalf are still available. A California court ruled: "Unexplained delay of approximately 140 days was unreasonable."

## Warrants Of Arrest

A warrant is a written order directing the arrest of a person issued by a court having authority to issue warrants. A warrant of arrest is usually directed to officers of the law but this is not a requirement. A warrant of arrest should contain facts sufficient to notify the defendant what offense he is charged with.

For federal offenses, a warrant of arrest upon a complaint is signed by a United States commissioner; whereas a warrant of arrest upon an indictment or information is issued by a federal judge and signed by the clerk of the court. A FBI agent could sign a complaint and a warrant for arrest would then be issued by the United States commissioner. A formal hearing would then be held within a short period of time, and the commissioner determines if there is sufficient evidence to warrant holding the defendant for action by a federal grand jury. If he finds there is insufficient evidence, he has the power to dismiss the complaint. If the matter is referred to the federal grand jury, bond is set and the defendant may be released from jail by posting a bond for the required amount. In due course of time, the federal grand jury will hear evidence presented by the United States Attorney and they have the choice of indicting the defendant or refusing to indict him which means he is free of all charges pending. If the defendant is indicted, he must then appear in person before a federal judge and plead to the charges contained in the indictment. He may plead "guilty" or "not guilty" or "nolo contendere." Nolo contenderE means "I did it but I did not have criminal intent." Most federal judges will advise the defendant that a plea of nolo contenderE is considered by the court to be the same as a plea of guilty. A plea of guilty eliminates a trial and the judge decides the sentence. For those that plead not guilty, their matter will be set down for a jury trial in the near future. A defendant may waive a jury trial, in which case his matter will be heard by the federal judge without a jury.

### Arrest Without Warrant

A felony is any serious criminal offense that is punishable by a penitentiary sentence of at least one year or more. A misdemeanor is a lessor or minor offense that is punishable by a fine or a county jail sentence for a maximum of one year. An arrest without a warrant is unlawful. However, there are always exceptions to the rule. The laws of the different states will vary and some provide that a felony arrest without a warrant, made on reasonable grounds may be justified.

The laws of many states provide that the commission of an offense in the presence of a police officer gives him the right to make an arrest without warrant. In a state in which arrest without warrant is governed by statute, the requirements must be closely observed by the arresting police officer. Some state laws provide that an officer may make an arrest without warrant when he reasonably believes that the person arrested is about to commit a felony.

## Citizen's Arrest - Arrest By Private Person

An arrest by a private person is frequently called "a citizen's arrest." The authority of a private person to arrest another without a warrant is more limited than that of an officer. In some states the subject of arrest by private persons is covered by statute. In some states a private person may arrest for any misdemeanor committed in his presence. In other states, the misdemeanor must also be a breach of the peace. As to any felony, it is not only the right but a duty of a private person to apprehend the offender.

## Drunkenness

Drunkenness in a public place is usually made an offense by state law or city ordinance, and a police officer is authorized to arrest without a warrant, especially if the intoxicated person is disturbing the peace. Operating a motor vehicle while under the influence of intoxicating liquor is an offense for which an officer may arrest without warrant, if it is committed in his presence.

## DWI - Driving While Intoxicated

Those of us who patronize the great American social institution, the cocktail party, and then drive our cars are subject to being stopped by a police officer for any reason. The officer smells an odor of alcohol and questions the driver on how much he had to drink. The reader is urged to be courteous and cordial to the officer inasmuch as sarcasm and belligerence can harm the situation. If you can recall, answer the question reasonably honestly. If you can't remember how many drinks you consumed, make a reasonable guess. The answer that is heard most often in court, when the defendant appears on the charge of DWI - "I had a couple of beers." Everyone present in the courtroom, from the judge on down, smile at that answer after hearing testimony about the erratic driving of the defendant.

If the police officer offers a blood test to determine the alcoholic content in your blood (and if your state law gives you a choice) decline the offer in a courteous manner. Some police officers tell the defendant that if the blood test is negative, he will drop all charges.

Turn down that not so generous offer because the police officer usually has a pretty good idea about the condition of his subject. In many states, the local law or custom provides that 150 milligrams is the dividing line in a blood test. If a defendant's blood tests over that amount, it is presumed that he was driving while intoxicated. If he tests under, the presumption is that he was not DWI. This is the amount of alcohol that is present in the bloodstream. Presumptions can be overcome but it is not easy. The obvious reason for not taking a blood test is that it furnishes evidence against yourself. If you refuse a blood test, the only witness usually available to testify against you is the arresting officer. If you take a blood test, the prosecuting attorney puts on a parade of witnesses that include the arresting officer, the technician that took the blood sample from your arm; and the laboratory technician who testifies as to the result of the blood test. Worst of all is the blood test result which is hard to argue against. Without the blood test, it results in a swearing contest in that the police officer says you were drunk and you say you were not drunk and the judge has a right to believe your testimony.

Some years ago, I participated in an unusual DWI case. The arresting police officer testified that my client did not appear to be drunk and that is why he charged him with reckless driving. He further testified that the longer my client stood in the city jail, the drunker he got. The police officer then charged my client with drunk driving in addition to reckless driving. Needless to say, justice prevailed and my client was found guilty of reckless driving but not guilty of driving while intoxicated. A conviction of DWI resulted in an automatic suspension of your driver's license for one year, in addition to a heavy fine. The moral is: NEVER FURNISH EVIDENCE AGAINST YOURSELF.

### Arrest For Nonpayment Of A Debt?

Years ago, the answer was yes but today the answer is no. Most of the state constitutions contain provisions which prohibit imprisonment for debt. Some state statutes permit arrest where the defendant has concealed or disposed of his property with intent to defraud his creditors. Some states permit arrest in contract actions for the recovery of money where the defendant is about to leave the state with intent to defraud his creditors. Since civil arrest is a drastic remedy the requirements are very strict.

## Right To Search?

Yes, the right to search the person of the one arrested is incidental to a lawful arrest. The officer may seize anything found on the arrested person or in his immediate control, if the item is unlawful. The officer may take from the arrested person anything that might endanger the officer's safety, or that of the public, or that might enable the prisoner to escape. However, the right to take property from an arrested person is limited.

In an unusual case, a New York court ruled: "Where an arrest was made on a warrant charging acceptance of a $3,000 bribe, the seizure of $74,000 in cash, together with securities of substantial monetary value, things not criminal in themselves and not identified as fruits or instrumentalities of the crime for which the arrest was made, was unreasonable under the Constitution, notwithstanding the government's argument that defendant's luxurious manner of life, contrasted with his meager salary, was evidence of other similar crimes."

## Riding With A Drunk Driver

In some states, it is a criminal offense for a sober passenger to ride with a drunk driver. The guilt or innocence of the sober passenger is later determined by the court's ruling as to the guilt or innocence of the driver who is charged with DWI. If the reader thinks this is a bad law and should be repealed, I agree with that opinion.

Some people who are celebrating and drinking, decide to take one drink with them when they enter their car. At the moment it sounds like a cute idea but it can boomerang. If the car is stopped by an officer for any reason, it is in violation of law to drink in a moving vehicle and the consequences can be serious. Don't invite trouble by violating the law. You can wait until you arrive at your home and then do all the drinking you wish.

A true incident occurred involving a young man and a young lady who decided it would be fun to drive around their city without either wearing any clothes. They ran a red light and were stopped by a police officer. He took them to the police station and charged them with indecent exposure. On his report, the officer wrote, "I searched both of the suspects and found nothing unusual."

*Minors Driving While Under Influence Of Alcohol*

Each state has its own laws pertaining to a minor. Recent federal legislation now permits young adults of 18 years of age, to vote in federal elections. The right to vote in state elections varies from 18 to 21. Similar variations occur with the right of a young adult, male or female, to drink alcoholic beverages.

A recent automobile accident death case in Darien, Connecticut received international publicity. The facts were that a birthday celebration took place in a private home and the parents of the celebrant served hard liquor to the young adult guests present, some of whom were minors and under the age permitted to drink by local law. As the evening wore on, one of the young men drove his car and had an accident and a young lady passenger was killed. The local authorities instituted criminal proceedings against the host parents and they were found guilty of contributing to the delinquency of a minor, under local law.

The legal problem involved is difficult to answer. Technically, it is against the law to serve alcoholic beverages to a minor. Yet as a practical matter, many of the young adults drink beer or other alcoholic beverages at their universities and if they are not served at home, they will obtain the beer or liquor on the outside. Under normal conditions, an attorney should not advise anyone to break the law. I have served beer in our home to young adult guests. When they are ready to leave, I urge the driver to be very careful in his driving and if there is any doubt, arrange for a friend to drive for him. If there is need, I have driven my young guest home.

The same admonition applies to all adults as well. Those of us that do imbibe, know that if there is any doubt as to our ability to drive being impaired, we should take a taxicab home or permit a friend to drive us. Alcohol reacts differently to the person drinking. Some can act drunk by merely smelling a cork of a bottle. Others can consume a fair quantity and react favorably while driving. A man I knew was a heavy drinker and he made it a habit to drive next to the curb at the rate of 10 miles per hour, while on his way home after a drinking night out. He always managed to get home but his habit was not a safe one.

Whenever a client advised of his arrest and being charged with DWI, I could not help but think to myself, "There but for the grace of God, goes I."

*If Arrested, Silence Is Golden*

More people have convicted themselves by voluntarily talking than have ever been convicted by the evidence presented in court by the prosecution. The cardinal rule among experienced criminals when arrested is "DON'T TALK." If the defendant does not talk, then the police and prosecution authorities have to produce evidence and present it in court.

Even recent rulings by the United States Supreme Court, requiring the arresting police officer to advise the suspect of his constitutional rights does not seem to stop some defendants from making statements and being "talk-talk" individuals and furnishing evidence that will help to convict themselves. This is truly amazing but people do like to talk and the police never counsel a defendant "not to talk."

Most police officers have been told by City Attorneys to advise criminal defendants of their constitutional rights. It could be the following or similar: "It is my duty to advise you of your constitutional rights. You are entitled to be represented by a lawyer of your choice or if you have no money, one will be appointed by the judge. You are not required to make a statement or say anything and anything you say can be used as evidence against you at the time of your trial. Do you understand?"

There is a vast difference between not talking and not being courteous. There is no reason for any person who is arrested lawfully in not behaving properly or in being sarcastic. The police officer has his job to do and you will fare far better by being polite and cordial. When asked the usual routine questions about your name, age, address, occupation; answer them in a courteous manner. In a borderline situation, the police officer may be in a position to help you. There is no percentage in antagonizing the officer for no valid reason. Those that are abusive can only make matters rougher on themselves. The average officer is a reasonable person and if you abuse him, he will become angry and try to get even with you in any way possible. I have seen many defendants help their defense in the courtroom when the police officer testifies truthfully: "The defendant was very courteous and cooperative at all times."

After answering the various routine questions, the officer should advise you of your constitutional rights. He may then ask if you desire to make a statement. You can then say in a polite manner: "No thank you" or "I would prefer not to talk" or "I want to telephone my lawyer" or a comparable statement. The rule in most communities is that any person arrested and charged with a criminal offense is entitled to make one telephone call. He may call a member of his family or his boss or his attorney. He is privileged to tell the person that he has been arrested and what offense he is charged with and the amount of his bond and the name and address of the jail where he is confined. Whether you think you are guilty of the offense alleged is aside from the point. You are still better off to remain silent. There will be plenty of time to discuss your problem with an attorney of your choice or even one appointed to represent you. When you are alone with your attorney you can then talk to your heart's content. If you are honest with your attorney and tell him everything there is to know, he will be in a better position to handle your matter, than if you omit important details.

The customary procedure in a criminal matter is to plead "not guilty" regardless of the facts. The plea of "not guilty" can always be changed later to "guilty" without suffering any penalty. Time is an important factor and many things can happen while your matter is pending. Your attorney may be successful in working out some sort of compromise with the prosecuting attorney.

The less a defendant talks to the police and prosecuting authorities, the harder it is for them to convict him. The more a defendant talks, the easier it is for the prosecution to obtain a conviction. Don't help convict yourself by being talkative.

## Should A Lawyer Defend A Guilty Person?

Some people criticize lawyers for defending a person charged with a serious crime when the newspaper publicity indicates clear guilt. Under the American system of justice, a person is presumed innocent until proven guilty. Every person is entitled to a fair trial and regardless of how horrible the crime or how bad a character the defendant may seem, he is still entitled to be represented by counsel and to a fair trial. We do but should not form opinions on the basis of newspaper headlines. The proper forum is the courtroom where legal evidence is presented and the defendant's guilt or innocence is determined by a jury or a judge. As a member of the legal profession, I am proud of the American system of justice, even though on rare occasions a defendant escapes punishment due to some technicality.

If, at the present time, the scales of justice have been tipped a bit too far in favor of the defendant due to recent rulings of the United States Supreme Court, they will be balanced in the not-too-distant future.

## What To Say If Arrested Outside of U.S.A.

With the advent of inexpensive air travel and charter tours, Americans of all ages are travelling more than ever before. A small percentage run afoul of the law in various foreign countries.

If arrested, don't say "I am an American citizen and I demand my constitutional rights." The foreign police are just as intelligent and informed as are American police. Frequently, the language barrier may create a problem but it doesn't help matters to be ornery with police in any country.

Basically, the old rule of being "Silent Cal" still prevails and other than being courteous, the less you say the better off you are. Better still, SAY NOTHING ABOUT YOUR ARREST PROBLEMS.

You can courteously ask to speak to the representative of the United States government, be it a consul, ambassador or lesser rank official. On rare occasions, American officials can possibly exert a bit of influence. More often than not, the American official has no influence and all he can do is notify members of your family at your request.

Those Americans who are stupid enough to violate the narcotic laws of foreign countries are begging for long sentence in a foreign jail that is not competing with a proverbial "Hilton Hotel." Foreigners who violate American laws receive comparable treatment in the United States.

# EMPLOYER AND EMPLOYEE

Under the old English common law, the legal relationship of one person working for another was called "Master and Servant." Americans do not like the word "servant." It just rubs them the wrong way for any employee to be called by that name. So in our industrial age we now use the term employee and employer. A New Jersey court ruled: "The essence of an employer-employee relationship is that there be a hiring for a fixed period of time, for fixed wages, and that the employee's work should be subject to the control and direction of the employer." The key to this relationship is the fact that the employer has control over the work to be performed by the employee.

The determination of whether a person is an independent contractor or merely an employee, depends upon the power of control which the employer is entitled to exercise over the person in question. The fact that a salesman is paid on a commission basis is not a decisive test to determine whether he is an employee or an independent contractor. If a salesman is employed by one company only and told which customers to call on and when, then he would be classified as an employee. A manufacturer's agent, who may represent many different companies, is not under the direction or control of any one company and is therefore classified as an independent contractor. As further evidence, his automobile insurance would be under his name only and not include any of the names of his various companies that he might represent. The fact that the parties agreed upon a flat fee and no deductions were made for witholding or income tax would indicate that the relationship was that of an independent contractor and not employee. If you are wondering what difference it makes to be classified as an employee or independent contractor, it can be very important in the event of an accident and injury to the person working on the job. If he is an employee, he is protected by insurance carried by his employer. If he is an independent contractor, he is basically on his own.

### Is A Lifetime Employment Contract Legal?

Yes, it is perfectly legal for the parties to enter into such a contract. Contracts for permanent or lifetime employment are legal and do not offend public policy. An Indiana court ruled: "A contract by a railroad company to give permanent employment to an injured employee in settlement of his claim is not against public policy." A Massachusetts court ruled: "A contract for permanent employment whereby one is induced to give up his own business and enter into the business of another is not unlawful or against public policy."

### May An Employee Quit?

Yes, an employee may quit at any time. It is considered decent and proper for the employee to give reasonable notice so that the employer may make other arrangements. The only exception could be if the parties had a written contract and the employee was leaving to go to work for a competitor. In this situation, the employer could file a lawsuit to stop the employee from working for a competitor. The employee cannot be prevented from earning a living by working for someone who is not in a competing business. Professional athletes sometimes get involved by trying to quit one team to play for another. The athlete may quit the game at any time but may not play for another team if his written contract provides otherwise.

### May An Employee Be Fired At Anytime?

In the absence of a written agreement providing otherwise, the employer may discharge the employee at any time. Again, it is considered the decent and proper thing for the employee to be given reasonable notice of the impending discharge, so that the employee can try to obtain other employment. The right to quit and the right to be discharged is a two way street and each side has equal rights.

Even in the case of a written contract, a university may fire its football coach at any time, however, the coach must be paid for the time remaining under his written contract of employment. If the coach received $1,000 per month, he is entitled to the same monthly payment but he is not entitled to a lump sum.

Legally, neither the employee nor employer are required to give notice. If there is a written employment contract that provides otherwise, the written contract would control the dispute.

Like any other contract, an employment agreement may be

broken for cause. Intoxication, incompetence, neglect of duty, disobedience of rules, insolence and many other reasons could be justifiable grounds for the employer discharging the employee, without any liability for his actions.

## How Much Must An Employee Be Paid?

In certain kinds of employment minimum wages have been established by law. Aside from this, the compensation for an employee is up to the parties involved. Some of the cases hold that "wages" are paid for manual labor or menial work, whereas "salary" is used for more important services. If you say, "So what!", I agree with you.

If the employee is not paid monies due, in addition to normal remedies of suing the employer, most states have a Labor Commissioner who handles unpaid wage claims. The state official does not charge for collecting the unpaid wages, whereas an attorney would charge for his services in collecting the money. If the boss goes into bankruptcy, the wage claim of his employees are not dischargeable in bankruptcy and they can still try to collect from him.

Vacation pay is usually the perogative of the employer. It is considered to be a bonus for the coming year and not a bonus for last year. If the employee notifies the boss that she is quitting immediately after her vacation, the boss has the legal right to refuse to pay for the vacation period. If the parties have a written contract that provides otherwise, the terms of the contract would naturally prevail.

## What About Trade Secrets And Confidential Information?

A former employee cannot use his former employer's trade secrets learned during his employment, even though there is no express contract precluding the use of such trade secrets. It matters not whether the secrets are secrets of trade or secrets of title, or any other secrets of the employer important to his interests. The fact that the confidential matter is not patentable or copyrightable does not disqualify it from protection. The United States Supreme Court upheld a ruling declaring that the communication of the language and form of proposed advertisements is not within the rule which prevents the wrongful use of confidential information.

A former employee may compete with his former employer just as a stranger may do so, or he may enter a competitor's employment. A former employee may not compete with his former employer fraudulently, by misappropriating trade secrets or confidential information.

Before leaving his employment, an employee may notify the employer's customers that he is severing relations with the employer, but he may not solicit them as customers for his new business or divert orders from his employer to his new business.

## What Duty Is Owed By The Employer To Employees?

The employer is legally obligated to furnish a safe place for the employee to work and to provide for his safety. The employer must warn his employees of conditions under which he is employed which are liable to result in disease. A federal court ruled: "Blindness and loss of health in one employed to gauge and measure sheets of polished steel under brilliant lights and unhealthful conditions are occupational diseases for which the employer is responsible."

## What Protection For Employees Injured On The Job?

All of the states have adopted laws which offer protection for any employee who is injured or killed while on the job. Unlike an automobile accident, where the claimant has to prove negligence on the part of "the other driver," no negligence need be proven in any industrial accident. The only requirement is that the employee was injured or killed while on the job. In some states, this protection is called "Workmen's Compensation Acts," in others it may be called "Employer's Liability Acts." The law may be enforced by the courts or by industrial accident commissions, but the result is the same. Workmen's Compensation Insurance is usually compulsory on the part of the employer and the injured employee is entitled to receive compensation in accordance with the schedule of benefits fixed by the compensation law. The employee is entitled to these benefits, regardless of any fault or negligence on his part. In an unusual federal court case in favor of the employee, it held: "An employer violates its duty to exercise ordinary care for the safety of its employee by failing to inform him of a tubercular condition disclosed by X-rays taken in its medical department, so as to enable the employee to seek medical treatment, even though the employer is under no obligation to have such physical examination made, since by remaining silent the employer permits the employee to rely upon a tacit assurance of safety despite its knowledge of the existence of danger."

*Fringe Benefits*

Some employers offer certain benefits to employees, over and above their agreed salary. These extra benefits are known as "fringe benefits." Some of the more common fringe benefits are free or low-cost medical insurance; free or low-cost life insurance; pensions; bonuses; stock-options and other similar type of benefits for the employee. Some years ago, Sears, Roebuck Company was commended for their employee pension plan which resulted in low-income retiring employees to receive greater money benefits than they received while they were active employees. The reason for this unusually favorable result, was that the Sears pension fund money was invested in Sear's stock and the stock did exceptionally well on the New York stock exchange.

Fringe benefits are not required by any state law and it is up to the employee and the employer to make their own arrangements. The same rule applies to stock-option plans. Some large firms, in an effort to keep their key personnel offer stock in the company at an agreed low price. If the stock goes up in value, the key-employee can take advantage of the stock-option and buy the stock at the lower price. If the stock price goes down, the key-personnel are privileged to ignore the stock-option. This procedure is perfectly legitimate and no hankypanky is involved.

*Bonding Of Employees*

Most employers deem it good business and advisable to bond employees that handle the company's money. The cost of the bond is always paid by the employer and there is no expense falling on the employee. This is called a fidelity bond and some employees think that their honesty and integrity is being questioned. The employee is wrong who has this thought because the fidelity bond is not bad for the employee, it is actually good. Any employee who handles the firm's money and who is bonded, can be proud of the fact that their past record and reputation is favorable, otherwise the bonding company would not have bonded them. It is a mark of distinction and not any reflection on their honesty. All banks and other financial institutions automatically require that any employee handling money be bonded. If there are any flyspecks or problems in the employees' background, it is usually discovered by the bonding company who make a very thorough investigation. Being bonded falls in the same category as being fingerprinted. If nothing is wrong, one should not object to being fingerprinted. Every time we read about some old time trusted bookkeeper who was caught with his hands in the employer's till, you hope that the employer was experienced enough to protect the company's money by having the employee bonded. If he didn't, he will have learned a lesson and bonds will be required by him in the future.

# HOW TO LOCATE AND MOTIVATE YOUR LAWYER

*Can I Act As My Own Lawyer?*

Yes, under the federal as well as state constitutions, every person has the right to handle his own legal matter and is not required to be represented by a lawyer. You can act as your own attorney in civil as well as criminal matters. It is up to each individual to decide if he or she is knowledgeable enough to properly present the case to a judge. In lower courts, such as Police Court or Small Claims Court, I have seen many litigants present their own case in a very creditable manner.

In California, Small Claims Court handles civil matters involving claims up to $500 and lawyers are not permitted to appear in behalf of a client. Each side presents his case and the judge even has toy cars so that each litigant can demonstrate how the other party was in the wrong. Justice is meted our promptly and the winning claimant does not have to share his award with an attorney. Most attorneys are delighted to have their client handle disputes involving limited sums of money, because the legal fees based on time are too expensive and are not justified.

If you disagree with the police officer who gave you a citation for failing to come to a complete stop at a boulevard stop sign, and you want to have a little fun and satisfaction, act as your own lawyer. The judge will listen to the testimony of the officer and then your story and the odds are favorable he will lean a wee bit in your favor if the testimony is close. The amount of the fine for this minor traffic violation does not warrant the time and effort of an attorney, not to speak of his charges.

If your legal problem is important, complicated and means a lot to you, hire the expert in the form of a qualified lawyer.

*How Do I Find A Lawyer?*

Locating a lawyer who is qualified to handle your matter is not quite as simple as it sounds. If you turn to the yellow pages under the listing of "LAWYERS" you will find any number of names that mean nothing to you. This is the age of specialization and every lawyer is not qualified to handle every field of law. If you had a medical problem, you would look for a doctor who specialized in the branch of medicine covering your ailment.

For those who have or know a lawyer, there is no problem. If the question involves a tax dispute, your attorney will tell you if he handles tax matters and if not, he will be honest enough to refer you to a tax specialist. Any attorney who attempts to bluff his way in any field of law in which he is not familiar, is being unfair to his client and somewhere along the line, the truth will out.

If you are new in the community and have a real estate or business problem, ask your banker who his bank uses and the bank attorney will be well qualified to represent you.

In larger communities, the local Bar Association maintains a list of lawyers who are qualified for certain fields of law and you will be referred to a qualified lawyer on the list. There is usually no charge for the service.

If you are poor or have limited funds and feel that you cannot afford to hire a lawyer, most larger communities have a Legal Aid Society for legal advice at no charge. Usually, the Legal Aid Society has lawyers available for needy people and they are financed by contributions from local lawyers and the United Community Fund.

Federal and state funds are now available to various legal organizations, to maintain neighborhood law offices for benefit of the poor and the needy.

Under recent rulings of the United States Supreme Court, every person charged with a felony which is a serious criminal offense, is entitled to be represented by a lawyer. If he cannot afford to hire his own the judge will appoint an attorney to represent him without charge. In some states, this privilege attaches to misdemeanors, which are less serious criminal offenses.

### Who Wants To Be A Lawyer?

EVERYBODY! If you have legal problems and need help, where should you go for answers? Some people think that the fashionable American cocktail party is an ideal time and place to propound legal problems to an attorney-guest present. I developed a stock answer to this procedure by advising the inquiring party that this was a "night call" and suggested a telephone call to my office during business hours, to arrange for an appointment. We have all learned that our family doctor charges much more for a house call at night than if we see him the next day at his office.

Other popular legal advisors who classify themselves as "general specialists" are bartenders; barbers; notary publics; justices of the peace; deputy sheriffs, etc. The designation of "general specialist" means that the person is an expert in every field. These people never say, "I am sorry but I do not know the answer to that problem."

The bartender has the advantage of a captive audience as well as listening to people who are influenced by the contents of the liquid they are consuming. He knows all about affairs of the heart; domestic problems and modestly confesses that there is very little that he does not know about. Some lawyers claim that the legal profession has benefitted tremendously by litigation resulting from "expert" advice given by the above group.

Many people would like to be lawyers without benefit of attending law school for three grueling years and then passing the bar examination for the particular state in which they intend to practice their profession. Contrary to the opinion of some people, a license to practice law is really not a "license to steal." Over a period of years, I have advised many young men and young women who have asked my opinion about studying law, that I recommend it highly even for those who later decide not to practice law. It is definitely worthwhile and is not time wasted; it will help the individual whether they wind up in the field of banking, insurance, mercantile, or any other line of business.

One of my favorite clients who later became a personal friend was an American of Greek descent. Gus was a loyal booster of mine and a leader in the local American-Greek community. He had brought a newly arrived Greek widow to my office, to assist her in probating her husband's estate. A dispute developed with other relatives of the dead man and a number of hearings resulted before the Probate Judge. My lady client did not speak English and either Gus or or some other friend would act as interpreter. I complained to Gus that at each of the court hearings, 20 or so well-meaning Greek-American friends were trying to act as junior lawyers in coaching me from the sidelines and that it would be much better if I were permitted to handle the case on my own. Gus replied, "Edward, you don't understand that every Greek is an automatic lawyer from the day that he is born."

## Why Don't Lawyers Give Clear Answers?

Some people have difficulty in understanding why the legal

profession in general and some lawyers in particular, are inclined to hedge and hem and haw when asked their professional opinion based upon a given set of facts. The law is not always that certain to enable the lawyer to give his opinion in a dogmatic manner practically guarantying favorable results. Any lawyer who says he can predict the outcome of a litigated lawsuit is either being untruthful or he lacks experience. When you stop to consider that the United States Supreme Court, the highest court in the land, is composed of nine justices and they seem to wind up with more 5 to 4 decisions than any other numerical count, you can appreciate the difficulty in predicting the outcome of a lawsuit. The law is a changing thing and legal reasoning has to change with modern life. For example, a landowner used to be told that he owned the land to the center of the earth and all of the sky above. Along came modern aircraft and we now understand that the landowner does not own the airspace above his land.

### Can Anyone File A Lawsuit For Anything?

Over a period of 25 years of active legal practice, I have heard hundreds of persons relate a set of facts and then ask, "Can he sue me" or "Can I sue him?" My answer has always been that anyone can sue another for any reason under the sun, but proving your case and prevailing in the court trial is something else again. The more you can stay away from the courthouse and litigation, the better off you will be. Lawsuits are expensive to defend against and even if you prevail in court, it is still costly. The old saying "A poor settlement is better than the best lawsuit" is still true. Experienced judges advise litigants to compromise and settle their differences because if they are not fair with each other, the judge will force them to be fair, by his ruling. Of course, we all realize that there are certain situations where there is no way of avoiding a lawsuit and in that case, the dispute must be litigated.

Even large companies are more inclined to settle claims by way of compromise because of the expense of carrying on lengthy lawsuits. Many contracts provide for disputes to be settled by arbitration, in order to avoid courts.

### Who Pays The Defendant's Attorney Fees If He Wins?

Unfortunately, there is no provision in American law as there is in Canada, that where the Defendant (the person being sued) prevails in the lawsuit, the Plaintiff (the person who filed the lawsuit) has to pay the attorney's fees of the winner.

## Can You Win A Lawsuit And Be A Loser?

Frequently, the winner of a lawsuit is actually a loser. Be sensible and practical, don't spend $500 to prove that you don't owe $100. Work out some reasonable compromise. If you are wealthy and stubborn and want to establish new law, some lawyer will handle your lawsuit and charge for his services. Many clients say they want satisfaction and are willing to pay for it. One client said, "I will pay $1,000 to teach that so-and-so a lesson." Believe it or not, with that statement, he named his own fee. Satisfaction can be expensive and sometimes it represents childish conduct instead of mature judgement.

## Why Do Lawyers And Lawsuits Take So Long?

The biggest complaint of the general public against courts and the legal profession is that it takes too long to bring their case to trial. This complaint is justified and the present situation of waiting for as long as 5 years in large cities for a jury trial is a denial of justice to the claimant. Justice delayed is justice denied. Chief Justice Warren Burger of the United States Supreme Court has suggested that juries be reduced from 12 to a lesser number and that steps be taken to speed up the court's docket. A notice from the 3 federal judges for New Mexico advised that civil juries will be reduced from 12 to 6. I applaud their decision and we all agree that 6 jurors can decide a case as easily if not easier than can 12. I hope that many other courts, federal as well as state, will follow suit in reducing the jury panel from 12 to 6. Some state court judges could emulate many federal court judges by working harder and longer.

## Lack Of Communication Between Client And Lawyer

Needless misunderstandings that arise between the Client and his or her Attorney are usually caused by a lack of communication between the parties. More often than not, it is the fault of the Attorney and not of the Client.

Cartoonists and gag writers have delighted for many years in referring to lawyers as "shyster," "mouthpiece," "sharpy," and even "crook." Every profession or group that is composed of thousands of members is going to have a few "bad apples" included. If you have had an unfortunate or unpleasant experience with a lawyer, it isn't fair to condemn the entire fraternity on the basis of a single experience. Each state has its own Bar Association and attempt to police their own lawyers through its Grievance Committee. This Committee is a group of lawyers who donate their time in a sincere effort to investigate all complaints against lawyers and if the lawyer is in the wrong, he can and will be punished. If his offense is serious enough the lawyer can be suspended from the right to practice law or he can even be disbarred, which means he can no longer hold himself out to the public as a lawyer or attorney. For a lawyer to be disbarred is nearly as bad as being sent to a penal institution. It is a horrible disgrace and if the lawyer was guilty of that type of misconduct, he deserves the punishment. Although many complaints are without foundation, every complaint is investigated to ascertain the true facts. A Client who accuses his lawyer of "selling me down the river" and cannot prove his charge, is being unfair to the lawyer. The lawyer who used his Client's money without authority and when called upon to repay it, says "I needed the money to live on and I can only repay it on the installment plan" has violated every canon of ethics and is deserving of being disbarred. Every law student is required to take a law course called "Ethics" and learns early in his legal career that a Client's money belongs in a trust account, separate and apart from the lawyer's personal funds and is not to be used under any circumstances. The bank teller with sticky fingers who only plans to "borrow" the bank's money and intends to repay the money tomorrow, has committed his criminal offense the moment he took the money from the cash drawer without authority. Replacing the money does not cancel the offense.

*Lawyers And Fees*

The most frequent complaint of Clients against Lawyers is that "he charged too much" or "he won't take care of my matter and tell me what is going on." Both complaints are justified and can be avoided by the lawyer discussing his fees and charges in advance and keeping his client posted on the status of his legal matter.

Most people who are dealing with a lawyer for the first time, have either been recommended to him by other satisfied clients or have met the lawyer previously. Some lawyers charge for the first consultation with the new client and others advise the individual there is no charge for the first discussion.

Many law firms and individual lawyers base their charges on hourly rates. They keep accurate records and bill the client for the amount of time spent on his legal matters. Most of the larger law firms charge more for the time of a senior lawyer with years of experience than they do for a junior lawyer with limited experience. When it comes time for a court hearing, it has become quite popular for two lawyers to be present, usually one is a senior lawyer and the other a junior lawyer. The charge per hour will vary so greatly that it is difficult to even venture a guess. Other lawyers will charge a flat fee for a simple divorce or preparing a simple will, etc.

In many communities, the local or state bar association have published a list of minimum fees to be charged by a lawyer for certain specified legal services. This is done not with the viewpoint of gouging the public but to provide a reasonable and adequate fee for the lawyer. It is described as a minimum fee and not a maximum fee.

Certain legal services are covered by the laws of each state. For example, fees for probating an estate of a deceased person are regulated by law. It is usually a certain percentage of the value of the estate and the percentage decreases as the amount increases. Statutory fees are usually provided in workmen's compensation lawsuits, or in some states, the judge sets the lawyer's fee.

When a lawsuit is filed on a note that provides for reasonable attorney fees, the judge determines the amount of the attorney fee award. Years ago, some California credit jewelry stores tried a horrible collection stunt that was stopped by the judges. The delinquent customer might have owed a balance of $25 and his contract with the store provided for an attorney fee of $100 if he failed to pay and his account was turned over to an attorney for collection. The judges properly ruled that a $100 attorney's fee on a $25 collection item was unconscionable and they substituted $5 as the attorney's fee and that stopped the racket. If the note or contract does not provide for the payment of attorney fees in the event of default and the item being referred to an attorney, the courts will not grant any attorneys fee. Most bank notes provide for a 10% attorney's fee and other forms will use reasonable attorney's fees and the judge sets the amount.

## Contingent Fees

Contingent attorney fees take place in connection with automobile accident cases or in collection of money. A person is injured in an automobile accident case which is sometimes called a personal injury case. He retains a lawyer to handle his claim against the other driver and his insurance company, if one is involved. If no insurance company is involved, it usually means the other driver is not very sound financially. In an automobile accident lawsuit the insurance company is not named in the lawsuit and in a jury trial, it is grounds for a new trial if the words "insurance company" is mentioned. If that sounds silly, I agree. Most lawyers who specialize in personal injury lawsuits will gamble on a favorable result, thus the name contingent fee. If the lawsuit is won, the lawyer gets paid his fee and if the lawsuit is lost, the lawyer gambled his time and does not get paid. Usually, the percentage of the recovery for the lawyer's fee will vary from 25% to 40%, depending upon the lawyer, the area and the seriousness of the injuries.

Some lawyers handle the collection of money on an hourly charge basis, while others are willing to gamble on a contingent fee, based upon collecting the money. If the money is not collected, the lawyer gambled his time and lost.

After the problem has been discussed in detail and if the client wants the lawyer to proceed to handle the matter, the question of fees ought to be covered. If the client doesn't say "How much do you charge for this type of divorce?" then the lawyer ought to say "To avoid any misunderstanding we should talk about my fees and how they are to be paid." Many people are too embarrassed to ask the lawyer what his charges will be. The best time to talk about charges and fees is at the beginning, rather than be shocked at the end. The highest compliment any lawyer can receive is to have a satisfied client recommend him to a friend with the comment "He charges pretty good but he does a bangup job."

## Can A Client Fire His Lawyer?

The Client has the power and the right to discharge his lawyer at any stage of the proceedings. However, the Client must be fair and pay the lawyer for the reasonable value of his services performed before he was discharged. The same rule applies to the medical profession. The patient and/or his family have the right to change their doctor at any stage of his services. Again, the doctor must be paid for the fair value of his services rendered. Like the legal profession, the medical profession have their state medical societies which include grievance committees to investigate complaints against doctors.

Many complaints have been made against lawyers where the client pays the agreed fee and then is unable to get the lawyer to perform. The lawyer who alibis about how busy he is, is not being fair. If the lawyer is too busy to render his services, he is obligated to advise the client, instead of accepting the fee. There are some lawyers who will waste time alibing to their client whereas it would be quicker for them to perform the chore involved. I ran into one lawyer who presented a new problem. He never did accept any money from his client but he did not complete the legal job that he undertook. Then the client went elsewhere and complained about the lawyer's failure to complete his work. The lawyer alibied that he was "too busy" which is a weak excuse.

Some clients think that their lawyer is too friendly with the lawyer on the other side. Some clients are really quite unreasonable and hard to please. They would like to see their lawyer get into a fist fight with opposing counsel to prove that he is a fighter and looking out for their interest. This is ridiculous and has nothing to do with the lawyer's ability to properly represent his client. With no intent to defend the legal profession, it is my considered opinion that very, very few lawyers ever take advantage of their client by making secret deals with the opposition. The same holds true of judges, and, although a few judges become involved, a high percentage of the judges are honorable men and women, trying to do the best job they can. Judges are human beings like the rest of us and have their strong points and weak points and emotions that affect their decisions.

If you lose faith in your lawyer, tell him so and find another. If you think your lawyer is incompetent or not doing his job the way you think it ought to be done, make a change. A lawyer cannot properly represent his client if there is an unfriendly feeling between them. Every lawyer has had the experience of being replaced and he should not be disturbed when it occurs. On occasions I was replaced and on many more occasions, I was retained to replace another attorney. This is the clients prerogative because after all he is the person paying the bill.

Obviously, the lawyer is not always at fault nor is the client always right. Some clients are really unfair, unreasonable, and unpleasant persons that cannot be pleased under any conditions. That is the type of client that most lawyers are happy to get rid of permanently.

## How To Motivate Your Lawyer?

Let's talk about clients and things they do that are unfair and annoying. A client who fails to keep his or her appointment promptly is taking time that could be used for another client. Time and knowledge are the two main factors that a lawyer has for sale. If you pay as agreed, your lawyer is going to do the best job he can in your behalf. If you are "bad news" and fail to pay, the lawyer loses his desire to do his best job for you. It is estimated that about 40% of a lawyer's income goes to pay his overhead and expenses.

A client who lies to his lawyer or fails to make a full disclosure of all of the pertinent facts is only hurting himself. Regardless of how black the picture may be, the lawyer can do you more good if he knows everything there is to know about your problem or predicament. Some clients don't lie but will tell a half-truth which is nearly as bad. We have all heard of the old saying: "There are two sides to every story." Someone added a third dimension and now say there are three sides to every story. In any disputed situation: "There is your side; there is my side; and there is the truth." A good example of why it doesn't pay to lie to your attorney occurred during a divorce hearing when my client claimed to be a bona fide resident of the state of New Mexico for more than one year before we filed his divorce complaint. His wife appeared in person and proved that he had filed for a California divorce six months earlier and claimed that he was a bona fide resident of the state of California. We were thrown out of court; I was embarrassed and my client was only fooling himself.

As a final tip to clients, I would suggest that they do not unnecessarily telephone their attorney day and night with unimportant details. There is very little that he can do in your behalf when you telephone him at his home in the evening. If there is an emergency or something truly important, a night telephone call is necessary and proper. In a friendly vein, don't make a pest of yourself to the point of annoying your attorney. It is his duty to act as your legal advisor but be reasonable in your demands. The ideal relationship between client and lawyer is one of respect and implicit trust flowing both ways.

# DICTIONARY
# OF LEGAL TERMS

## A

**ABANDONMENT**
To release claim or forfeit rights — as in the case of a homestead.

**ABEYANCE**
Pending or temporarily suspended. Such as an action held in abeyance.

**ABSTRACT OF JUDGMENT**
Record of a court judgment. Creates lien when recorded.

**ABSTRACT OF TITLE**
A digest or summary of documents or records affecting title to property.

**ACCELERATION CLAUSE**
Provision inserted in a mortgage or trust deed note causing it to become payable at once, in a lump sum under certain conditions — in event property is sold, leased or delinquent payments.

**ACCEPTANCE**
Giving consent to an offer — as when seller agrees to an offer to purchase.

**ACCESSION**
Acquiring title to unauthorized improvements to your land.

**ACCOMMODATION PAPER**
An act of trying to help a friend by co-signing his note at a finance company or bank. A good way to lose a friend.

**ACCRETION**
Addition to your land as by deposits from a stream or lake.

**ACKNOWLEDGMENT**
A formal declaration before a notary public or other qualified officer, in signing a document, that it is your voluntary act.

**ACQUISITION**
The process by which property is procured — through purchase, inheritance, gift, foreclosure, etc.

**ACRE**

An area of land containing 43,560 feet

**ACT OF GOD**

A disaster inflicted by nature such as an earthquake, unusual flood, tornado or hurricane.

**ACTION TO QUIET TITLE**

A lawsuit to determine status of title to land. Often to remove a defect or cloud on the title.

**ACTUAL NOTICE**

Notice given by open possession and occupancy of property.

**ADDENDUM**

Something to be added.

**AD HOC**

A committee arranged for a special purpose.

**ADMINISTRATOR**

A man appointed by a court to take charge of an estate of a deceased person who left no will. If a lady were appointed, she would be called the administratrix.

**ADULT**

A person who has reached an age established by law to attain certain privileges, such as the right to vote, to enter into binding contracts, etc. Persons of lessor age are minors.

**AD VALOREM**

Based upon the value — property taxes for example.

**ADVERSE POSSESSION**

Openly holding possession of land under some claim of right which is opposed to the claim of another.

**AFFIANT**

One who makes a sworn statement, such as an affidavit.

**AFFIDAVIT**

A sworn statement in writing before an officer authorized to administer oaths.

**AFFIRMATION**

A solemn declaration — usually by one opposed to oaths on religious grounds.

**AGENCY**

Act of representing a principal in the capacity of an agent.

**AGENT**

One who is authorized to represent another person, as in a real estate transaction.

**AGREEMENT OF SALE**

A written contract whereby buyer and seller agree on terms of the sale.

**ALIAS**

An assumed name.

**ALIEN**

A resident who is a citizen of a foreign country.

**ALIENATE**

Act of transferring title to property.

**ALIENATION CLAUSE**

Provision in a mortgage or trust deed providing for lump sum payment if the property is sold.

**ALLUVIUM**

Deposit of soil on or adjoining property, as by flow of a river or stream, or by tides.

**AMERICAN STOCK EXCHANGE**

The second largest stock exchange in the United States. Their requirements are not as rigid as the New York Stock Exchange.

**AMICUS CURIAE**

A friend of the court. Usually an attorney authorized to file a brief in a case that he did not originate.

**AMORTIZE**

Pay off debt in installations; or gradual recovery of an investment.

**ANCILLARY PROCEEDINGS**

Like a branch reporting to the main office. Usually occurs in probate court when property is located in more than one state.

**ANNEXATION**

Adding land to another unit. Such as bringing a tract within the limits of a city.

**ANNUITY**

Money paid annually or other agreed periods.

**ANTICIPATORY BREACH**

An announced violation of contract that permits a lawsuit before the completion date of the contract.

**APPRAISAL**

An expert opinion as to value based upon facts and experience.

**APPURTENANCE**

A thing or right which attaches to or becomes incident to the land, so as to become a part of the realty. A house, fence, etc., which, when the land is conveyed, goes with it without special mention in the deed.

**ARBITRATION**

A substitute for court proceedings to settle disputes between parties to a contract.

**ARCHITECT**

A professionally trained person who plans buildings and sometimes is employed to oversee their construction.

**ASSESSED VALUE**

Value placed on property by the county assessor as basis for the levy of taxes.

**ASSESSMENT (SPECIAL)**

Levey against particular properties for cost of improvements which particularly benefit them. (Sewers, sidewalks, drains, etc.)

**ASSESSOR**

An official, usually county or city, who determines the value of property for tax purposes.

**ASSIGN**

To endorse over to another, such as a promissory note or lease.

**ASSIGNEE**

One to whom property or a right is transferred.

**ASSIGNOR**

One who assigns or transfers a property or right to another.

**ASSUMPTION OF MORTGAGE OR TRUST DEED**

Taking title to property and assuming personal liability for payment of existing notes for which the property is security.

**ASSUMPTION OF RISK**

You know all there is to know about the danger.

**ATTACHMENT**

Seizure of property by court order in connection with a pending lawsuit.

**ATTESTATION**

Witnessing the signing of a will or other legal document.

## ATTORNEY IN FACT
A person to whom a power of attorney is given authorizing him to do specific acts for another.

## ATTRACTIVE NUISANCE DOCTRINE
A theory of law that anything that attracts children does not require proof of negligence. It used to be the ice man and now could be a construction project.

## AUTHORIZATION TO SELL
Commonly called a listing by real estate brokers.

## AUTHORIZED CAPITAL STOCK
The amount of common stock specified in the articles of incorporation.

## AUTOPSY
Examination of a dead body.

## AVULSION
Sudden removal of land by flowing water.

## AWARD
The decision of the arbitrators. The same as a judge's ruling.


## B

## BALLOON PAYMENT
Usually an extra large payment on an installment note at the time it is payable in full.

## BANKRUPTCY
A federal court legal proceeding to aid those that are unable to pay their obligations when they fall due.

## BANKRUPTCY PETITION
The required form to be filled out and filed in federal bankruptcy court by those who seek relief from financial problems.

## BASE AND MERIDIAN
Principal survey lines in an area from which townships are numbered.

## BENCH MARK
Permanent marker placed by surveyors at an important point, upon which local surveys are based.

## BENEFICIARY
One who is a recipient of benefits; such as a lender of money secured by a trust deed.

**BEQUEATH**
To leave property by will.

**BEQUEST**
What is bequeathed by will — an inheritance.

**BID**
An offer by a contractor to build a certain structure for a fixed price.

**BIGAMY**
One spouse too many.

**BILATERAL CONTRACT**
A contract by which both parties agree to perform certain acts.

**BILL OF SALE**
Document which transfers ownership of personal property.

**BILLS OF LADING**
Paper evidence of title that represents the goods that are described in it.

**BILLS AND NOTES**
Abbreviation for a bill of exchange and a promissory note. A check is one of many examples of a bill of exchange that are used in daily business transactions.

**BINDER**
A preliminary agreement for sale of real estate requiring a deposit, and providing for a formal deed or contract at some future date.

**BLANKET MORTGAGE**
A single lien covering two or more lots or parcels of land.

**BOARD OF DIRECTORS**
A group of persons that manage a corporation.

**BONA FIDE**
In good faith — honest.

**BOND (SURETY)**
A pledge to pay a sum of money in case of failure to fulfill obligations, inflicting damage, or mishandling funds. Usually written by a bonding company for a fee.

**BONDABLE**
An employee who is able to obtain a bond to protect the employer. Also a contractor who is able to do the same for his customer.

**BONDS (CORPORATE)**
Evidence of indebtedness of a corporation which is secured by its general assets.

**BOOK VALUE**
The value of a property as carried on the owner's accounts.

**BOOT**
A profit gained in exchange of properties, not reflected by cash, upon which income tax is not deferred.

**BREACH**
Failure to perform a duty or fulfill an obligation.

**BROKER LOAN STATEMENT**
A statement of charges to be made in connection with a loan, for information of borrower.

**BUILDING RESTRICTIONS**
Laws or ordinances requiring sound construction for protection of health and safety.

**BULK SALES LAW**
State law requiring that the sale of a business be advertised beforehand, for protection of creditors.

**BUSINESS OPPORTUNITY**
A going business, including physical assets, good will and perhaps a property lease.

**BYLAWS**
Rules for internal management of a corporation within its charter's limits.

## C

**CAPITAL GAIN**
Profit from increase in value of an investment. If held more than six months, it becomes taxable at a lower rate.

**CAPITALIZATION**
In appraising, using a predetermined interest rate and the net earnings of a property as a basis of computing value.

**CASHIER'S CHECK**
A check drawn by a bank on its own account and signed by the bank's official.

**CAVEAT EMPTOR**
Means "Let the buyer beware." Dealing "at arms' length." Used car dealer selling a jalopy "as is."

## CD (CERTIFICATE OF DEPOSIT)
A receipt for a time deposit of money left with a bank at an agreed rate of interest.

## CERTIFIED CHECK
A customer's check that is guaranteed by his bank to be good when presented for payment.

## CERTIFIED FINANCIAL STATEMENT
A statement of assets and liabilities that is confirmed by the person's or firm's certified public accountant.

## CHAIN OF TITLE
Detailed account of all actions and events affecting a title to land as far back as the original government patent, if possible.

## CHANGE ORDERS
A variation in the plans and specifications of the architect that require a written memo.

## CHATTEL
Personal property; moveable property.

## CHATTEL MORTGAGE
A mortgage on personal property.

## CLOSING STATEMENT
A final accounting in closing a transaction. Mandatory for real estate brokers.

## CLOUD ON THE TITLE
Anything affecting clear title to property. Term usually used in connection with minor nuisance items that must be eliminated by quitclaim deed or quiet title lawsuit.

## CODICIL
A change in a will.

## COLLATERAL SECURITY
Additional sums or things of value posted to guarantee fulfillment of a principal contract.

## COLLUSION
A secret arrangement to defraud someone.

## COLOR OF TITLE
A title which appears to be good on the surface, but actually is not good.

**COMMERCIAL ACRE**

What remains of an acre after allowing for deductions for streets, alleys, etc. Something less than an acre.

**COMMERCIAL PAPER**

Notes assigned in the course of trade, bills of exchange, etc.

**COMMINGLING**

Situation where husband or wife has confused separate property with community property to the extent it cannot be separated.

**COMMON LAW MARRIAGE**

A man and a woman living together as husband and wife without benefit of marriage. Frequently no protection for the female.

**COMMON STOCK**

A printed certificate that represents the ownership of a corporation.

**COMMUNITY PROPERTY**

That property acquired by husband and wife from time of marriage onward as a result of their joint efforts.

**COMPACTION**

Tamping of filled ground to make it more suitable for building. Done extensively in subdividing of hilly ground.

**COMPARATIVE ANALYSIS**

Appraising a home or lot by comparing it with others of similar qualities with known recent sales prices.

**COMPETENT PARTIES**

Persons mentally fit; legally capable of entering into a contract.

**COMPOUND INTEREST**

Earnings on the original investment and the accummulated interest therefrom.

**CONDEMNATION**

Ruling by a public agency that property is not fit for use. Also refers to taking of private property for public use by right of eminent domain, and paying the fair value.

**CONDITIONAL SALES CONTRACT**

The purchase of personal property on contract, usually on the installment plan. Buyer does not receive title until he has made all payments called for by the contract.

**CONDITIONS**

Limitations imposed in a deed

## CONDOMINIUMS

Apartments or other types of properties in which the owner has fee title to the part actually occupied, with an undivided interest in areas used by all occupants.

## CONGLOMERATE CORPORATIONS

A group of companies that have been merged into a single ownership and are usually engaged in non-related business.

## CONSIDERATION

Something of value to induce a person to enter into a valid contract. The consideration for a gift between husband and wife or parents and children can be love and affection.

## CONSPIRACY

An agreement between two or more persons to commit an unlawful act.

## CONSTRUCTIVE NOTICE

Notice given by the public records, as opposed to actual notice.

## CONTIGUOUS

Adjoining, touching. As two contiguous parcels of land.

## CONTINGENT FEE

A gambling fee by an attorney based upon favorable result of collecting money.

## CONTRACT

Agreement to do certain things, or not to do them.

## CONTRACTOR

One who is licensed to build or erect a home, building, or other structure for another.

## CONTRIBUTORY NEGLIGENCE

The fault of negligence of the claimant that weakens or defeats his claim against the alleged wrongdoer. One who enters a dark building under construction may be guilty of contributory negligence.

## CONVENTIONAL LOAN

A loan not guaranteed or insured by a governmental agency. Usually made by banks, insurance companies and savings and loan associations for home mortgages.

## CONVERTIBLE STOCK

Designation where stock is changed into another class or into other obligations of the corporation.

**CONVEYANCE**

Transfer of title from one person to another. This is accomplished by the use of a deed.

**COOPERATIVE APARTMENT HOUSE**

Each occupant owns his apartment by receiving a deed to an undivided interest in the entire property.

**CORNER INFLUENCE**

In appraising, the additional value given to a corner lot due to its advantages, especially in business property.

**CORPORATE CHARTER**

Articles of incorporation that give the corporation the right and power to do many things over a period of years.

**CORPORATE MERGERS**

In a humerous vein, big fish eating little fish. Usually, the larger corporation buys all or the controlling interest in a smaller corporation and controls its fate.

**CORPORATE MINUTES**

A detailed written record of what transpires at meetings of the stockholders and also of the board of directors of a corporation.

**CORPORATION**

A legal creation authorized to act with the rights and liabilities of a person.

**CO-SIGNOR**

One who guarantees that if his friend who borrowed money does not pay as agreed that the good guy will get stuck.

**COST PLUS CONTRACT**

An agreement that the owner will pay the cost of all labor and materials plus a certain profit to the contractor.

**COUNTY RECORDS**

A recording system for documents maintained by each county as provided by state law.

**COVENANT**

Agreement in a deed to control the use and acts of future owners. Used also in other instruments such as leases and conditional sales contracts.

**CPA (CERTIFIED PUBLIC ACCOUNTANT)**

A skilled professional accountant who has been licensed by his state after passing a difficult examination. He is to the accounting profession what the MD is to the medical profession.

**CREATURE OF STATUTE**

A subject covered by state law in its entirety as enacted by the state legislature.

**CREDITOR'S COMMITTEE**

A group of creditors who decide if the debtor's petition for an extension of time or compromise of his obligations shall be permitted. This is handled under Chapter XI of the federal Bankruptcy Act.

## D

**DAMAGES**

Compensation the court may award to a person who has been injured physically or financially by another.

**D/B/A**

Abbreviation for "DOING BUSINESS AS" — used in lawsuits to identify a trade name. John Jones, d/b/a Highway Motors.

**DEBENTURES**

An unsecured note given by a corporation for money it has borrowed on a long term payback.

**DECLARATION OF HOMESTEAD**

Document recorded to declare a homestead under state law.

**DECLARATION OF RESTRICTIONS**

A list of restrictions to a tract imposed by a subdivider and recorded.

**DECREE**

A decision by a court or others authorized to make decisions. Frequently mispronounced, as if spelled degree.

**DEDICATION**

Acceptance of gift of land from an owner by a city or county for particular use by the public.

**DEED**

A written instrument which conveys title to real estate.

**DEED OF RECONVEYANCE**

Deed given by a trustee under deed of trust when loan is paid.

**DE FACTO AND DE JURE CORPORATIONS**

A de facto corporation although irregularly formed, exercises corporate rights under color of law. A de jure corporation is one which has been created in compliance with all legal requirements.

**DEFAULT**

Failure to perform a duty or keep a promise, such as to make payments on a note.

**DEFENDANT**

Persons who are being sued in a civil lawsuit.

**DEFICIENCY JUDGMENT**

A judgment awarded by a court against a person when after foreclosure the security for the loan does not realize enough money at a sale to pay the balance of the loan.

**DELIVERY**

Formal transfer of a deed to the new owner, without the right to recall it. Essential to a valid transfer of title.

**DEPOSITION**

Sworn testimony by way of questions and answers given outside of the courtroom in a pending lawsuit. Preliminary to the actual trial.

**DEPRECIATION**

Loss of value to property from any cause.

**DEVISE**

Gift of real estate by will.

**DEVISEE**

One who inherits property by will.

**DISCHARGE IN BANKRUPTCY**

A document that legally excuses one from being forced to pay certain obligations listed in his bankruptcy schedule that are legally dischargeable.

**DISCOUNTING BILLS**

Paying bills promptly when due and thereby earning a discount. Builds up good credit.

**DISGORGE**

A creditor who has been favored by a bankrupt debtor at the expense of all other creditors and he is ordered to return the money to the trustee in bankruptcy.

**DIVERSITY OF CITIZENSHIP**

A citizen of one state becoming involved in a lawsuit with a citizen of another state.

**DIVIDENDS**

A payment of a portion of corporate profits to its stockholders. Also payment by a bank to its depositors as interest for use of their money.

**DOMICILE**
Place of residence. In court proceedings, residence is a matter of intent.

**DONEE**
One who receives a gift.

**DONOR**
One who makes a gift.

**DOWER**
Interest of wife in her husband's estate after his death. Not used much in community property states.

**DRAFTSMAN**
One who is trained in the skill of drawing plans. Frequently employed by architects for drawing plans and specifications.

**DUMMY DIRECTOR**
A figurehead in the formation of a new corporation who has no duties to perform.

**DURESS**
Unlawfully forcing someone to do an act against his will by use of force.

**DWI (DRIVING WHILE INTOXICATED)**
Commonly called "drunk driving." One who is charged with the criminal offense of driving a motor vehicle while under the influence of alcohol to an extent prohibited by law.


E

**EARNEST MONEY**
A deposit of money to bind an agreement or an offer.

**EASEMENT**
The right or interest of one person in another's property.

**ECONOMIC LIFE**
Life of a building during which it earns enough to justify maintaining it.

**EGRESS**
A means of leaving property without trespassing.

**EMANCIPATION OF A MINOR**
A legal proceeding to permit one under age to transact business as an adult.

**EMINENT DOMAIN**

The right of government to take private property for public use, provided it serves a necessary public use and fair compensation is paid to the owner.

**ENCROACHMENT**

Building in whole or in part on another's property.

**ENCUMBRANCE**

A debt on property. Anything that burdens the title to property.

**ENDORSEMENT**

The signing on the back of a check or note for the purpose of transfer.

**ENDORSEMENT IN BLANK**

Signing to transfer rights to a check or note without qualification, making endorser equally responsible for payment.

**ENDORSEMENT WITHOUT RECOURSE**

Signing to transfer a check or note in this manner makes no guarantee to future holders.

**ENJOIN**

Forbid or prohibit.

**EQUITABLE OWNER**

One who has hypothecated his property. He has conveyed title in trust perhaps, but retains the right to use and enjoy the property.

**EQUITY (OWNER'S)**

Value of owner's interest in property in excess of the lien's against it.

**EQUITY OF REDEMPTION**

Owner's right to redeem property after foreclosure sale for a period provided by law.

**ESCALATOR CLAUSE**

Provision in a lease whereby the rents increase under certain conditions, such as every year, or based upon a periodic appraisal of the property.

**ESCHEAT**

Process by which property reverts to the state for lack of private ownership. Bank accounts that lie dormant for a number of years, with no apparent owner alive, are subject to escheat laws.

**ESCROW**

The depositing of papers and money with a third neutral party along with instructions to carry out an agreement. Such as the transfer of title to a house.

## ESCROW HOLDER
One who undertakes to carry out escrow instructions.

## ESTATE
The interest of a person in property; as to real property, the degree, quantity and extent of his interest.

## ESTATE FOR LIFE
Use of property only during the life of the person given the interest; after which it reverts to the original estate or others designated.

## ESTATE TAX (FEDERAL)
A tax on estates of deceased persons in excess of an exemption specified by law.

## ESTATE AT WILL
A lease which may be terminated at will by either party.

## ESTATE FOR YEARS
Another term for a lease or leasehold estate.

## ESTIMATOR
A person who is skilled in the cost of construction to determine the amount the contractor should place in his bid to the owner.

## ETHICS
A standard of moral practice and fair play.

## EUTHANASIA
A good death.

## EXCHANGE AGREEMENT
A contract for the exchange of properties.

## EXCLUSIVE LISTING
An authorization to sell which gives sole right to sell to one real estate broker. He is entitled to his brokerage fee even if the owner finds his own buyer.

## EXECUTE
To sign and consent to carry out an agreement to completion.

## EXECUTOR
Man named in a will to handle and dispose of an estate. If a woman is named for the same purpose, she is called EXECUTRIX.

## EXEMPTION STATUTES
Laws that protect property from creditors in connection with attachment or bankruptcy or other legal proceedings.

**EXPERT WITNESS**

One who testifies in a lawsuit who is not directly involved in the dispute but is qualified by reason of experience or educational background.

**EXTRAS**

Anything that is ordered by the owner after construction has started that was not included in the original contract.

## F

**FAMILY CORPORATION**

One whose stock is owned and controlled by immediate members of a family with no stock available to the general public.

**FEDERAL HOUSING ADMINISTRATION (FHA)**

Federal government agency, which insures loans on residential property.

**FEDERAL SAVINGS AND LOAN ASSOCIATION**

A financial institution that is chartered by the federal home loan bank board in Washington, D.C. and whose accounts are insured by an agency of the government.

**FEE SIMPLE ESTATE**

Highest and best estate possible.

**FELONY**

A serious crime punishable by a sentence of more than one year in a state penitentiary.

**FICTITIOUS NAME**

A name which does not identify the person. As indicated by John Jones, doing business as Highway Motors.

**FIDELITY BOND**

The dictionary says: "The quality or state of being faithful." A bond to protect the employer against employees who embezzle money.

**FIDUCIARY RELATIONSHIP**

A position of trust and confidence requiring loyalty.

**FINANCING STATEMENT**

A list of assets and liabilities which means a list of what you own and what you owe. Required by banks and other financial institutions before they will lend money.

**FINDER'S FEE**
Money paid to a person who furnishes information helpful in arranging a loan or completing a deal.

**FIRST MEETING OF CREDITORS**
A bankruptcy court proceeding held in the courtroom of the Referee in Bankruptcy to question the bankrupt debtor.

**FIXTURES**
Things which are attached to property which cannot be removed as ordinary personal property, because they become a part of the realty.

**FORECLOSURE**
The sale of pledged property to cover a defaulted debt.

**FORFEITURE**
Loss of a deposit or earnest money for failure to perform.

**FOUNDATIONS**
Nonprofit corporations that are formed for charitable or educational purposes.

**FRANCHISES**
A right granted by a state to a newly formed corporation. Sometimes used to denote a food type of franchise sold by a national company, authorizing a purchaser to use their brand name and recipe.

**FRAUD**
Causing loss of property due to use of deceit, cheating, false promises, etc.

**FREEHOLDER**
Owner of land in fee.

**FRONT FOOT**
The measure of land along the street frontage. Used as a unit in pricing business property.


## G

**GARNISHMENT**
A court proceeding whereby a creditor attaches the wages or bank account of the debtor.

**GENERAL LIEN**
One which may attach to all property of a person, such as a judgment or a tax claim.

**G I LOANS**

The government guarantee of loans to veterans of various wars in connection with their purchase of a home with certain limitations.

**GIFT DEED**

A deed for which the consideration is love and affection, rather than money.

**GIFT TAX (FEDERAL)**

A tax on gifts over a certain amount with exemptions.

**GOBBLEDYGOOK**

Wordy and generally unintelligible jargon.

**GOING PUBLIC**

A corporation whose stock had previously not been made available to the general public and is now being offered to the public for the first time. Ford Motor Company stock was held by the Ford family for many years before going public.

**GOOD WILL**

The intangible value that a business has built up over a period of time.

**GRANT DEED**

Instrument used to convey title to land. Carries implied warranties.

**GRANTEE**

One who acquires title to property by deed.

**GRANTING CLAUSE**

Clause in deed stating "I grant" or "I convey." Essential to a valid deed.

**GRANTOR**

One who conveys title to property by deed.

**GROSS INCOME**

Total income from a business or property before deducting expenses.

**GUARANTEE OF TITLE**

An opinion on the condition of title based upon a search of the official records, and backed by a fund to compensate in case of oversight or negligence.

**GUARDIAN**

A person or bank appointed to act for a minor or incompetent.

# H

### HABEAS CORPUS
A court order to bring a person before the judge.

### HARMLESS ERROR RULE
When a trial court judge commits an error and on appeal, the appellate court says that the trial court judge's error did not materially affect the defendant's rights or the law of the case.

### HEAD OF A FAMILY
One who is responsible for dependents. Not necessarily a married person.

### HEIRS
Those who obtain property upon death of another, either by will or by operation of law.

### HOLDER IN DUE COURSE
One who in good faith takes a note for value and without knowledge of any defects, in the course of business.

### HOLDING COMPANY
A super corporation which owns or controls such a dominant interest in one or more other corporations that it is able to dictate their policies.

### HOLOGRAPHIC WILL
A will entirely handwritten and signed by the testator or testatrix.

### HOMESTEAD
A home upon which a declaration of homestead has been recorded. Gives certain protection against judgments.

### HYPOTHECATE
To pledge property as security for a debt, but retaining its use. As in connection with a mortgage loan.

# I

### IMPLIED WARRANTY
A warranty assumed by law to exist in an instrument although not specifically stated. As in a grant or warranty deed.

### IMPOTENCY
Inability to have sexual intercourse.

### IMPOUNDS
Monthly payments to mortgage company by the mortgage borrower to pay for annual taxes and insurance premiums.

**IMPROVEMENTS**

Things built on land which become part of it.

**IMPROVEMENT ACTS**

State laws providing for the installation of improvements in certain districts, such as street widening and paving, installation of sewer lines and storm drains, etc. The cost is usually assessed against the properties benefited.

**INCOMPATIBILITY**

Ground for divorce when a couple do not get along.

**INCOMPETENT**

One who is unable to manage his affairs because of feeblemindedness, senility, insanity, etc.

**INDEMNIFY**

Guarantee against loss — as by an insurance policy. Same as a guarantor.

**INDORSEMENT**

A name signed on the back of a check or note.

**INGRESS**

A means of entering a property without trespassing.

**INHERENTLY DANGEROUS**

A type of danger that is an essential part of something, requiring special precautions to be taken to prevent injury.

**INHERIT**

To obtain property as an heir.

**INHERITANCE TAX (STATE)**

Tax on estate of deceased resident.

**INJUNCTION**

An order of a court to restrain against certain acts in connection with a pending lawsuit or one adjudicated.

**INSOLVENT**

Inability of a person to pay his debts. Where liabilities exceed assets.

**INSTALLMENT NOTE**

A note which provides for payment of a certain part of the principal at stated intervals.

**INSTRUMENT**

A document in writing creating certain rights to its parties or transferring them.

**INTEREST**

The rental charge for the use of money.

**INTEREST TABLE**

A table giving the amount of annual interest on various sums of money at different rates of interest.

**INTERSTATE COMMERCE**

Involving two or more states in the United States.

**INTESTATE**

Death without leaving a will. The dead person is called a testator or testatrix, indicating male or female.

**INTRASTATE COMMERCE**

Involving one state only.

**INVITEE**

One who has a perfect legal right to be on the premises where the accident occurred.

**INVOLUNTARY BANKRUPTCY PETITION**

A document filed by three or more creditors in federal bankruptcy court, claiming that the debtor person, firm or corporation is unable to pay their bills when due and is therefore bankrupt.

**INVOLUNTARY LIEN**

A lien placed against property without the owner's consent. Taxes and assessments are examples.

**IOU (I OWE YOU)**

A written acknowledgement of a sum of money owed to another. Similar to a note except that a note contains a promise to repay at a certain time.

**IRREVOCABLE**

That which cannot be recalled or revoked.

**IRRIGATION DISTRICT**

A district created by law to furnish water. It is a quasi-political district having governing features similar to counties and cities.


J


**JOINT NOTE**

A note signed by more than one person. All have equal responsibility for payment and must be sued together.

## JOINT AND SEVERAL NOTE

Same as a joint note, but makers may be sued either jointly or individually in event of default.

## JOINT TENANCY

Equal ownership by two or more persons under four essential unities. It features right of survivorship. If one dies, his interest goes to the survivor or survivors.

## JOINT TENANCY DEED

A deed which names grantees as joint genants. Very popular for married couples.

## JUDGMENT

A court's final decree. Often involves awarding a sum of money.

## JUDGMENT PROOF

Applies to persons who have no assets to satisfy a money judgment.

## JUNIOR LIEN

A lien which is subordinate to another lien which has prior claim on the security. The prior lien holders can collect before the junior lien is satisfied.

## JURISDICTION

The right given by law by which courts, commissions, etc., enter into and decide cases.

## K

## KEY MAN INSURANCE

Life insurance protection paid for by management to cover the cost of replacing a man important to the organization. Sometimes used as a fringe benefit for the key man.

## L

## LACHES

Sleeping on your rights which results in failure to secure legal relief because of waiting too long.

## LAND CONTRACT

An agreement whereby land is sold, usually on an installment basis, and buyer does not receive a deed until the contract is paid out.

## LAND DESCRIPTIONS
A description of land recognized by law. One based on government survey or surveys based on it.

## LANDLORD'S LIEN
The landlord's right to hold the tenants property as security for unpaid rent.

## LAST CLEAR CHANCE
The final opportunity to avoid the accident, even though the other party was on the wrong side of the road.

## LATENT DEFECTS
A defect being unknown and not discoverable by inspection.

## LEGALEZE
The author's slang definition of technical language used by certain judges and members of the legal profession.

## LEGAL HYBRID
A cooperative apartment because the stockholder-tenant possesses both stock in the corporation as well as a lease with the corporation.

## LEGAL RATE OF INTEREST
Varies in different states. Used to be about 6% or 7%, however, some states have increased the legal rates recently.

## LEGATEE
Recipient of a legacy or bequest; an inheritance.

## LESSEE
A renter under a lease.

## LESSOR
A landlord or owner who has leased his property.

## LETTERS OF CREDIT
A written authorization from your bank to other banks all over the world permitting you to draw money to be charged against your bank. Your bank will then charge your account.

## LIABLE
Responsible under the law.

## LICENSEE
A person who is authorized to be on the construction project. A license gives one the right to walk over another's land.

## LIEN
An encumbrance against property making it liable for a debt.

**LIFE ESTATE**
Right to use property for your lifetime only.

**LIMITED PARTNERSHIP**
A type of partnership with limited liability.

**LINE OF CREDIT**
The amount of money your bank will permit you to borrow.

**LIQUID ASSETS**
Those readily convertible to cash.

**LIQUIDATE**
To sell off property at best available price to secure cash.

**LIQUIDATED DAMAGES**
Extent of damages agreed upon in a contract in event of default.

**LIS PENDENS**
A recorded notice to advise persons interested in certain property that a lawsuit is pending which may affect title to it.

**LISTING**
A contract authorizing a real estate broker to buy, sell or lease certain land under specified terms and conditions.

**LITIGANTS**
All parties to a lawsuit.

**LOCO PARENTIS**
One who stands in place of a parent.

# M

**MAJORITY**
The age at which a young man or lady becomes an adult, according to law.

**MARGINAL RELEASES**
Entry on the margin of an official record book showing that a claim has been paid.

**MARKETABLE TITLE**
Title to real estate which is free and clear from any reasonable objections.

**MARKET PRICE**
The going price of equivalent properties based upon recent sales.

## MARKET VALUE

The best price a property would bring in dollars if freely advertised for sale for a reasonable time, to find a buyer who is fully informed on the possible uses of the property.

## MASTER PLAN

A plan for future physical development of a community.

## MATERIAL FACT

A fact, which if known to the parties, might seriously affect their decisions in a transaction.

## MAUSOLEUMS

A filing cabinet for dead bodies above ground.

## MECHANIC'S LIEN

A lien right provided by law whereby persons who have furnished labor or materials may make legal claim for their money against the property.

## MENACE

Use of threats to induce one to enter into a contract.

## MESNE PROFITS

Mesne means intermediate. Profits from a property during a period when a rightful owner is wrongfully deprived of the earnings.

## METES AND BOUNDS

A method of describing the boundary lines of a parcel of land.

## MILLER ACT

A federal law that protects those who furnish labor or materials used on a federal building project. Federal law prohibits the filing of a lien against the government, thus this substitute protection by way of the Miller Act.

## MINERAL, OIL AND GAS LICENSE

Special license to deal in such lands.

## MINORS

Young men and women who have not reached a legal age to vote or to enter into legal contracts. The laws of each state will vary.

## MISCEGENATION

Prohibition of a person marrying one of another color.

## MISDEMEANOR

A lesser crime than a felony. Sentences may be to county jail for less than one year or a fine or both.

## MONEY LEFT ON THE TABLE

Difference in money between the successful bidder on a highway construction job and the second low bidder.

**MONTH TO MONTH TENANCY**

When rent is paid by the month. The usual arrangement for renting houses.

**MORATORIUM**

A law suspending liability for paying a debt and granting more time for payment.

**MORTALITY TABLES**

Established procedures for determining life expectancy. Important in lawsuits to determine how long the claimant would have lived if he had not been struck by the car.

**MORTGAGE**

An instrument which makes property security for the payment of a loan.

**MORTGAGEE**

One who lends money secured by a mortgage.

**MORTGAGOR**

An owner who borrows money on a note secured by a mortgage.

**MULTIPLE LISTING**

A cooperative listing for the sale of real estate taken by a real estate board, which permits any member of their group to find a buyer. Brokerage fees are then split.

**MUTUAL CONSENT**

An essential to a valid contract.

**MUTUAL FUNDS**

An organization that invests other person's money and charges for their services. They claim to be experts in the field of investments.

**MUTUAL MISTAKE OF FACT**

An error or misunderstanding of a material fact that exonerates both parties to a contract.

# N

**NATIONAL BANK**

Chartered and authorized to engage in the banking business by the Federal authorities. Each account is federally insured by an agency of the government.

**NEGLIGENCE**

Doing something wrong or failing to do something that is required to be done.

**NEGOTIABLE INSTRUMENT**
Those which are commonly transferred by endorsement in the course of trade; such as checks and drafts.

**NEGOTIABLE NOTE**
One capable of being assigned in the ordinary course of business.

**NET INCOME**
Remaining income from business or property after proper charges and expenses are deducted.

**NET LISTING**
One which provides that real estate agent get his commission over and above a net sum to the seller.

**NEW WORTH**
The difference between your assets and liabilities. What you own and what you owe.

**NEW YORK STOCK EXCHANGE**
The largest association of stockbrokers in the world where trading in securities is accomplished under an organized system.

**NOLO CONTENDERE**
A substitute for a plea of guilty in a criminal matter. "I did it but I did not have criminal intent."

**NONPAR VALUE OF STOCK**
Corporate stock that is issued without placing any value on the shares. Usually occurs in a family corporation.

**NON-PROFIT CORPORATION**
A company that is organized for purposes other than earning money. It could be educational or charitable. Happens to some firms on an involuntary basis.

**NOTARY PUBLIC**
Person authorized by law to take acknowledgements and oaths.

**NOTICE OF ABANDONMENT**
Notice filed when work is discontinued on an unfinished job.

**NOTICE OF COMPLETION**
Document filed to give public notice that a building job is completed.

**NOTICE OF DEFAULT**
Notice filed by owner of a trust deed with the county recorder that borrower has defaulted and foreclosure proceedings may be started.

## NOTICE OF INTENDED SALE

A notice to be recorded when a business is sold, to give notice to creditors and to the public.

## NOTICE OF NON-RESPONSIBILITY

A notice provided by law, which when recorded, is designed to relieve an owner from liability for work or materials used on his property without his authorization.

## NOTICE TO QUIT

A three day notice to a delinquent tenant to pay up or surrender possession of the premises.

## NSF CHECKS

Abbreviation for "Not Sufficient Funds." Returned by the issuer's bank because there is not enough money on deposit to cover the check. The popular slang expression is "A HOT CHECK."

## NSL (NO STOCKHOLDERS LIABILITY)

A state corporation that limits the liability of its stockholders to the original amount they contributed to the new corporation.

## O

## OBLIGEE

The owner of the property and the building to be constructed is called the "obligee" under the bond issued by the bonding company.

## OBLIGOR

The bonding company that issues the construction bond is called the "obligor."

## OFF-SALE LICENSE

State liquor license issued to sellers of "packaged goods" to be taken from the premises.

## OFFSET STATEMENT

Statement of an owner or lien holder as to present status of a lien — the remaining principal balance on the note, interest due, etc.

## ON-SALE LICENSE

License to sell alcoholic beverages for consumption on the premises, such as cocktail bar, beer hall, etc.

## OPEN LISTING

A non-exclusive listing given to one or more real estate brokers. It may be oral or written and the first agent to get owner's acceptance to an offer earns the entire commission.

## OPTION
A written instrument which, for a consideration, gives one the right to buy or lease a property within a stated time on the terms set forth.

## OPTIONEE
One who secures an option right.

## OPTIONOR
An owner who gives an option.

## ORAL
Verbal or spoken; not in writing.

## ORDINANCE
A law enacted by a city.

## ORIGINAL OR PRIME CONTRACTOR
The contractor who contracts with the owner to do the overall building job for an agreed price.

## ORIGINATION FEE
A charge made by a financial institution in connection with making a new loan.

## OUTLAWED CLAIM
A claim is outlawed or barred by the statute of limitations when the claimant delays bringing suit beyond the time limit allowed by law.

## OVER THE COUNTER
Corporate stocks that are not listed on any stock exchange, but are sold by stock brokers "over the counter." The companies involved are usually smaller and it is not always easy to sell stock over the counter because the buyers are not as numerous as when stock is sold through a large stock exchange.

## OVERHEAD
The standard expenses of operating a place of business that are not chargeable to a particular part of the work.

## OWNER'S EQUITY
What a property is worth over and above the liens against it.

## P

## PAID-UP CAPITAL
The amount of cash with which the new corporation is going to start their business.

**PAROL EVIDENCE**
Oral or verbal.

**PARTIAL RELEASE CLAUSE**
Clause in a mortgage or trust deed which provides for removal of certain property from the effect of the lien upon payment of an agreed sum. Subdividers must have these if their tract is subject to a "blanket lien."

**PARTIAL SATISFACTION**
An acknowledgement in writing that a part of a claim or judgment has been paid. Usually filed with the clerk of the court.

**PARTNERSHIP**
A contract between two or more persons to unite their property, labor or skill, or some of them, in prosecution of some joint or lawful business and to share profits and losses in certain proportions.

**PARTY WALL**
One built on the dividing line of property for use of both owners.

**PAR VALUE**
The value placed on new stock about to be issued. This is determined by its incorporators.

**PATENT**
An original conveyance of lands by the federal government. Title is granted by letters patent.

**PAYOR AND PAYEE**
The payor pays the sum due on a note, and the payee receives the money.

**PENDENTE LITE**
A court order effective while the case is pending.

**PERCENTAGE LEASE**
A lease providing for rental based on the dollar volume of business done. Usually based on gross sales with an agreed minimum rental.

**PERFORMANCE BOND**
A guarantee that the contractor will perform the contract and also pay all bills for labor and material.

**PER SE**
As such.

**PERSONAL PROPERTY**
Moveable property; that which is not real property.

**PLAINTIFF**
One who brings a civil lawsuit.

## PLAN OF ARRANGEMENT
A written proposal filed in federal bankruptcy court by an insolvent debtor for an extension of time and a compromise payment of his obligations.

## PLANS AND SPECS
Abbreviation for "plans and specifications." These are usually prepared by an architect and are vital to the construction of any structure.

## PLEDGE
A deposit of personal property to secure a debt.

## POINTS
In the language of the money lending business, a point is one per cent of the amount of the loan. Bonuses and commissions are often expressed in "points."

## POLICE POWER
The power vested in the state to enact and enforce laws for the order, safety, health, morals and general welfare of the public.

## POLYGAMY
Too many spouses; a glutton for punishment.

## POSTNUPTIAL PROPERTY SETTLEMENT AGREEMENT
A written agreement between husband and wife, after their marriage, specifying their property rights for the past and future.

## POWER OF ATTORNEY
Authority given in writing by one person for another to act for him.

## POWER OF SALE
A right given to a trustee to sell property under deed of trust if the borrower defaults.

## PREFERENTIAL PAYMENT
Money paid by an insolvent debtor to a creditor in violation of bankruptcy law because it was made within four months of the filing of his bankruptcy petition. The money has to be returned to the trustee in bankruptcy for benefit of all of the creditors.

## PREFERRED STOCK
Corporate stock that is entitled to priority over common stock in the distribution of profits.

## PRENUPTIAL PROPERTY SETTLEMENT AGREEMENT
Written contract between husband and wife to be, before their marriage, dividing and agreeing to their ownership of property in the event of death or divorce.

**PREPAYMENT PENALTY**

A charge for paying off a mortgage balance ahead of schedule where the mortgage so specifies.

**PRESCRIPTION**

A means of obtaining title to property by long open possession under some claim, in defiance of owner's rights.

**PRESUMPTION**

A fact assumed by law which must be proved to the contrary.

**PRIMA FACIE**

On its face; presumptive.

**PRIMARY MORTGAGE MARKET**

Making original loans.

**PRINCIPAL**

One who employs an agent.

**PRIOR IN TIME IS PRIOR IN RIGHT**

Rights established by prompt recording, ahead of others who failed to record their lien or mortgage or other instrument promptly.

**PRIORITY**

Being first in rank, time or place.

**PRIVITY OF CONTRACT**

Lack of agreement, understanding or connection between the parties involved in the dispute.

**PROBATE COURT**

A special court that handles estates of persons that have died. Also all disputes that involve estates.

**PROBATE SALE**

Sale to liquidate the estate of a deceased person.

**PROMISSORY NOTE**

Written promise to pay a sum of money at a definite future time.

**PROOF OF CLAIM**

A special form that is filed in probate or bankruptcy court to substantiate a claim for money claimed to be owed by the decedent or bankrupt debtor.

**PROPERTY**

In general, anything capable of ownership.

**PROPERTY MANAGEMENT**

A branch of the real estate business.

**PROPERTY SETTLEMENT AGREEMENT**
A written agreement usually used in connection with a pending divorce action. It divides the property of the husband and wife as well as other matters.

**PRORATION**
In any transaction involving land, to divide taxes, interest, etc., proportionately between the parties, as in closing an escrow.

**PROXY**
The authority to act for another.

**PROXY FIGHTS**
A battle for control of a corporation by owners of its stock granting to another the right to vote his stock.

**PUBLIC LIABILITY INSURANCE**
Protection against claims for the injury or death of one or more persons.

**PUBLIC UTILITY**
A private company giving public service, such as water, gas or electricity.

**PURCHASE MONEY MORTGAGE**
One given as part of the purchase price when buying property. The note it secures is given to the seller instead of cash to meet the required down payment.

## Q

**QUASI-PUBLIC CORPORATION**
A corporation which has been given certain powers of a private nature. The local gas company is given the right to exercise eminent domain.

**QUIET TITLE**
A lawsuit to determine status of title; to remove a cloud on the title.

**QUITCLAIM DEED**
Deed by which the grantor releases any claim or interest in a property he may possess. It says in effect, "Whatever interest, if any I have, I give to you."

**QUORUM**
The number of persons required to be present for corporate business to be legally transacted. For a stockholder's meeting, a quorum means a majority of the voting stock issued and not a majority of the actual bodies of the stockholders.

R

## RANGE
A strip of land running north and south and six miles wide, established by government survey.

## RECONVEYANCE
Transfer of title to a former owner, as when a trustee under a deed of trust reconveys title when the note is paid in full.

## REDEMPTION
Reacquiring property lost through foreclosure within the prescribed time limit.

## REFEREE IN BANKRUPTCY
An attorney who is appointed by the federal judges of his district to act as an official to preside over bankruptcy court. He is sort of a junior federal judge with limited power in his bankruptcy court.

## RELEASE CLAUSE
Provision in a trust deed or mortgage to release portions of the land from the lien upon payment of an agreed amount of money. Subdividers, who sell individual lots, are required to have these.

## REQUEST FOR NOTICE OF DEFAULT
Acknowledged request filed with the county recorder by holder of a junior lien so he may be notified of actions of prior lien holders.

## RESCISSION OF CONTRACT
To set aside or annul a contract, either by mutual consent or by court order.

## RESERVATION
A right withheld by a grantor when conveying property.

## RESIDENCE
Sounds simple like where do you live. In the courtroom it can become very technical and very important. It is a matter of intent.

## RES IPSA LOQUITOR
Translated from latin it means "the thing speaks for itself." A legal doctrine that eliminates the vital requirement of proof of negligence under certain circumstances.

## RESOLUTION
A written approval of the board of directors of a corporation authorizing its officials to take some action of importance. Examples could be, who is authorized to sign corporate checks or the purchase of real estate by a corporation, etc.

**RESTRICTION**
A limitation on the use of property, usually imposed by a previous grantor.

**RETAINAGE**
The portion of a percentage of the monthly payments made by the owner to the contractor for construction work completed. It is withheld until the construction contract has been completed.

**REVERSIONARY INTEREST**
The right to an estate or its residue after present possession is terminated. As with a life estate.

**RIGHT OF FIRST REFUSAL**
The choice of buying an interest or land itself under specified terms and conditions. If the right is not exercised, then the owner is privileged to sell to others.

**RIGHT OF SURVIVORSHIP**
The right of a joint tenant to the interest of a deceased joint tenant.

**RIGHT OF WAY**
An easement to pass over, or maintain services, on property or a particular part thereof.

**RIPARIAN RIGHT**
Rights of a landowner to use the water on, under or adjacent to his land.

**RUNNING DESCRIPTION**
Tracing the boundaries of a tract by giving distances, angles and points around the edges. A metes and bounds description.

S

**SANDWICH LEASE**
A sublease which is subject to an original lease, the sublessee having further sublet the property. He holds an "in between" lease.

**SATISFACTION**
An instrument executed by a lien holder declaring that the debt has been paid. When recorded, it discharges the lien from the records.

**SEAL — CORPORATION**
A round metal device that contains the name of the corporation, the state of its incorporation and the date it was incorporated. Required on all real estate matters.

## SEC (SECURITIES EXCHANGE COMMISSION)

A federal agency that polices the sale of stocks and other securities to residents of states other than the home state of the corporation involved. Their requirements are tough, however, they effectively protect the gullible public from phony speculative investments.

## SECONDARY MORTGAGE MARKET

The dealing in trust deeds and mortgages already in existence.

## SECTION OF LAND

A standard land measurement containing 640 acres, or one square mile.

## SECURED CREDITOR

One who holds collateral as protection that his obligation will be paid. If the debtor does not pay as agreed, then the creditor can foreclose on the collateral.

## SECURITY DEVICE

An instrument or contract which results in real estate being made security for money owed, such as a trust deed, real property sales contracts, etc.

## SECURITY FUNDS

Funds deposited by lessee to protect lessor if a default occurs. These are trust funds.

## SEPARATE PROPERTY

That property which is owned and controlled separately by either husband or wife, as distinguished from community property.

## SETBACK ORDINANCE

Local law requiring owners, when building, to keep improvements a certain distance from land boundaries.

## SEVERALTY OWNERSHIP

Sole ownership — as by a single person.

## SHERIFF'S DEED

One given by the sheriff upon court order when property is sold to satisfy a judgment.

## SIGNING BY MARK

Making a mark or an "X" by a person unable to sign his name. The mark usually has to be witnessed by two persons.

## SINGLE PERSON

One who has never married or whose marriage was annulled.

## SOLVENT

Able to pay all debts when they become due.

**SPECIAL ASSESSMENT**
A legal charge against property for improvements which benefit it.

**SPECIAL MASTER**
A person appointed by the judge to take charge of and sell property at a public sale and report the results of the sale to the court for necessary approval. Usually an attorney.

**SPECIFIC LIEN**
A lien affecting one particular property.

**SPECIFIC PERFORMANCE**
Court order requiring a person to do what he has agreed to do in his contract.

**SPOUSE**
Either husband or wife.

**STATE CHARTERED BANK**
A financial institution that is incorporated and approved by its own state. It is not subject to federal regulatory bodies and its accounts are not federally insured.

**STATUS QUO**
The existing state of affairs. In a dispute, leaving the parties in the same position they were in originally.

**STATUTE**
A law enacted by a legislative body.

**STATUTE OF FRAUDS**
A state law requiring certain agreements to be in writing to be enforceable at law.

**STATUTE OF LIMITATIONS**
A state law limiting the time in which certain court actions may be brought.

**STATUTORY DEDICATION**
Surrendering land for public use when required by law; as for streets in a subdivision.

**STATUTORY FEES**
Attorney fees set by law.

**STERILITY**
Inability to bear children.

**STOCK CERTIFICATES**
Written or printed evidence of ownership of a certain number of shares in a corporation.

## STOCKHOLDER-SHAREHOLDER
There is no difference between the two terms. One who owns stock in a corporation.

## STOCKHOLDER'S MEETING
Meetings called by a corporation for the purpose of electing directors and transacting other business requiring the consent of the stockholders.

## STOCK OPTION PLAN
Offers to key employees and officials of a corporation to buy stock at an agreed price on an optional basis. If the price of the stock goes up, you exercise your option, otherwise you forget it.

## STOCK SPLITS
Dividing up of the outstanding shares of a corporation into a greater number of units. Sometimes done when the price of a stock is too high for the average investor to buy.

## STOP PAYMENT ORDER
Written instruction to your bank not to pay a certain check that you issued and which has not yet been presented for payment.

## STRAIGHT NOTE
One payable in a lump sum and not in installments.

## SUBCONTRACTOR
A builder or contractor who enters into an agreement with the prime contractor to build some part of the entire structure. The plumber, electrician, roofer, heating and air conditioning are typical examples.

## SUBDIVISION MAPS
When approved by the governing body and recorded they are the basis for good legal description.

## "SUBJECT TO" A MORTGAGE
Language used when buyer does not assume personal liability for payment of a mortgage or trust deed note against a property he buys.

## SUBLEASE
A lease given when the original lessee in turn sublets.

## SUBMISSION AGREEMENT
A written provision that if a dispute arises which the parties are unable to settle, the matter will be referred to a board of arbitrators.

## SUBORDINATION CLAUSE
Clause in a junior mortgage or trust deed enabling the first lien to keep its priority in case of renewal or refinancing.

## SUBPOENA

A court order commanding a person to appear in court at a designated time and place. Failure to appear could constitute contempt of court.

## SUBROGATION

The right to stand in another's shoes by virtue of paying him money on his claim. This occurs when the insurance company pays for the repairs on your car and tries to collect their loss from the other party involved in the accident.

## SUBSTANTIAL PERFORMANCE

When a certain portion of a construction contract has been completed. There is no set percentage of completion required, it will vary with the facts of each case.

## SURETY

One who becomes a guarantor for another person.

T

## TANGIBLE PROPERTY

Personal property which has substance and can be manually delivered from one person to another.

## TAX DEED

One given when land is sold by the state for non-payment of taxes.

## TAXES (REAL ESTATE)

A levy on property by political subdivisions, such as county, city, school districts to pay for government administration and services.

## TENANCY IN COMMON

Ownership of equal or unequal undivided interests in property by two or more persons, without right of survivorship.

## TENANCY AT SUFFERANCE

Occurs when a lease expires and owner permits tenant to continue in possession on a temporary basis. Usually one month at a time.

## TENANT IN PARTNERSHIP

Interest in property held as a partner.

## TERMITES

Wood devouring insects. Enemies of home owners.

## TESTAMENTARY GIFT

When a will provides for a gift.

**TESTATOR AND TESTATRIX**

One who makes a will. Testator is a man. Testatrix a woman.

**THIRD PARTY BENEFICIARY**

A laborer, materialman, or subcontractor who is protected by a performance bond taken out by the general contractor, even though they are not named in the bond.

**TIGHT MONEY**

A situation that exists when the demand for money is greater than the supply. Banks durn down applications for loans by good customers because they are temporarily out of loanable funds.

**"TIME IS OF THE ESSENCE"**

Necessary provision in contracts. Contemplates prompt performance by the parties within the time limits set forth.

**TITLE**

Evidence of ownership and lawful possession.

**TITLE INSURANCE**

Protection to a property owner against loss because of defective title. Policies are written by title companies and cover all hazards.

**TITLE SEARCH**

An accurate check of the courthouse records to determine if title to land has been affected by the filing of any instrument. This work is usually done by experienced personnel of the title companies.

**TOPOGRAPHY**

The character of the land's surface, such as level, hilly, etc.

**TORT**

A civil wrong other than a crime. An automobile accident is a good example.

**TOWNSHIP**

A unit of land six miles square, or 36 miles. Established by government survey.

**TRADE NAME**

A name used by someone engaged in business, other than his own personal name. Jones Motor Company or Pacific Motor Company are both trade names for John Jones, the owner.

**TREASURY STOCK**

Corporate stock that has been issued and paid for, but has later been reacquired by the corporation by purchase, donation, forfeiture, or other means.

**TRESPASSER**

One who enters upon the lands of another unlawfully.

**TRUST DEED [DEED OF TRUST]**

A conveyance of title to a trustee to be held until a loan secured by a note is paid, at which time title is reconveyed.

**TRUST FUNDS**

Money that belongs to another that is being held for a particular purpose. Should be kept separate and apart from the holder's regular funds.

**TRUSTEE**

A person or corporation which holds title in trust pending repayment of an obligation or the rendering of a service. In connection with trust deed, holds title until note is paid in full.

**TRUSTEE IN BANKRUPTCY**

An official appointed by the Referee in bankruptcy to take charge of the bankrupt person's estate.

**TRUSTEE'S DEED**

One given by a trustee when foreclosed property is sold.

**TRUSTOR**

Borrower on a trust deed note.

**TURNKEY JOB**

An agreement to complete a structure for a fixed price.


U

**ULTRA VIRES**

Acts of a corporation that are beyond its legal powers as provided in its charter.

**UMPIRE**

Not the baseball variety. A person selected by a board of arbitrators to decide the matter in controversy when the arbitrators are unable to agree.

**UNDIVIDED INTEREST**

A partial interest in a whole property, merged with the interest of others.

**UNDUE INFLUENCE**

Taking advantage of a person because of his weakness or distress.

**UNIFORM COMMERCIAL CODE**

A comparatively new law requiring filings with the Secretary of State of security devices making personal property loans secured liens.

**UNIFORM SIMULTANEOUS DEATH ACT**

Where husband and wife died in a joint disaster leaving community property, and evidence indicates that they died simultaneously, then one-half of the property goes to the husband's family and the other one-half to the wife's family.

**UNILATERAL CONTRACT**

One which imposes an obligation on one party only; exchange of a promise for an act.

**UNISSUED STOCK**

Corporate stock that has been authorized but has not been issued.

**UNIT OWNER**

A person who buys an apartment in a condominium.

**UNITED STATES SUPREME COURT**

The highest court in the United States. Its nine justices decide litigation that involve constitutional questions. They select or reject matters their court will hear.

**UNITIES**

Essential such as to a joint tenancy, the unities being time, title, interest, and possession.

**UNLAWFUL DETAINER**

Failure of a tenant to vacate after being notified that he is in default.

**UNSECURED CREDITOR**

One who has extended credit without obtaining any collateral as security. Typical examples could be the drug store; the grocery store; the department store; the dress shop; and all of the public utilities.

**URBAN PROPERTY**

City property.

**URBAN RENEWAL AND REDEVELOPMENT**

Plan to improve substandard areas in populated communities.

**USE TAX**

A sales tax on goods purchased from out of state.

**USURY**

Charging an illegal rate of interest.


# V


**V A LOANS**

A mortgage loan made to a service veteran which is insured or guaranteed by the Veterans Administration.

**VALUATION**
Appraising. Estimating the worth of property in money.

**VEHICULAR TRAFFIC**
Street or highway traffic.

**VENDEE**
The buyer.

**VENDOR**
The seller.

**VERBAL LISTING**
A listing not reduced to writing.

**VERIFICATION**
Confirmation of the truth of a document by sworn statement.

**VEST**
To bestow upon, such as title to property.

**VETERAN'S ADMINISTRATION**
A federal governmental agency, which among other services to veterans, insures or guarantees repayment of home loans borrowed by veterans.

**VETERAN'S TAX EXAMPTION**
A property tax exemption given to certain qualified veterans or their widows.

**VOID**
Having no binding effect at law.

**VOID AB INITIO**
Void from the beginning.

**VOIDABLE**
That which may be declared void, but which is not void until so adjudged by a court.

**VOLUNTARY LIEN**
A lien placed on property through the voluntary act of the owner, such as when he makes a mortgage loan.

## W

**WAGE EARNER'S PLAN**
A petition filed in federal bankruptcy court by a debtor who is financially involved, for an extension of time in which to pay his debts in full. A sincere attempt to avoid an ordinary type of bankruptcy.

**WAIVE**

To relinquish; to surrender the right to require anything.

**WAREHOUSE RECEIPT**

A written instrument that represents that certain goods are in the hands of a warehouseman. It is a symbolical representation of the property itself.

**WARRANTY DEED**

A deed which recites certain warranties that are guaranteed by the seller or grantor.

**WASTE**

Abuse of property by a tenant or someone holding a temporary interest, such as a life estate, which results in a loss of value.

**WATER TABLE**

Depth of natural underground water from the surface.

**WILL**

A legal document to distribute property after death.

**WOMEN'S LIBERATION MOVEMENT**

Latest demands by the female of the species for equal pay and greater equality with men.

**WORKMANLIKE MANNER**

An artisan performing his chores in a skillful manner. The test is what type of work would be done in his own area and not in New York or Chicago.

**WORKMEN'S COMPENSATION INSURANCE**

Protection furnished by the employer for benefit of his employees in the event they are injured or killed on the job.

**WRIT**

A written document issued by a court commanding a person to do certain acts, or sometimes to refrain from doing them.

**WRITING OFF A BAD DEBT**

Cancellation of a debt when the creditor is convinced that he cannot collect from the debtor. The creditor is then entitled to a tax credit due to his loss in writing off his chances to collect his money.

**WRIT OF EXECUTION**

A court order that property be seized and sold to pay a judgment.

## Z

**ZONING**

Control of the use of land by county or city authorities; power to limit property to specific use.

Jocaly, David MAY 29 1973

Frost, Frederick JUL 6 1913

Berkowitz Mollie AUG 1 1973

Tannenbaum B 8/27/73

Talmi, Elizabeth 8/30/73 —

Scheeman, Harry OCT 2 1973

Smith, Barry, 10/26/73

Haesloop, M. DEC 3 1973

Jalonese, Phyllis DEC 26 1973

White, Jeannette JAN 28 1974

Lang, Richard 3/4/74

Sheldon, Ruth 3/1/74

Finley, B 3/22/74

Levinson, L. MAY 7 1976

Hilliard, L. JAN 28 1983

Swift. V. FEB 2 1990

Lanao, J. FEB 26 1991